£2.00

D1631253

The Verderers and Forest Laws of Dean

Dr Cyril Hart

The Second Viscount Bledisloe, QC

John H. Watts, Esq

Alderman F. G. Little

Today's Verderers

THE VERDERERS and FOREST LAWS OF DEAN

(With notes on the Speech House and the Deer)

CYRIL HART

Senior Verderer

DAVID & CHARLES : NEWTON ABBOT

ISBN 0 7153 5289 X

Set in 11/12 pt Baskerville
and printed in Great Britain
by Clarke Doble & Brendon Ltd, Plymouth
for David & Charles (Publishers) Limited
South Devon House Newton Abbot Devon

Contents

Forest Organisation
Forest Officials
Forest Courts
Beasts of the Forest
Hunting
The Sheriff and Common Law

References

The Verderers to 1282
The Forest Eyre of 1282
The Pleas of Vert
The Pleas of Venison
Vills which did not come fully
Cases before the King or Parliament
The Regard
Illicit trade in venison and vert
The clergy as malefactors
The extent of Dean Forest
Chases, Parks, Warrens and Groves
Gifts of Venison
Religious Houses as Beneficiaries
Military Equipment in St Briavels Castle in 1275
The Prorogation of the Eyre
The Financial Aspects
Conclusions

List of Illustrations

List of Plates

*Most of the photographs which are not acknowledged
in the list were taken by or for the author*

List of Figures

List of Illustrations

Principal abbreviations used in References

(The source is the Public Record Office where not stated
otherwise)

BGAS	Bristol & Gloucestershire Archaeological Society
BM	British Museum
Bodl	Bodleian Library, Oxford
C	Chancery Papers :

      C47 Chancery Miscellanies
      C53 Charter Rolls
      C54 Close Rolls
      C60 Fine Rolls
      C62 Liberate Rolls
      C66 Patent Rolls
      C77 Welsh Rolls
      C99 Chancery, Forest Proceedings

Cal	Calendar
CNFC	Cotteswold Naturalists' Field Club
E	Exchequer Papers :

      E32   Treasury of Receipt, Forest Proceedings
      E101 Accounts Various
      E112 Bills and Answers
      E134 Depositions by Commissions
      E146 Forest Proceedings
      E178 Special Commissions of Enquiry
      E372 Pipe Rolls

F	Forestry Commission Records
GRO	Gloucestershire Records Office
HMC	Historical Manuscripts Commission
IPM	Inquisitions Post Mortem
Lansd	Lansdowne (Manuscripts)
R	Roll
SC6	Ministers' and Receivers' Accounts
SP	State Papers Domestic
Tsy	Treasury

Preface

Forest was land not necessarily belonging to the king, but preserved by him for his hunting and subject to his will under special laws enforced by forest officials and courts. The Royal Forest of Dean in west Gloucestershire is among the few remaining ancient tracts of forest designated by William the Conqueror. It was a hunting ground of the Saxon, Norman, and Angevin kings, also of their relatives, favourites and churches. Forest law, harsh in early days, was administered to protect the king's 'beasts of the forest', namely deer and wild boars. Today the election of verderers 'to guard the vert and the venison' is the only remnant of the ancient forest administration : there are four of them in Dean, and they constitute the Verderers' Court, which is still held at the Speech House in the centre of the Forest. Their court of attachment was for long synonymous with the unique 'court of speech'. Only the verderers of Dean continue to be elected (under the supervision of the sheriff) and to hold office according to ancient custom : the verderers of the New Forest and Epping Forest have been reconstituted under modern statutes.

The first of three objectives in writing this book was to relate the history of Dean's verderers. The other two were to give an account of forest law and its administration, and to record the repeals made therein by the Wild Creatures and Forest Laws Act 1971. The opportunity has been taken to add information on the Speech House and on the deer which happily are again an ornament to the Forest. Furthermore, much has been included of the interesting rolls of the Dean Eyre and its Regard of 1282 —for the reason that they are among the richest sources of our knowledge both of the persons whose lives were set in the Forest, and of the relations subsisting between them and the Crown.

Forest and forest law are fascinating subjects. To some people they conjure up pictures of men in green tunics, with bows, arrows and hunting horns, enjoying the chase. It is opportune to write on the subjects because the 1971 Act noted above has abolished any prerogative right of the sovereign to wild creatures (except royal fish and swans), and has abrogated forest law ex-

B

cept in so far as it relates to the appointment and functions of verderers. Two of the main achievements of the Act are the repeal of obsolete and unnecessary enactments and the simplification and modernisation of the law relating to ancient forests.

In this book I have written only briefly on the privileges in Dean of common, pannage and estovers—for comprehensive information on which the reader is referred to my *Commoners of Dean Forest* (1951); and the peculiar mining rights are discussed in *The Free Miners* (1953). Likewise, the inquirer for information on the history of Dean as a timber producing Forest, or in regard to its industrial past is referred respectively to *Royal Forest* (1966) and *The Industrial History of Dean* (1971). It is to be hoped that the whole will enable the reader to gain a comprehensive appreciation of the rich history of the Royal Forest of Dean, now some 24,000 acres, and thereby to derive additional pleasure from a visit to this delightful part of Britain.

C.H.

Chenies
Coleford
Forest of Dean
Gloucestershire GL16 8DT

1 July 1971

One: Forest: Its Organisation, Officials and Courts

Forest Organisation

In early times dense woods were avoided by man as dangerous and unpleasant, but he used the less dense parts to live near and hunt in, and from them he took wild animals, and wood for tools, fencing, dwellings and fuel. He cleared stretches of trees to provide for cultivation land enriched by humus and often by wood-ash from natural and purposeful fires. His swine fattened on acorns and beech mast, and his cattle, horses, and possibly sheep, browsed the trees and grazed the natural and induced clearings. Later, more permanent cultivation succeeded the old 'shifting system', dung and marl were used as a fertiliser instead of wood-ash, and the plough replaced the hoe.

By Saxon times, villagers looked to manorial and royal woods as sources of food, fuel and timber, and of sustenance of domestic animals. Kings and their relatives and favourites valued the woods as a source of pleasant and fruitful hunting. How much law relating to woods was inherent in Saxon administration is unknown, but Cnut laid heavy penalities on those who unlawfully hunted, and Edward the Confessor shared in the enjoyment of the chase.[1] Already there were sylvan hunting preserves, yet woods were also thought of in terms of the number of swine that could be fattened on their mast in the autumn. The Norman conqueror confirmed the lands preserved for hunting; and whether they were wholly clothed with trees, or only partially covered—as was usually the case—the territories were called 'forest' and were protected by forest officials. Under William I 'there was a rapid and violent extension of forest land',[2] and he 'preserved the harts and boars, and loved the stags as if he were their father'.[3] The royal monopoly created something like a nature reserve which afforded free movement, shelter, and food for deer and other desirable wild animals, and which harboured useful hawks and falcons in their eyries, and bees for their honey.

Thus the institution of forest was established by William, the innovation being due to the love of hunting (*venatio*) which in the Norman kings amounted almost to a passion. Forest consisted in preserves in certain well-wooded counties where there were adequate coverts and good pasture for the 'venison'—a term which embodied 'the beasts of the forest'—the red deer, the fallow deer, the roe, and the wild boar, and later the meat thereof. To those preserves the king went to forget his cares in the chase; there he enjoyed quiet and freedom : consequently those who committed an offence against forest lay themselves open to his personal vengeance. Punishment was no concern of the ordinary common law courts, but depended entirely on the king or those to whom he delegated. Forest had its own customary (and, later, written) laws, not based on the common law of the realm; and the vital distinction in the countryside was between forest, subject to forest law, and land which lay outside.

The word forest probably comes from *fera*, wild beast, *e* being changed to *o*; thus forest owed its origin to sport. Such territory chiefly comprised woodlands, but also included pasture, arable and villages. It must not be confused with the royal demesne, because there were royal woods which were not forest, and on the other hand, forest often comprised estates which were the property of subjects, high and low. But forest belonged to the king in the sense that it was created (afforested) for his benefit, and within its limits none save himself and those authorised by him might hunt or harm venison, on pain of severe penalties, sometimes preceded or followed by long imprisonment. Furthermore, forest law protected vert (*veridis*, green) or 'green hue', that is to say trees, undergrowth, and herbage—capable of serving as cover or food for the wild beasts. Forest was later defined as consisting of 'four things . . . vert, venison, particular laws, and privileges, and of certain meet officers appointed for that purpose, to the end that the same may the better be preserved and kept for a place of recreation and pastime, meet for the royal dignity of a prince';[4] and, again, of 'eight things . . . soil, covert, laws, courts, judges, officers, game, and certain bounds'.[5]

For an explanation of the intricacies of forest and its laws historians have had recourse chiefly to the *Dialogus* of Richard

Fitz-Neal,[6] the Assize of Woodstock (1184), the Forest Charter of 1217, and the much later treatises of Manwood[7] and Coke.[8] Modern scholarship has thrown more light upon and clarified the general subject : Turner[9] has laid all students of forest history under his debt; Bazeley[10] added much on the extent of forest; and Petit-Dutaillis[11] made a notable summary of the whole. More recent scholarship has added information.[12] Nevertheless, the last word has by no means yet been said : for instance, there is reason to doubt whether the administration or incidence of forest law was really so harsh as has been asserted.[13]

In the reign of John, the chief barons were considered to have a certain interest in forest, because, said the king, 'We hold our forest and beasts not to our own use only but also to that of our loyal subjects',[14] and barons traversing forest were granted licence to take some venison. Apart from royal permission to hunt, some favoured subjects had grants of chases, parks, warrens, woods, and groves. The chases and woods were generally part of forest which had been alienated by charter; but the grant did not involve complete deforestation, because forest law (at least in part) was maintained for the benefit of the recipient. The parks, on the other hand, were not under forest law, and they could be enclosed. The warrens were unenclosed tracts on a lord's demesne where he hunted other game than the beasts of the forest.

Nobody had a right, without royal permission, to appropriate any of the vert. Even for grantees of a wood within forest, the right of cutting trees was restricted lest the cover should be reduced to the detriment of the beasts. Any grantee who exceeded customary or granted rights was fined for waste (vastum) at the chief forest-court—the eyre—until the damaged wood had become rehabilitated by coppice shoots or seedling growth. If trees were uprooted to turn woodland into arable a fine was imposed and the occupier had to pay a composition or rent on every crop raised on this 'assart'. Furthermore, there was the offence of 'purpresture'—the unlawful occupation of the king's land, though the word was used increasingly to signify an encroachment of any sort. The offender was fined, and might continue his encroachment only by an additional payment, generally an annual one.

The supervision of all activities within forest, including the regulation of the inhabitants' privileges of common, pannage (feeding of swine on acorns and beech-mast), and estovers or 'botes' (chiefly firewood, timber, and other necessaries), came to be exercised by a system of courts and many officials—functionaries appointed by the king, officers elected or appointed, as well as others who held their posts by hereditary right. Above all was the chief justice of forest, one north and another south of Trent, who above his normal duties was expected to join with other itinerant justices to hold the forest eyre (from *iter, in itinere*). In charge locally was usually the ferm-paying warden, whose office was often combined with that of constable of a neighbouring castle.

The social, economic, legal, and political effects of the forest system were far-reaching. Forest comprised a large part of the realm; and those portions of it which were woodland swarmed with deer and boars, which even in time of famine it was unlawful to touch. Forest was still subject to the operation of common law and of the custom of the realm : consequently perpetrators of civil crimes, ie those which had nothing to do with forest law, were still held liable to be brought to justice under common law. Furthermore, forest was a fruitful source of revenue to the king. Besides judicial fines there were sums accruing from pasturage, pannage, encroachments, and assarts. There were also benefits in kind : timber for boats, bridges, and castles; and venison for the king's larder and as a source of his gifts to favourites, churches, and trusty servants.

The Assize of Woodstock (1184), which embodied in part some earlier formulation of customary and legal practice regarding forest, is the earliest surviving set of regulations enacted to preserve 'the peace of the king's venison (*pax venationis suæ*)'. At least from the reign of John, kings were subjected to persistent baronial agitation for deforestments together with the relaxation of the severity of forest law, and in *Magna Carta* (1215) a beginning was made by John to reduce forest and to restrain oppression by its officials. The relevant articles were expanded in 1217 by Henry III into the separate Charter of the Forest. The most famous article is 10, dealing with punishments : 'No one shall henceforth lose life or members for the sake of our venison.' Henceforth the Angevin kings through their officials normally contented themselves with the imprisonment of offenders and the exaction of fines. Most of the excesses which were remedied in

1217 had sprung up since the accession of Henry II, but the most offensive afforestations, attributed to Richard and John, were at once annulled, with the exception that those of Henry II were deforested only so far as they had been of injury to landowners. However, the Charter granted only part of the benefits hoped for in 1215, and the extraordinary jurisdiction over forest remained. The inhabitants were still oppressed, subject to irksome restrictions, and liable to heavy individual or collective fines. Nevertheless, several of the evil forest oppressions from which they had suffered were suppressed by law, and some deforestations might be expected.

By 1227 Henry III was dissatisfied with the results of the perambulations of forest which followed the confirmation two years earlier of the Forest Charter.[15] He took the view that all land afforested before the death of Henry I (1135), even if it had since been deforested, was forest within the terms of the Charter, and that recent perambulations had wrongly deforested many areas satisfying this test. He summoned the knights in batches from groups of shires to account for the decisions and forced them to acknowledge their errors—much to the indignation of the barons. The king compromised, the storm died down, and in the next few years Henry deforested many areas but exacted in return heavy fines from the inhabitants.

Forest continued to be both a source of income to the king and to provide some benefits to the inhabitants. It was also a source of temptation both to those living therein or nearby and to those who guarded it. Land for cultivation was taken at the expense of vert, and buildings were set up; the privilege of estovers was sometimes exceeded; trees and undergrowth were stolen; and charcoal was illegally made. Though moderate grazing and pannage were permitted, the woodlands and pastures were sometimes 'overburdened' with cattle and horses.[16] Venison was furtively taken. Offenders included paid and unpaid officials, clergy and laymen, nobles, and commons. The administration of forest law irritated most of the populace, whose general resentment against the system was inflamed by the behaviour and exactions of some officials. But the picture of royal oppression, avarice, and self-indulgence, which charters and rolls of forest eyres have been taken to present, obscures a brighter and more human aspect of forest life. Not all forest officials were harsh

and tyrannical: often they were local men who might sometimes sympathise with the trespasser and were perhaps even
loath to enforce rigorously the law they were expected to
administer.

The king wished to maintain his forest, but his subjects demanded its partial curtailment. Henry III was striving for the
enjoyment of his possessions; he was reluctant to lose the proceeds of forest justice, rents, food for his table, profits from the
sale of woodland produce, satisfaction and prestige from gifts
of venison and timber, and freedom to grant to religious houses,
and others, territorial gifts, or to reward supporters with lucra-
tive offices or occasional hunting. His attempts to prevent inter-
ference with his prerogative are shown by inquests, especially
the great inquest of Robert Passelewe in 1244 regarding encroachment on forest.[17]

The nobility led the renewed clamour for partial deforestation.
In 1258 the earls and barons complained that Henry had re-
forested lands no longer within the bounds of forest. But the
struggle was not ended during his reign, and under Edward I
forest created since the accession of Henry II still remained. In
1277[18] Edward announced his resolve ostensibly to keep the Forest
Charter inviolably, and ordered a great inquisition in forest south
of Trent, not only to repress excesses but also to make perambulations accord with the Charter. The officials were 'to make a
just perambulation', namely that made in the time of 'the lord
King Henry our father, which has not yet been impugned', but
the king commanded that no executive measures were to be taken
without reference to him. In effect, Edward granted a perambulation but resolved that the extent of forest should remain as fixed
by his predecessor. His subjects refused to be satisfied with this
illusory concession.

Similar inquiries instituted by Edward[19] were usually met by
grievances. In 1278, if Manwood[20] is correct, the *Consuetudines
et Assise de Foresta* were issued,[21] which summarised the custom
and law concerning trespass in the vert and on the venison, the
procedure of the courts, and the obligations of both inhabitants
and officials. The articles safeguarded the king's prerogative, but
the pressure against the forest system, and for some deforestment,
was going on in 1282 when the war in Wales intervened; and the
struggle was not renewed until 1297 (*infra*).[22]

One of the largest extents of forest was that of Dene (later Dean) in west Gloucestershire, more fully discussed in Chapter 2.

Forest Officials

At the head of forest administration *(Fig 1)* were two chief justices, one north and another south of Trent. Being quite unable to exercise an adequate supervision of the actions of forest officials, they were dependent on the evidence supplied by them.[23] Much of the contemporary maladministration escaped their ears, and even such directions as they issued might be disobeyed. Though the justice's visits were infrequent, the fear of him exercised some restraining force on the inhabitants. One of his principal duties was to authorise the release on bail of prisoners who for forest offences were detained in custody. (In Dean, incarceration was usually in St Briavels Castle—*Plate p 67*—but sometimes in Gloucester Castle.)

The itinerant justices, or justices-in-eyre, comprised usually the justice of forest for the relevant province and three other justices, who from time to time were expected to visit each area of forest. They had extensive powers, but could be over-ruled by the king. Bishops, sheriffs, and constables had to produce offenders before them; and earls and barons could be made to answer before the king or parliament for irregular or evil deeds of themselves or their subordinates.

Each particular tract of forest was usually administered by a ferm-paying warden, through a deputy, who often had the custody of a local castle (in Dean, this was St Briavels Castle). Few of the wardens devoted close personal attention to their custody, because many of them resided elsewhere and some were engaged on national business: their deputies, living locally, shouldered a great burden. The duties which the warden was expected to perform whether in person or by deputy, were many and various. Although unauthorised to hold forest pleas he was generally responsible locally for the administration of forest law; and grants of exemption from it or release from the immediate consequences of infringing it were addressed to him by the king or his justice. Evil-doers to the venison were committed to his keeping, as well as offenders against common law. He was responsible for receiving beasts found slain, and for taking charge of cattle and pigs discovered feeding unlawfully. He ensured that no trees or undergrowth were cut and no clearings were made without due authority. He appointed some at least of the foresters, and was called to account if they proved unsuitable. He produced offenders and their *mainpernors*, ie those who stood bail, when requested by the justices to do so. He released on writ offenders after they had found pledges; and he had to answer if any had been released without authority. He looked after woods temporarily taken into the king's hands. He received the fines exacted for vert and other offences during the interim of eyres, and took possession of waggons and oxen used by transgressors. Besides ordering that the deer were supplied with sufficient natural food in hard winters, he arranged for the catching, salting and despatch of venison requisitioned by the king; and he executed the royal grants of venison and timber. The foregoing duties were in addition to those of custodian of the castle, and the collection of Crown rents and dues of many kinds. Occasionally, his duties extended to extraneous matters (in Dean, the warden was ordered in 1281 to take Flaxley Abbey under the king's special protection, and to administer its revenue, on account of the financial difficulties into which it had fallen[24]). Obviously the constable-warden, through his deputy, was of great value to the Crown.

In most large areas of forest there were one or more hereditary foresters-of-fee, who helped to conserve the vert and the venison. They held the office with its perquisites as an hereditary fief. Each had charge of a bailiwick, an extensive district of forest (in Dean, *vide Fig 3*, the nine bailiwicks were those of Abenhall, Bearse, Bicknor, Blakeney, Bleyth, Dene, The Lea, Ruardean, and Staunton). The foresters-of-fee held certain land by the service of keeping their bailiwick, with one or more foresters under them, and of paying for the land and bailiwick a fixed annual sum to the king. They enjoyed many forest privileges, including those of minerals, falcons and sparrowhawks, estovers, nuts, pannage, and herbage. The forester-of-fee of Abenhall in Dean claimed that he (and his ancestors since the Conquest) held the bailiwick and the land 'in fee of the king and rendered 20s for the former and 9s for the latter' on the following terms:[25]

He ought to find two sergeants for guarding the bailiwick, and if the King goes to war he will come on a horse with a hauberk, with bows and arrows to do the King's command within the bounds of the Forest. And he will have from him wardship, heriot and marriage. And he claims in his bailiwick housebote and heybote by view of the verderers and of their bailiff. And he claims iron ore and sea-coal if it is found in his bailiwick. And he claims eyries of falcons and sparrowhawks, but the eyries of hawks belong to the King. And he claims dead and dry wood for himself and his men without waste, free pannage for himself and his men, windfall in his bailiwick, common for himself and his men in the Forest for all their beasts. Furthermore, he and his ancestors have been wont to have their dogs running for wolf and fox outside the covert. This he has had and used, himself and all his ancestors, since the Conquest of the land. And he claims nuts in his bailiwick when they fall. And after St Martin's when the King will take tallage for pannage he takes after-pannage. And when the King's men gather chestnuts for him in his bailiwick he will have two who then shake down. Towards Christmas the trunk of an oak for his fire. And when the King gives any timber-tree in his bailiwick he will have the lopping and stump. And he claims a pig or 2s at St Martin's when the King takes his pannage in his bailiwick.

It was the duty of foresters-of-fee to search for evil-doers in their respective bailiwicks and to bring those found before the verderers (infra). Each was obliged to keep his roll of attachments to present to the itinerant justices, and each appointed his foresters apparently with the consent of the warden. They had to answer for their misdeeds and for those under them. They had the duty of felling trees and underwood for the king's deer to browse in hard winters.

Sergeants-of-fee were men of local importance with hereditary rights of holding lands in forest. In Dean, at least one sergeant held his land by charter of the king, rendering yearly a rose at midsummer and by performing the service due to the king as expressed in his charter.[26] Usually in Dean they were eight to twelve in number, and their land, usually 12 acres, was stated to be 'in St Briavels'. They had to help guard the vert and the venison, and to attach offenders;[27] but unlike the foresters-of-fee

they had not charge of a specific bailiwick of forest but helped
to keep watch over the whole of it. They enjoyed certain forest
privileges, claimed in Dean to be : [28]

> Housebote to maintain their houses, and a tree trunk at
> Christmas by view of the constable, foresters and verderers,
> and heybote and bote of dead and dry wood without view,
> and common for their beasts throughout the Forest except
> the forbidden lawns of the same, and quit of pannage.

Woodwards acted as foresters in granted woods within forest.
They had to be sworn before the itinerant justices, under penalty
of the wood being taken into the king's hands. Although employed by the grantee, the woodwards were expected to protect
the king's venison and to prevent waste of trees and undergrowth
within their care.

Foresters were appointed by the grantee of a wood, or by
foresters-of-fee, or by the warden. They took their oath before
the verderers, and shared with the other officials the duty of
guarding forest and apprehending evil-doers to vert and venison.
On occasion, foresters themselves transgressed, causing their spon-
sors to be brought to judgement. There were two kinds of
forester : first, those on horseback, or riding forester (referred to
as either *forestarius chiminarius* or *forestarius eques*); second, the
foot, or walking forester. (In Dean there is a record of venison
having been secretly sold to a burgess of Bristol in exchange for
green cloth of Ireland for summer tunics for foresters.[29])

Each forest had as a rule four agisters, chiefly concerned with
arranging and collecting money for the agistment of cattle feeding in the king's demesne woods, pastures and lawns; and for
regulating pannage. They were included in the general summons
to the eyre 'with all agistments', that is the list of people putting
animals into forest. Beasts of the plough were allowed to graze
on the king's demesne (except the 'forbidden lawns') subject to
customary restrictions. They were not allowed in the forest during the fortnights before and after Midsummer Day respectively,
a period which was known as the Defence or Fence Month
(*Mensis Uetitus*) when the deer were supposed to be fawning.
Another restricted period was that called Winter Heyning when
the pasture was scanty and reserved for the deer. In Dean an

Act of 1667 (see Chapter 3) specified the time of the Fence
Month as the fifteen days before and the fifteen days after 24
June, and the time of the Winter Heyning as the period from
11 November to 23 April. However, both close seasons have been
abolished by an Act of 1971 (see Chapter 8). Pigs exercising pannage were agisted in the king's demesne woods from 25 September until 22 November inclusive in every year, and a few pence
were paid for each pig agisted. Goats were expressly prohibited,
and there is no evidence to show that sheep were admitted to be
'commonable animals'.

Regarders were somewhat apart from other officials in forest.
They were usually twelve knights appointed by the king, and
charged with a temporary commission of inquiry. Before each
eyre, the newly appointed regarders made a tour of the relevant
forest, embodying an intensive and far-reaching investigation to
discover answers to a series of questions known as 'Chapters of
the Regard'. The chief chapters were those of assart, waste, and
purpresture; others concerned the pasture in the demesne, woods
held under grant, the eyries of hawks and falcons, honey, forges,
minerals (usually iron ore and coal), ports, boats, weapons, and
dogs. The resulting regard was placed before the itinerant justices.

In all forest there were officers called verderers (*viridarius*),
usually four in number, who were responsible to the king. The
office of verderer is a title derived from vert (discussed *supra*).
The verderers were (and in Dean, uniquely, still are) elected
in the county court by the freeholders of the county under the
supervision of the sheriff on receipt by him of a writ from the
Crown called '*de viridario eligendo*'. Their duty was to guard
the vert and the venison, and their chief work was that of holding their court of attachment (*infra*). Their symbol of office was
an axe. The qualification of a verderer was the possession of land
within forest,[30] good health,[31] and freedom from other engrossing
duties.[32] They received no salary, and no perquisites were
attached to their office (other than, in later times, a buck and a
doe annually[33]). By custom they were not liable to be put on
assizes and juries.[34] When elected they held office for life unless
they were removed by the king because they were incapacitated
by age or illness, or by reason of insufficient qualification.

About every forty days the verderers held their court of attachment where they regulated the taking of estovers, and, under their

30

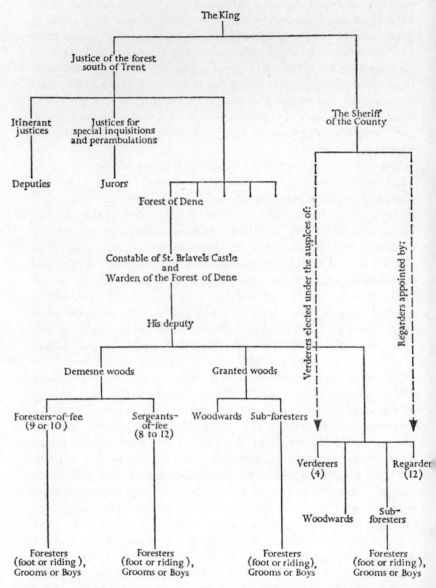

Fig 1. A diagrammatical presentation of forest administration in Dean in the thirteenth century

power to levy fines up to 4d, disposed of simple vert offences. They enrolled the names with their pledges of those accused of more serious trespass against vert, and of all those against venison, for presentation at the next eyre. They took the oaths of foresters, and were called to account if they accepted insufficient pledges or transgressed in any other way. Furthermore, they had to answer queries on many matters relating to incidents within private woods as well as elsewhere in the forest.

On some occasions the king's orders for replacement of a verderer were not complied with, and renewed orders had to be issued some years later.[35] On the death of a verderer 'his heir had to bring in the rolls of his ancestor's time'.[36] Furthermore, 'if the verderer alien his lands or die seised, and no man brings in the rolls, then the land by the law of the forest shall be seised by the sheriff, which the verderer had, until the rolls be brought in, and if they be lost, then till he make his fine and have his *ouster le main*'.[37] The unpopularity and burden of such office during part of the thirteenth century are illustrated by the charters of exemption produced in 1282.[38] Comprising men of local and county standing, trying to keep a fair balance between the interests of the king and the inhabitants, and receiving little reward beyond local prestige, the verderers fulfilled an exacting office. Furthermore, they shared with the regarders the preparation of evidence for the eyre. Writers in later centuries gave their interpretation of the office; Manwood wrote in 1598:[39]

It is to be understood that there are most commonly in every one of the King's forests within this realm, four officers of the forest, called verderers (which ought to be esquires or gentlemen of good account, ability, and living) which are wise and discreet men, and well learned in the laws of the forest.

A verderer is a judicial officer of the King's forest chosen by the King's writ in the full county of the same shire within which the forest is, and sworn to maintain and keep the assizes of the forest, and also to view, receive, and inroll the attachments and presentments of all manner of trespasses of the forest, of vert and venison.

The office of a verderer is almost like the office of a coroner in some points: for as a coroner by the law is to view the dead body . . . so a verderer is to view the wild

beasts of the forest slain or sore wounded, or hurt, then upon
notice thereof given unto the verderers or unto one of them,
he ought to repair to the same wild beast that is so slain,
killed, or hurt, and there cause an inquisition to be made by
the four neighbouring villages in the forest, to know how
the same wild beast was killed, and by whom, as it doth
appear by the Assizes of the Forest, Article 7. And so a
verderer in that respect is like unto a coroner.

Of the method of appointing a verderer, Manwood added : [40]

Even as a coroner is chosen by the King's writ in the full
county, so is a verderer also : for when any of the King's
verderers of his forest is dead, then upon certificate thereof
made unto the King in his Court of Chancery that one of
the verderers [named] of the forest of [named] is dead, the
King thereupon doth grant a writ *de viridario eligendo*
directed to the sheriff of the same shire within which the
forest is, where is to be chosen a verderer, commanding him
in his full county to chose another verderer in the place of
him that is dead. . . . By which writ it appears that a verderer shall be chosen in the full county, in the same manner
as a coroner is, by the freeholders. So that when the sheriff
has received the King's writ aforesaid for the choosing of
another verderer, and that he by virtue of the same writ in
his full county has caused the freeholders there to elect a
wise, discreet, sufficient and able man to serve in the said
place of a verderer, and the same sheriff has given unto him
an oath according to the tenor of his writ, then this election
of such a new verderer together with his name must be certified into the Court of Chancery by the same sheriff in his
return made of the same writ. And in this sort a verderer
is made, and otherwise than this no man may be made a
verderer of any forest of the King.

Manwood set out the form of the oath to be taken by a verderer after his election : [41]

You shall truly serve our Sovereign Lord the King in the
office of a verderer in the forest of [named]. You shall to
the uttermost of your power and knowledge, do for the profit
of the King, so far as it doth appertain unto you to do so.
You shall preserve and maintain the ancient rights and

franchises of his crown. You shall not conceal from His Majesty any rights or privileges, nor any offence either in vert or venison, nor any other thing. You shall not withdraw or abridge any defaults, but shall endeavour yourself to manifest and redress the same; and if you cannot do that of yourself, you shall give knowledge thereof unto the King, or unto his justice of the forest. You shall deal indifferently with all the King's liege people. You shall execute the laws of the forest, and do equal right and justice, as well unto the poor as unto the rich, in that appertaineth unto your office. You shall not oppress any person by colour thereof, for any reward, favour, or malice. All these things you shall to the uttermost of your power observe and keep, so help you God.

He then explained the duties of a verderer : [42]

A verderer ought to view the vert and venison of the forest. . . . If an oak, being over vert within the forest, be felled or cut down out of the King's demesne woods, the same oak is to be apprised by the view of the verderers. Also . . . the verderers ought to inroll their apprisement and view in their roll. And the verderers ought to take inquisitions of matters of the forest, and of trespasses of the forest, as well of vert as of venison; and those inquisitions they must inroll in their roll likewise, and also certify the same before the Lord Justice in Eyre of the Forest at his next coming into the forest to hold the general sessions of the forest. And also the verderer's office in some cases is to judge of offences and trespasses that are committed and done within the forest, as of trespass in vert, the value thereof being under the sum of four pence . . . whereby it doth appear that the office of verderer is a judicial place or office.

Today, the verderers of Dean are the only survivors of the ancient forest administration (see Chapter 8).

Forest Courts

There were two kinds of forest courts—the verderers' court of attachment, and the eyre of the itinerant justices. The court of

c

attachment, held by the verderers in each forest about every forty days, was so called because its chief function was to view and record attachments made by forest officials : *attachiamentum* was the obligation to appear. The jurisdiction of the court was small : it could adjudicate only in minor vert offences, and then impose fines to a limit of 4d. It had no authority to try cases relating to the venison. Such offences were usually first investigated in special local inquisitions (*infra*). All cases concerning venison, and important cases relating to vert, were enrolled together with names of pledges, in readiness for the coming of the itinerant justices. At the court the verderers received the oaths of newly appointed foresters, and regulated the taking of estovers. Thus its functions were rather administrative than judicial. (In Dean the court became known, uniquely, as the Speech Court—hence the Speech House, the name of the Crown building, now an hotel wherein the verderers' court is held.)

The swanimote, sometimes referred to as a court, was a forest assembly authorised to enable the forest officials including the agisters to superintend and regulate the pannage of pigs in the king's woods in the autumn and to remove cattle during the Fence Month and the Winter Heyning. The term *swanimote* later became applied loosely and vaguely to courts of attachment and to some infrequent forest inquisitions. In Dean, *swanimote* poses problems; for instance, two interpretations may be placed upon the following extract in the roll of the justices in eyre of 1282 :[48]

And because the pleas of vert have been hitherto unduly pleaded and presented in the swanimotes, the constable, foresters and verderers are instructed that henceforth attachments for vert should be rightfully made and pleaded, and touching each person attached for vert two safe pledges should be taken and enrolled, and that each forester-of-fee should have with him the roll of all the attachments for vert and venison to be presented to the justices.

Firstly, it may be that *swanimote* was used as a synonym for the court of attachment; or, secondly, the meaning may be that a swanimote in the original sense existed and that attempts had been made to plead vert cases therein : if so, they had been unduly pleaded and presented there, and henceforth attachments should be rightfully made and pleaded in the court of attachment, whence the serious offences were to pass to the justices. Nevertheless the whole matter is obscure, because the same roll refers elsewhere to courts of attachment, and of foresters being presented before the verderers at the swanimote. Still later, when treated as a court, the swanimote was held three times in every year, and was presided over by the verderers. (Two of the cases at the last eyre for Dean, held at Gloucester in 1634, were initiated by presentments of the swanimote,[44] while two rolls are extant covering the years 1673–84 for swanimotes held before the verderers:[45] obviously the swanimote had, at least temporarily, assumed the rôle of the court of attachment.)

On occasion, special inquisitions were used to enquire into any matter concerning forest. For the purpose, usually twelve or twenty-four jurors were sworn in. The inquisition usually concerned poaching of venison—an offence which involved the neighbouring vills in trouble. If a deer was found dead or injured, an inquisition to discover the offender had to be held by the four vills nearest to the scene of the crime. Poachers detected by the inquisition, or discovered in the act, were generally committed to gaol by the verderers until they had found sureties for their appearance before the itinerant justices. Trespassers on the vert were not kept in detention until after their third attachment.

The justice seat in eyre, that is the court of the itinerant justices for forest pleas, *justiciarii itinerantes ad placita foreste*, was expected to be held from time to time in each forest. The justices, persons of some eminence, always included one of the two chief justices of forest. The visitations were arranged by royal writ nominating itinerant justices to hear and determine the pleas of the forest in a particular county or group of counties. In the twelfth century the eyres were usually held once in three years, since the regards (*supra*) took place at that interval and were prepared in readiness for the coming of the justices. Later the intervals became longer. For Gloucestershire, evidence has been found for eighteen forest eyres before 1282;[46] intervals of eleven and twelve years separate the last three eyres of Henry III; and a period of twelve years elapsed before the 1282 eyre. The rolls (in Latin) of only the last three eyres (1258, 1270 and 1282) survive.[47] That of 1282 has been fully transcribed, studied, and commented upon.[48] (This was the last certain eyre for Dean except one held in 1634—see Chapter 3.)

Much business was transacted at the forest courts in the twelfth and thirteenth centuries, the period when forest law was most rigorously enforced. In Dean it has been estimated that some £12,000 in fines were imposed during the period 1155–1307, an average of £75 per annum.[49] Some 35 vills are mentioned as attending courts in the years 1247 to 1282. Details of the eyre of 1282 are given in Chapter 2.

Beasts of the Forest

There were four beasts of the forest—the red deer, the fallow deer, the roe, and the wild boar. In Dean during the twelfth and thirteenth centuries, fallow deer seem to have formed the majority: some 850 bucks and does are mentioned in grants of venison alone. Gifts of red deer were less common, some 200 head in all appearing in the Close Rolls of the period; only 34 head of roe are mentioned. During the same two centuries, at least on fifty-four occasions venison was despatched from the Forest to the Court. In twenty-two cases the number of beasts sent is specified: of the total of 1,185, 58 were described as harts or hinds, 615 as bucks or does, and 512 as boars, wood boars (aper silvestris), wood pigs, pigs, and sows.[50] The total number of animals furnished by the Forest for the royal table was probably well over 2,000.

Of wild boars, Dean seems to have been unusually rich. John commanded that the Forest was to be agisted on the skirts, not in the middle, or in places where the wild boars congregated; Henry III's order on one occasion was for twenty boars, and on another for twenty boars and sixty wild sows. Henry's demands may have seriously reduced the stock in Dean: in 1247, he commanded his huntsmen not to take any more boars, yet for his Christmas dinner in 1254 he ordered a hundred boars and wild sows.[51] The boar appears only infrequently after 1267; there is only one entry relating to it in the eyre roll of 1270, and only three entries of boars and of three sows appear in the eyre roll of 1282 (see Chapter 2).

In 1282, fallow and red deer were far the most numerous; roe deer are mentioned in only six cases presented at the eyre. The foresters-of-fee were wont and bound to fell in their bailiwicks, on the warden's instructions, trees and undergrowth for sustaining the deer during hard winters. During 1275–80 twenty-two oaks and one beech for this purpose were felled in Mailscot and Coverham.[52] In the snow that occurred in the winter of 1281–2, there were felled in one of the nine bailiwicks (Abenhall) seventy oaks besides underwood which included holly and hazel. The regarders when asked by the itinerant justices if the deer might have been sustained by underwood alone, answered 'yes'.

Wolves were kept in bounds,[53] but in 1281 they were harming the deer around Hope Mansel and elsewhere whereupon Richard Talbot was given licence to hunt the fox, the cat, the wolf and the hare throughout the king's Forest of Dean, and to catch by nets or in any other way the wolf there, so long as he did not take of the deer or course in warrens belonging to the king or any other person.[54] In the same year, a writ of aid was given for Peter Corbet, enjoined to take and destroy all wolves throughout England.[55]

The warden, through his deputy, supervised arrangements for the catching, salting and despatch of the venison ordered by the king for his own use or as gifts,[56] of which some in 1282 are noted in Chapter 2. In the same chapter, instances are given of the methods used by poachers.

Hunting

There is some doubt whether the designation of territory as forest was entirely the result of the king's love of the chase. Royal visits to Dean were few, and they were not solely, and were sometimes not at all, for hunting.[57] William the Conqueror appears to have visited the Forest more than once if that is the correct interpretation of the chronicler's words '*Rex autem Gulielmus erat in Dana silva ibique pro more venatui vacabat*'; he was certainly in Dean in 1069. Henry I was at Newnham-on-Severn at sometime before 1107. There is some evidence of visits by Henry II in 1158, 1164 or 5, and 1179. John was a more frequent visitor—in 1200, 1207 (three days), 1209, 1212 (three days), and 1213 (three days). Henry III was at St Briavels in 1226, 1229 (three days), and 1232; he may have been there in 1256, and was certainly at Flaxley on 27 July that year. This is the last royal visit of which traces have been found. The Forest does not appear in the *Itinerary of Edward I* : though he must have passed it often enough, he seems to have been too busy to find sport therein, at any rate for more than the briefest of seasons. No doubt there were several occasions, more especially in the twelfth century, when the king's hunting has left no record.

However, though Dean was rarely hunted in person by the king, his prerogative and his prestige were frequently satisfied by the numerous gifts and supplies which he requisitioned through his huntsmen and the constable. For example, in 1260 Henry III commanded his huntsmen, Henry and William de Candovre, to take in Dean eighty swine and thirty hinds, and in 1267 sixty does, sixteen hinds and sixty wild boars.[58] The constable had to receive and aid the king's huntsmen, but their wages appear only occasionally on his accounts : Hiche, the king's hunter in 1220, received 12d (5p) a day for himself, two horses, and two boys; and 9½d (4p) a day was allowed for eighteen dogs and lime-hounds on the same occasion.[59] The constable paid for the salting and despatching of the venison, and deducted the cost from his ferm or from the revenue which passed through his hands.

The king gave to his relatives and friends permission to hunt in Dean; and during the reign of Edward I there are several records of their hunting, chiefly in the woods of Mailscot and of Coverham, which adjoined a place called King's Perch (*cf* to-day's Perch Lodge).[60] Edmund, his brother, hunted therein for five days in the seventh year and for eight in the eighth year of the reign; Gilbert de Clare and Roger de Mortimer three days and four days respectively in the eighth year; and William de Valence, brother of the king, five days in the fifth year. These and similar hunting expeditions, and the ravages of the few remaining wolves, gradually reduced the number of deer and boars, and further depletion was caused by the furtive depredations of the inhabitants.

The Sheriff and Common Law

The sheriff quite probably served as a restraint upon the forest officials, but beyond this he had little connection with forest so far as its law was concerned. His most important duty in respect of forest was the making of arrangements for the eyre when ordered to do so by the king's writ, following receipt of which he summoned 'the archbishops, bishops, abbots, priors, earls, barons, knights and all free tenants having lands or tenements within the metes of the forest', as well as representatives of forest vills and all forest officials. During the eyre he had the responsibility of producing on writ defaulters and malefactors dwelling in his county when ordered to do so by the itinerant justices. On occasions he had to collect the issues of lands taken into the king's hands. He had, too, the duty of superintending the election of verderers. (In Dean alone, the sheriff of Gloucestershire still has this duty.)

The sheriff was more concerned with common law, the code that kept the ordinary peace, which forest, with its laws, courts and administration, did not supersede or replace.[61] The ordinary malefactor, the felon and the murderer, were subject to common law administered by the sheriff, coroner, justices, and other officials in the manorial, hundred, county, or King's courts.

References to Chapter 1

1   *A. S. Chron*, 'E', s.a. 1086 (equals 1087)
2   Douglas, D. C., *William the Conqueror*, 1964, 372
3   Darby, H. C., 'Domesday Woodland', *Econ Hist Rev* 3, 1950, 42
4   Manwood, John, *Treatise of the Lawes of the Forrest*, 1598, f.1
5   Coke, Edward, *Fourth Part of the Institutes of the Laws of England*, ed 1644, 289
6   Fitz-Neal, Richard, *Dialogus de Scaccario*, ed Hughes, Crump, and Johnson, 1902
7   Manwood, op cit
8   Coke, op cit
9   Turner, J. G., *Select Pleas of the Forest*, Selden Society, 1901
10 Bazeley, Margaret L., 'The Extent of the English Forest in the 13th Century', *Trans Roy Hist Soc*, 4th Series, IV, 1921, 140–72
11 Petit-Dutaillis, C., *Studies and Notes Supplementary to Stubbs' Constitutional History*, II : The Forest, 1935, 149

12 (a) Neilson, Nellie, 'The Forest', Ch IX of *The English Government at Work 1327–36*, 1940
    (b) Wright, Elizabeth C., 'Common Law in the Thirteenth Century English Royal Forests', *Speculum*, III, Apl 1928, 2, 166–91
    (c) Stenton, Doris M., *English Society in the Early Middle Ages (1066–1307)*
    (d) Pettit, P. A. J., *The Royal Forests of Northamptonshire*, 1968

13 Hart, C. E., M.A. Thesis, University of Bristol, iii, iv
14 Turner, op cit, 138
15 Powicke, M., *King Henry III and the Lord Edward*, 1947, 71
16 Hart, C. E., *Royal Forest*, 1966, 14
17 See many references in Neilson, op cit, 395, n.2
18 C.66, 1272–81, 237
19 Turner, op cit, lxix, n.4, and 66
20 Manwood, op cit, 8. *Cf* Turner, op cit, xxxvii, n.4
21 *Statutes of the Realm*, I, 243
22 Petit-Dutaillis, op cit, 207, 219
23 Hart, M.A. Thesis, loc cit, xli–lvi
24 C.66, 10 Edw I, m.22; *Cal C.66*, 1281–92, 2
25 E32/32
26 C.53, 1257–1300, 165, 12 April 1271
27 *I.P.M.*, 45 Hen III, 20; 13 Edw I, 8; 19 Edw II, 32; E32/32, m.4
28 E32/32, m.4
29 E32/30, m.12d
30 C.54, 5 Edw II, m.28
31 Ibid
32 Ibid 19 Edw I, m.3, 14 Edw II, m.8
33 In Dean the verderers for some centuries received a fee doe and a fee buck, and on one occasion in 1656 they each received £10 (Wade's A/cs in SP18, 1656–7, 130, 155, No 102)
34 Turner, op cit, xx; *Rot Litt Claus*, I, 486
35 C.54 11 Hen IV, m.18; 13 Hen IV, m.8. For appeal against unlawful discharge, see Manwood, op cit, 352
36 Coke, op cit, 312
37 Ibid
38 E32/30, m.28d
39 Manwood, op cit, ed 1615, 188–9
40 Ibid op cit, 189–90

41 Ibid 190
42 Ibid 190b
43 E32/30, m.39
44 Gloucester City Liby, L.F.6.2, fos 3, 5
45 GRO, D36
46 Bazeley, Margaret L, 'The Forest of Dean in its Relations with the Crown during the twelfth and thirteenth centuries', *BGAS*, 1910, 214–16
47 E32/28, 29, 30
48 Hart, M.A. Thesis, loc cit
49 Bazeley, op cit, 'The Forest of Dean . . .', 94, 96
50 Ibid, 87, 88
51 C.54, 39 Hen III, i, m.3
52 E32/322
53 E32/30, m.6, 10d, 13, 25d, 38d
54 C.66, 1272–81, 429
55 Ibid 435
56 E32/30, m.16, 17, 22
57 Hart, *Royal Forest*, 15, n.87
58 C.54, V, 3; IV, 4; C.62, VI, 1267–72, 28
59 E372, 36 Hen III
60 E32/332
61 Wright, op cit, *Common Errors in History*, 2nd Series, 1947, 7, 8

Two: The Forest Eyre of 1282 and the Verderers to 1633

In *Domesday* (1086) no account was given of the central portion of the territory between the Severn and Wye in west Gloucestershire which later became known as the Forest of Dean. The king's demesne woods and pasture lands were simply referred to as 'forest', without a name but associated with the lands called 'Dene' (now represented by Mitcheldean, Abenhall, and Littledean). Forest extended up to some 100,000 acres (*Fig 2*), and although not delimitated in *Domesday*, in the north-west it extended in to Herefordshire, including the wood of *Rosse*, and some woodland pertaining to the manor of Cleeve, one mile south-west of Ross-on-Wye. Hewelsfield, and Wyegate between St Briavels and Newland, was 'by command of the King in his forest'. Churcham and Morton towards Gloucester were 'in the forest', and 'the Church had its hunting there in three hayes, in the time of King Edward [the Confessor]'. One virgate of Little Taynton lay 'in the forest'. This and other information in the same survey confirms that much of the territory between the two rivers as far north as the neighbourhoods of Ross-on-Wye, Newent and Gloucester was designated forest.[1] Its administration at the time of the survey was under William fitzNorman: 'The same William holds in Dene 2 hides and 2 virgates and a half. Three thegns, Godric, Elric and Ernui, held them in the time of King Edward . . . [who] . . . granted these lands quit of geld for keeping the forest.' At some time before 1130, the financial responsibility for the whole of the Forest of Dene (later, Dean) passed into the hands of the fitzNorman family. From *c* 1130 the administration was centred at St Briavels Castle (*Plate p 67*), and in Stephen's reign William of Dene was confirmed in his *ministerium* or service of the Forest.[2]

During Stephen's wars, supervision passed to Miles, sheriff of Gloucestershire, to whom Matilda later granted the Forest and castle, but in 1155 they were resumed by Henry II who placed them in the custody of ferm-paying constable-wardens who had the co-operation of many forest officials, as related in Chapter 1.

The Verderers to 1282

The earliest allusion to the office of verderer of the Forest of Dean is in 1216,[3] when the verderers together with other forest officials were ordered to be intendant and responsible to the new warden, John of Monmouth. A similar order in 1224 was addressed to

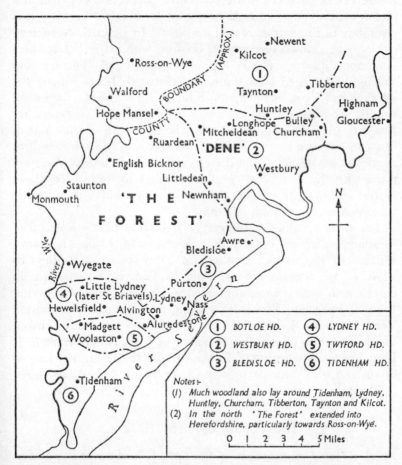

Fig 2. 'The Forest' and its neighbouring Hundreds at Domesday (1086)

them in connection with the constableship of Roger de Clifford.[4] The verderers' status in Dean was sometimes different from those in other forests, in as much as their duties and powers, and their contact with the Crown, were on occasion curtailed and over-shadowed by the constable-warden, though it is not fully evident how far they were subordinate to him. Usually verderers were apart from the normal administrators of forest—elected (as now in Dean alone) under the supervision of the sheriff—and often acting as a restraint on the warden and his subordinates in the interests of the Crown. It was the practice of the king to keep the verderers informed of his orders for gifts or sales of trees and undergrowth.[5] All removals or use of trees were 'by view and testimony of the verderers and foresters'.[6] In Dean the verderers' duties were unusually complex because within the Forest there was much mining of iron ore, and a little coal. The ore was smelted and forged with the aid of charcoal, hence among the inhabitants there were many miners, furnacemen, forgemen, smiths, woodcutters, and charcoal-burners. The verderers re-leased to the Free Miners trees for the timbering of their mines. On one occasion they arbitrated between the constable and an aggrieved inhabitant;[7] and there is only one instance of disagree-ment with the constable,[8] and one with a forester-of-fee,[9] both in the interests of accused persons. The verderers occasionally acted in a manner similar to coroners.[10]

The earliest named verderers[11] are those in 1221—Richard of Westbury, Richard of Blaisdon, Richard of Aston [Ingham], William of Helyun [of Lassingham], and Ralph of Rodley. In 1246, of the aforementioned only William of Helyun was in office, with new colleagues—Henry Haket, Philip Bauderun, John of Bykerton, Walter of Pulton, and William of Dunny.[12] Verderers who joined in the eyre of 1258[13] were Haket, Bauderun, John of Bykerton, Walter of Pulton, and William le Bret. Verderers who joined in the eyre of 1270[14] are not named in the roll, but those of subsequent years are named hereunder (*passim*).

The Forest Eyre of 1282

Much detailed information on the operation of forest law is con-tained in the Latin roll (*Plate p 50*) of the eyre held for Dean in

1282,[15] for which the preliminaries began with Edward I's writ to the sheriff of Gloucestershire 25 November 1281 :[16]

Touching the eyre for the pleas of the forest : summons :

The King to the sheriff of Gloucestershire greeting. Summon by good summoners the archbishops, bishops, abbots, priors, earls, barons, knights and all free tenants having lands or tenements within the metes of our forest in your jurisdiction, and from each vill of your county being within the metes of our forest four men and the reeve and the foresters of the vills, and all others who are wont and ought to come before our justices for the pleas of the forest, that they be at Gloucester in the octave of St Hilary next coming before our beloved and liege Luke de Tany, Adam Gurdon, Richard de Crepping and Peter de Lenche whom we constitute our justices in eyre for this turn for the pleas of the forest in the said county to hear and do what we command touching those things which belong to the aforesaid pleas. Also cause to come before the same our justices all our foresters and verderers both those who now are and those who have been foresters and verderers after the last pleas of the forest, with all their attachments both of vert and venison which after the last pleas of the forest have arisen and have not yet been determined, namely both of those attached who dwell within the metes of the forest and of those who dwell outside the forest.

And cause to come before the same our justices the regarders of your jurisdiction so that they have there their Regard marked with their seals, and all our agisters of the same your jurisdiction with all agistments. And have there the summoners and this writ.

Witness, the King at Westminster 25 November [1281]

Acting on the writ, the sheriff arranged for the making of a regard (infra) by regarders who are named in Appendix I. Another writ, 15 December 1281, gave notice that William Beauchamp, the earl of Warwick, Patrick de Cadurcis, Thomas bishop of Hereford, and the abbot of Tintern were, fortunately for them, quit of summons.[17] The aforementioned Luke de Tany, justice of forest south of Trent, Adam Gurdon, Richard de Crepping, and Peter de Lenche were appointed itinerant justices 18

January 1282. Tany, justice of forest south of Trent since 10 June 1281, had previously been constable of Tickhill and Knaresborough—about which time as 'a fierce man' he had beheaded some of his captives after conviction, but in 1270 had obtained a stay of any proceedings which might be taken against him. He had been seneschal of Gascony *c* 1271. Gurdon, keeper of the forest of Alice Holt, had previously been forester of Woolmer in Hampshire, 'one of the leaders of the South', and castellan of Dunster. De Crepping and de Lenche were justices in other parts of the country. The notification of their appointment reads :[18]

> Touching itineration for the pleas of the forest.
>
> The King to the archbishops, bishops, abbots, priors, earls, barons, knights, foresters, verderers, agisters, regarders and all others in Gloucestershire, greeting. Know that we constitute, set apart and appoint our men Luke de Tany, Adam Gurdon, Richard de Crepping and Peter de Lenche for itinerating for this turn for the pleas of the forest in the aforesaid county. And so we order you that to the same our liege men as our justices in eyre for the pleas of the forest there, in all things belonging to those pleas, you be attendant and answerable as in other eyres for the pleas of the forest in the aforesaid county is customary to be done. In witness whereof etc.
>
> Witness, the King at Hayles 18 January [1282]

There was much concern in Dean in the winter of 1281 when, after a period of almost twelve years, the belated order for the holding of the eyre was made known. It began at Gloucester 20 January 1282. During the following ten weeks some one thousand people attended before the four itinerant justices; they included those who had offended since the last eyre, in 1270, and their many pledges, as well as several dozen relevant officials, named in Appendix I. With so many local people involved, the eyre was for several months the main concern of all in Dean— both high and low, clergy and laymen, nobles, and commons. It can be conjectured with what worry and trepidation many of the offenders and their pledges made the arduous journey to Gloucester to await trial and judgement. The mass of evidence enrolled by the verderers in their courts of attachment, and the

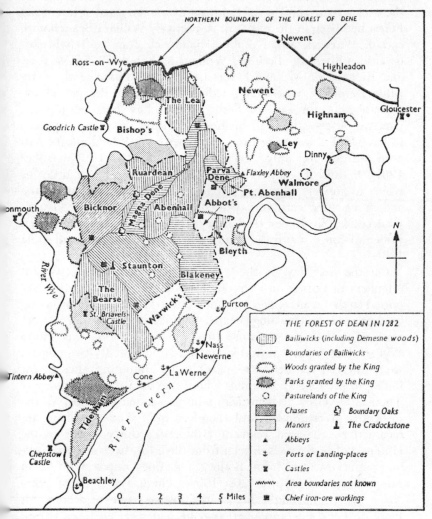

Fig 3. The Forest of Dean in 1282. It should be noted that the lower triangle formed by the two rivers up to the Cone and across to the Wye formed part of the Marchership of Striguil

detailed information in the regard (*infra*), were presented to the justices, who had to deal with business which had arisen during the twelve years 1270 to 1281, during which the wardenship of the Forest had been in the hands of respectively William Beauchamp, earl of Warwick and Ralph of Sandwich. The earl (with his deputies Osbert de Berford, William le Blund, Philip Wyther, and Richard de Muleford) was frequently accused at the eyre, while Ralph of Sandwich (holding for part of the period the office of escheator south of Trent) seems to have been left in comparative peace—although his deputy Walter de Snappe appears to have had a worrying time. Because Grimbald Pauncefot had been warden for only two months (appointed 16 November 1281), he and his deputy, Alexander of Bicknor, had little for which to answer. The justices had not only to bear in mind the actions of three constable-wardens but also those of de Tany's predecessor, Sir Roger de Clifford the younger, who had been justice of forest south of Trent from 1 August 1270 until June 1281.

On the first day of the eyre, 20 January 1282, fifty-eight offenders in respect of venison 'offered themselves', ie they reported to the justices, and two men offered themselves for having transgresssed by burning heath. Twenty-seven offenders were essoined, ie excused, because they were dead; one was Philip Wyther, late deputy constable and verderer. Seventy-two persons were amerced for defaults—possibly for non-appearance or for failing to produce an offender whom they had pledged; one was Thomas Deversey of Ruardean who was stated to be before the justices at Westminster and therefore quit. The defaulters are recorded by the four relevant Hundreds: thirty-two from the Hundred of St Briavels, fifteen from Bledisloe, twelve from Westbury, and thirteen from Botloe. The fines imposed on them ranged from 6d (2½p) to 20s (100p). Thomas de Pirie of Worcestershire was brought before the justices, one of whom, Sir Peter de Lenche, complained that he had received threats from him to life and limb. However, Thomas pledged peace to Sir Peter and found four pledges, one being Grimbald Pauncefot, warden of Dean.

An early act of the justices was the receipt of names of attorneys duly appointed to answer for their clients; among those thus represented were some of the abbots and priors of the neigh-

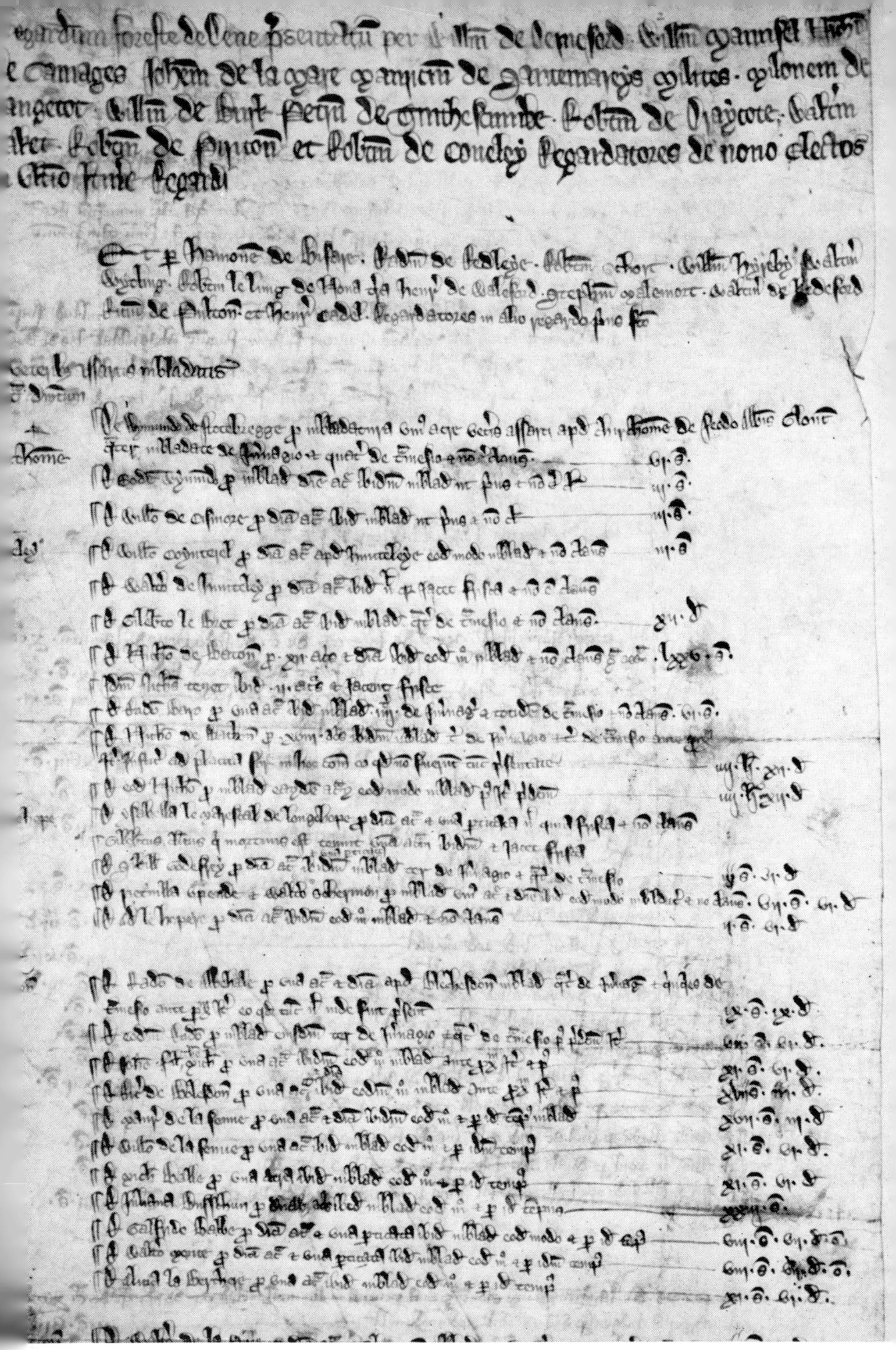

Page 49 The Regard for Dean of 1282: The beginning of the roll

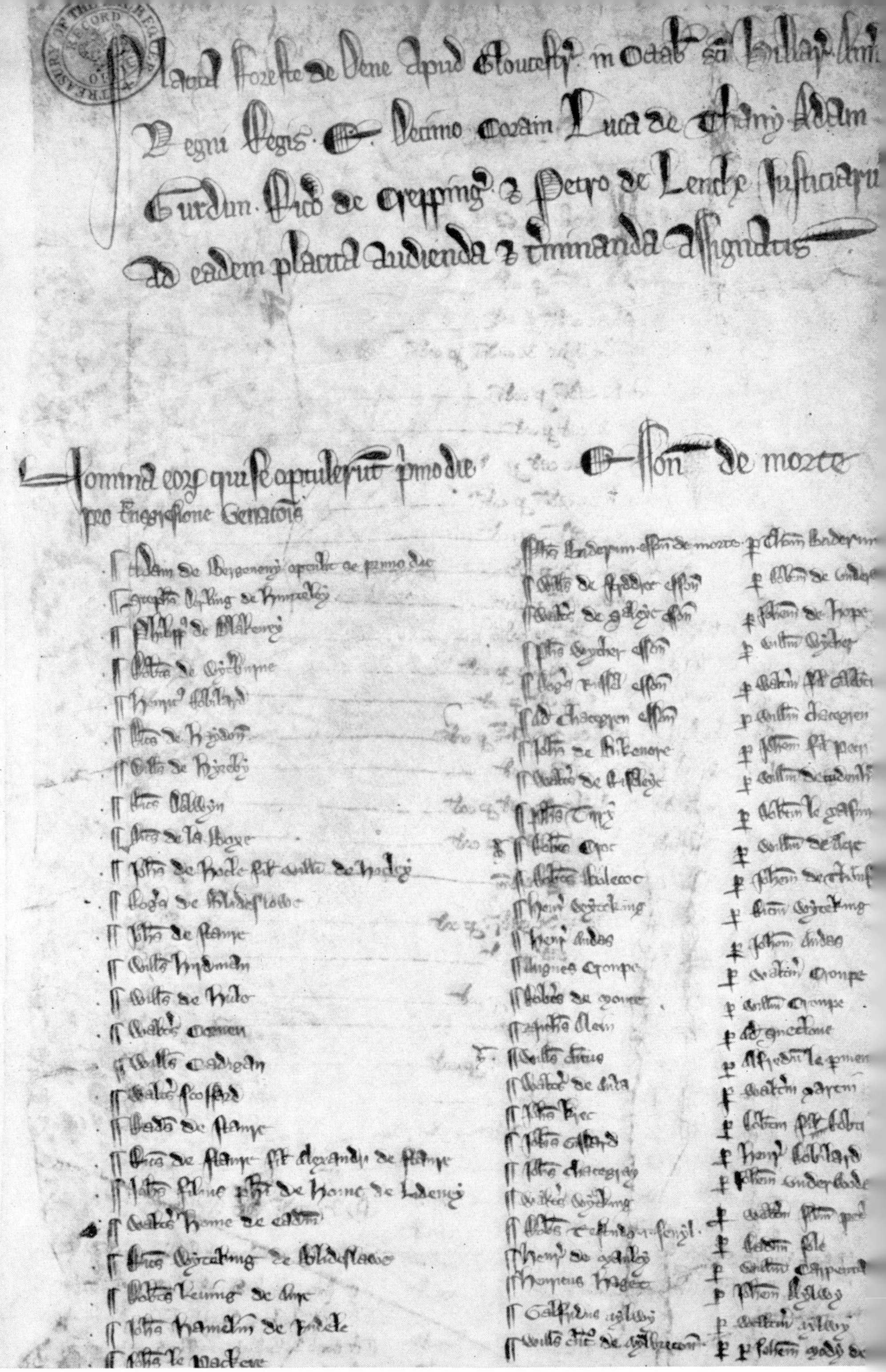
Placita Foreste de Dene apud Glouc' in Octab' sancti Hillarii Anno Regni Regis E. decimo coram Luca de Thany, Adam Gurdun, Ricardo de Crepping et Petro de Lenche Justiciariis ad eadem placita audienda et terminanda assignatis.

Nomina eorum qui se optulerunt primo die pro Transgressione Venacionis

Esson' de morte

Page 50 The Eyre for Dean 1282: The beginning of the roll

bourhood, foresters-of-fee, and sergeants-of-fee. The earl of Warwick, who had much land at Lydney, put in his place (*ponit loco suo*) someone 'to answer touching all things concerning which or of which he might be charged for the time when he was constable and warden', ie from at least 25 January 1271 to 28 September 1276. The same earl was ordered by the justices to cause those who had been his four deputies to attend on a given day. A day was likewise stated for the attendance of freeholders (*libere tenentes*) and representatives of vills.

THE PLEAS OF VERT

The vert offences in the roll number over four hundred; numerous lesser cases, involving fines up to 4d (1½p), had previously been adjudged by the verderers. Three hundred and seventy-two of the offenders were fined sums ranging from 6d (2½p) to 4 marks (£2.66), the analysis being :

Fine

		£	s	d
1	24s (£1.20)	1	4	0
139	6d (2½p)	3	9	6
90	12d (5p)	4	10	0
78	20d (8½p)	6	10	0
27	40d (16½p)	4	10	0
10	2s (10p)	1	0	0
5	5s (25p)	1	5	0
2	3s (15p)		6	0
3	4s (20p)		12	0
11	½ mark (33½p)	3	13	4
1	4s 8d (23½p)		4	8
3	1 mark (66½p)	2	0	0
1	20s (100p)	1	0	0
1	4 marks (£2.66)	2	13	4
372		32	17	10 (£32.89)

In addition, £13.91 had previously been received, chiefly by the deputy constables, making a total of £46.90. Of the remaining forty offenders, the fine on one is illegible, three were 'in mercy' (ie liable to punishment at the justices' discretion), one 'had nothing', one was a fugitive because of a venison offence, two were noted as 'fined elsewhere', one was 'condoned', another

D

pardoned, two were poor, four were to be answered for by the earl of Warwick, eight were dead, and sixteen were absolved. In many cases the punishment inflicted seems very slight; for example, two offenders, who apparently made their living by illegally transporting timber and wood to Bristol were fined 6s 8d (33½p) and 1s (5p) respectively; they would have been dealt with more severely if they had not been poor. Other habitual evil-doers were fined from 20d (8½p) to 5s (25p) each. The penalty for carrying off an oak from the royal demesne was 3s 4d (16½p), little more than the average selling value. The comparatively severe levy of 4 marks (*supra*) was imposed on Adam the reeve of St Briavels who, when carrying the seal as one of the appointed sellers of wood, had induced John the clerk of Dene to create a diversion by sounding his horn, while he, Adam, fraudulently sealed an oak. The same reeve was fined 10s (50p) for having had two charcoal pits for a week in the Defence Month. The damage done by charcoal-burners generally appears in forest rolls under the heading of 'waste', but under the heading of 'vert' there was a case in which an offender, attached for making charcoal in the king's wood of Haywood for two days without a warrant, was fined 2s (10p), in addition to 2s 4d (11½p), the value of the charcoal.

The language in which the pleas of vert are recorded is formal; often the nature of the offence is not fully stated, and the trespasser is merely stated to be liable for a small sum of money for vert (*pro viridi*). Where the offence was committed in the king's demesne, the additional words *in dominico* were entered; sometimes offences are stated to have occurred *extra dominico*. In other cases the fine is simply *pro plegio*—presumably where pledges have failed to produce or restrain a trespasser. Some offenders were fined both for vert and for pledging. Among those misdeeds given more explicitly were: cutting branches (*exbrancatura*), for a sapling (*bletrone*), for uprooting an oak, for a beech, for underwood (*viridi de subbosco*), for assarting thorns, for barking a lime, and for lopping a beech. Five cases concerned sealing of oaks with false seals. A misdeed perpetrated by night was treated as more serious than one by day.

On occasion it was acknowledged on the roll that the deputy constable had, quite rightly, received fines exacted during the interim of the eyres. Two verderers were fined 12d (5p) concerning pledging; the same two, with another verderer, were in mercy because they took insufficient pledges for attachment for vert in the king's demesne, by which the king had suffered serious loss. Two verderers although not fined, were recorded as having altered their roll 'insofar as they took out the names of the living and put in the names of the dead, as is apparent in their rolls'.

There are cases where waggons, boats, and oxen had been temporarily confiscated, together with goods which were the object of attachment: an offender fined 20d (8½p) for taking an oak by night had paid the deputy constable 36s (£1.80) for the tree, the waggon and six oxen; a second, attached with two loads of charcoal in the demesne by night, paid 11s (55p) for the price of the charcoal and two horses; and a third had paid 6d (2½p) because he did not have the price of the horses which he pledged. In a fourth case two offenders were before the justices 'for the price of a certain boat which belonged to a certain unknown Welshman, and wood found in the same, whence the pledges were 12s which the constable received and for which let him answer'; a note followed, reading 'Alibi—because they did not have before the justices the price as they had pledged'.

Another case concerned six offenders, each fined 6d (2½p), attached with four waggons and thirty-two oxen carrying four oaks from the king's demesne in the bailiwick of Blakeney— 'which oaks Henry Mauley then rector of the church of Awre, who is now dead, had said he claimed as housebote and heybote for the houses belonging to his church, and for which he found pledges to answer before the justices, and now on the first day he was essoined for death; but because it is in no way clear to the justices that any rector there was entitled to have such a delivery of right by which the same could not be claimed or warranted, therefore by the decision of the justices the aforesaid transgressors and their pledges are in mercy; and let all likewise answer touching half a mark of the price for the four oaks'. Sales of wood were inquired into, and there are two instances in the roll of the official sellers receiving acquittances for money properly paid to the warden.

Four men were before the justices because they had kept goats grazing 'within the covert of the forest against the assize and the defence'; no penalties were recorded, but the constable and the other officials were instructed not to allow any goats in the Forest.

The reeve of St Briavels was charged with embezzling at least 20s (£1.00) which he took for pigs agisted. Two men were fined 20s (£1.00) for building a house in the demesne.

The greatest causes of destruction of vert were the commission of 'waste' by the grantees of woods or by the foresters-of-fee in their bailiwicks, and by charcoal-burners and owners of small furnaces (bloomeries) and forges. Eight offenders, one of whom had since died, were named for taking wood for charcoal-burning from the king's demesne, and from the woods of Ross and Penyard of the bishop of Hereford, and from the Hope Mansel wood of the abbot of Gloucester. The names of the seven surviving offenders were each preceded by an illegible note of the fine. Three offences concerned malefactions in the wood of Walter of Huntley, in Richard Talbot's wood of Hope (Longhope), and in Alvington—a wood under grant to the prior of Llanthony, an Augustinian house in Monmouthshire; the justices dealt with these cases proving that their jurisdiction extended to woods granted within forest. One of the king's woodwards was presented for a transgression he made in the demesne. Two of Talbot's woodwards were fined for destruction in his wood of Hope, for which he, too, was called to account. The abbot of Tintern's wood of Harthill, taken into the king's hands because of a misdeed of his woodward, was released on payment of ½ mark (33½p). The Pleas of Vert end with the following incomplete memorandum :

Be it remembered that William Beauchamp, earl of Warwick answers nothing of a Court of Attachment of vert [lac] touching the custody of the bailiwick of the Forest of Dean, to wit, after the octave of Easter in the fourth year of King Edward [I] up to the Thursday next [lac] of St Lawrence of the same year—whereupon there is to be a conference. And Ralph of Sandwich answers nothing of attachment touching vert from the feast of St Michael of the same year [illeg] of the same bailiwick up to the Ash Wednesday next following, to wit in the fifth year.

THE PLEAS OF VENISON

These serious offences, which cover eighteen membranes of the roll, were many and varied, and ranged over the whole of the twelve-year period from the last eyre, in 1270. The first offence enrolled commenced with the words, 'It is presented and proved (*conuictum*) by the foresters-of-fee, the sergeants-of-fee, and the verderers'; all are named in Appendix I. Subsequent enrolments commence with the abbreviated phrase, 'It is presented &c.' Walter de Snappe joined in or answered concerning those offences perpetrated during the time he was deputy to Ralph of Sandwich.

The first venison case concerned an offence perpetrated jointly by a groom and two sub-foresters of the forester-of-fee of Blakeney bailiwick. The groom was attached on the night of 5 July 1271 with half a deer; the other half was found by the verderers the following day in the lodgings of his two accomplices. All three, as well as the owner of the lodgings who received the two foresters, were imprisoned by the deputy constable at St Briavels who eventually released them on bail of his own accord and apparently without writ. By the coming of the justices the two foresters were dead, the groom was not to be found and was put in exigence, the first of two stages in outlawry (*infra*), while the receiver was fined 2 marks (£1.33) and made to find pledges for his future good behaviour. Four vills which did not make full inquisitions as to the killing of the deer were in mercy, and their fine was noted as 'elsewhere', while the forester-of-fee who appointed the two foresters was to be adjudged. The constable, in this instance the earl of Warwick, answered concerning the releasing of the offenders by his deputy: his explanations were not accepted, but because he was a baron the justices could do no more than leave his judgement to the king (*infra*). This résumé is sufficient to give an indication of the complications of cases concerning venison, and the amount of detailed investigation and recording involved. The long delay in bringing the malefactors to judgement meant that full justice often could not be done. Many had died, some while in prison awaiting the advent of the justices. One had been killed while being captured; one had been hanged—presumably for a common law offence; and another was in the prison of the archbishop of Canterbury. Many offenders are noted as 'remaining in prison', while one offender had lain in Gloucester prison for two and a half years. Another offender was not brought to judgement because he was in the Holy Land.

When an offender was 'attached for venison' an inquisition was made by the four neighbouring vills, and he was put in prison to secure his appearance at the forest eyre. Usually the prison was that at St Briavels but sometimes that at Gloucester. The offender could subsequently apply for a writ, obtainable only from the king through his justice of forest or the sheriff of the county, whereupon he was delivered by the deputy constable to pledges pursuant to such a writ, the charge for which was from ½ mark (33½p) to 20s (£1.00). It is obvious from several presentments that poor offenders were unable to raise such sums. Furthermore, there must have been considerable difficulty in obtaining pledges who would make themselves responsible for producing the accused at the next eyre : those who undertook this obligation ran great risk of incurring fine on one plea or another, such as the elusiveness of persistent malefactors. The pledge was recorded simply 'that from henceforth &c'; however, one pledge reads *quod de cetero non erit malefactor nec receptator predictorum malefactorum nec aliorum in foresta.* One hundred and fifteen offenders obtained 759 pledges for their future good behaviour. Twelve was the usual number of pledges required, but by the time of the eyre often only eight, nine, ten or eleven, are mentioned —the others presumably being deceased or not found. Sometimes the constable or his deputy had released offenders without a writ, and the constable was asked to explain the irregular action. In the roll there are fines on 313 people relating to pledges who had failed to produce their man or had been unable to prevent him from continuing his ill deeds; even if such offender was dead, his mainpernors were fined a range of from 12d (5p) to 1 mark (66½p), the analysis of the total being :

	Fine	£	s	d
12	collectively	2	0	0
5	collectively		3	0
208	12d (5p)	10	8	0
54	20d (8½p)	4	10	0
3	2s (10p)		6	0
17	40d (16½p)	2	16	8
13	½ mark (33½p)	4	6	8
1	1 mark (66½p)		13	4
313		25	3	8 (£25.18)

Thirty-two others were named, of whom ten were dead, thirteen were pardoned, while nine are not defined. If the trespasser had never been attached, or, having been attached failed to appear at the eyre, the constable-warden, or the sheriff of the district in which the offender lived or had property, was ordered to cause him to appear—sometimes on a stated day, but usually 'from day to day'. If the trespasser could not be found and had no property by which he could be distrained, the justices directed him to be exacted in the county court, and if he failed to appear in due course, he was outlawed: the usual form was *exigatur et utlagetur*—'let him be exacted and outlawed'. If the trespasser was in holy orders (*infra*), the direction from the justices was to the bishop of his diocese, but if he had no benefice he was exacted and outlawed as if he were a layman.

When the trespasser appeared, if the presentment was in proper form, the justices usually adjudged that he be sent to prison for the purpose of securing payment of his fine, and the record usually continued: 'Afterwards . . . being brought out from prison, he made fine'; sometimes the enrolment of a plea ended with the words 'he is detained in prison'. The final stage after paying fine was for the trespasser to obtain a fresh group of pledges to hold themselves responsible for his future good behaviour. Sometimes the fine is not legible in the roll, but is shown on another membrane recording lists of fines; such lists supplement the deficiencies in this respect of the enrolment of the pleas of venison. It would seem that the clerk commonly began enrolling the proceedings of the eyre before they were actually concluded. Frequently trespassers were pardoned because they were poor, and the justices seem to have taken into consideration the time which a prisoner had spent in gaol before he had been released by writ to pledges until the next eyre.

Members of the whole hierarchy were transgressors. Constables, knights, foresters, woodwards, sub-foresters, burgesses (of Monmouth and Bristol), and reeves were among the malefactors of venison. Constables were not the only officials who had to answer for the deeds of their deputies: foresters-of-fee were called to account for their foresters, owners of private woods for their woodwards. It was not only the perpetrator of an offence against venison who was attached; so was anyone who was privy (*consenciens*) to the malefactions. To be an inciter was as wrong as actually taking venison. Even to take venison which had been killed by wolves or in other ways was an offence. The number of venison offenders whose cases were concluded by the time the eyre was prorogued, 12 April 1282, was 228. Of these, 29 were dead, 5 were not found, and the position of 14 not defined; of the remainder, 36 were put in exigence, 11 were sent to prison, 4 were quit by the king's writ, 14 were pardoned of the king's alms because they were poor, and 8 were to answer before the king or parliament. The remaining 107 were fined thus:

		£	s	d
	Fine			
2	2s (10p)		4	0
23	20s (£1.00)	23	0	0
22	40s (£2.00)	44	0	0
10	100s (£5.00)	50	0	0
11	½ mark (33½p)	3	13	4
12	1 mark (66½p)	8	0	0
1	1½ marks (£1.00)	1	0	0
10	2 marks (£1.33)	13	6	8
1	2½ marks (£1.66)	1	13	4
6	5 marks (£3.33)	20	0	0
3	6 marks (£4.00)	12	0	0
1	10 marks (£6.66)	6	13	4
1	12 marks (£8.00)	8	0	0
4	collectively 15 marks (£10.00)	10	0	0
107		201	10	8	(£201.53)

For a single offence of taking, receiving or selling venison the fine ranged from 20s (£1.00) to 2 marks (£1.33); accustomed malefactors were made to pay at least two or three times more, sometimes as much as 100s (£5.00). The two fines (*supra*) of 2s (10p), were on people who took venison which had been mauled by wolves. The presentments only rarely give information as to the methods of taking venison. Usually various types of dog, hound, and mastiff had been used. Other offenders had used bows and arrows, crossbows (*balistis*), nets (*retibus*), snares (*laqueis*), and 'other engines' (*ingeniis*). In some cases, the death of the deer had been caused by wolves, or by drowning. Five, hunted by the household of Edmund the king's brother, were afterwards found torn in pieces by swine (*porcis delacerate*), while nine others were wounded by the household of William de Valence (half brother of Henry III), but survived. One offender was attached with fifty hides of fawns. On occasion the venison is noted as having been taken 'in the time of grease' (*temporus pinquedinis in autumpno*). *Pinquedo*, the season for hunting the hart and the buck, extended from 3 May to 14 September. The word *pinquedo* should be translated as 'grease', the period during which the harts and bucks were hunted being known as 'the time of grease'.

VILLS WHICH DID NOT COME FULLY

The four vills neighbouring the place of the malefaction had the irksome duty of making inquisition whenever an injury to the venison was made known. Sometimes these inquisitions were made on the same day as that on which a court of attachment was held; but it was the usual practice for the inquisition to be held before the verderers and foresters soon after the offence had been discovered. Twenty-one vills were fined for not coming fully, ie either for not answering the justices' summons to appear on a fixed day or for not finding out all that the justices wished to know. Another vill, Hewelsfield, though twice in mercy for the same offence, was not fined. It is not possible to tell from the roll how often attendance of vills had been required during the period, but there are over a hundred entries relating to venison offences in the roll : these do not of course correspond exactly with the number of inquisitions held; in some cases it is obvious that no inquisition had been needed, because the crime was patent. Fines for not coming fully usually ranged from ½ mark (33½p) to one mark (66½p), but there are three instances of the fine being 40d (16½p). The fines on 21 vills amounted to £8 10s (£8.50), 3 being fined 40d (16½p), 12 fined ½ mark (33½p), and 6 fined 1 mark (66½p). There is no means of estimating the number of residents in a vill among whom the fine was distributed, or the means of raising the amount of the fine, for instance whether a levy was made by a reeve or a bailiff.

CASES BEFORE THE KING OR PARLIAMENT

The justices dealt out summary punishment to offenders, referring only pleas in which earls and barons were concerned for a further hearing before the king (*coram rege*) or before parliament : the privilege of 'trial by peers' had been reserved to earls and barons in *Magna Carta*. Among the cases concerning venison thus referred were those of Sir John Tregoz (a baron), Humphrey de Bohun earl of Hereford, Hugo Lovel, and Richard de Riparia. The justices had especial difficulty in connection with matters concerning Roger Bigod earl of Norfolk and Suffolk (earl Marshal and Marcher Lord of Striguil—later Chepstow), and concerning William Beauchamp earl of Warwick (late warden of the Forest). As to the earl of Warwick, the justices ordered him to produce on a day stated his four deputies to answer for the time he was warden touching the many persons attached who were released from St Briavels Castle with insufficient pledges; and to answer for his deputy, William le Blund who placed in office as forester in the bailiwick of Blakeney a man who proved to be an accustomed poacher, and for appointing a riding-forester who took venison. To ensure that the earl fully answered, the justices ordered the sheriff of Gloucestershire to take into the king's hands all the earl's lands and tenements, goods and chattels so that neither the earl nor another through him might lay hands on the same, and that he, the sheriff, answer touching the issues. The earl was given a day to come before the justices, and a marginal note *venit* implies that he appeared either in person or by attorney. The matters were to be referred to the king, together with certain actions of the abbot of Tintern. These and other cases referred by the justices were never proceeded with on account of the Welsh War. Edward I issued instructions for all legal proceedings to be stayed concerning those who were following him to Wales. The two earls mentioned above, besides Lovel, de Riparia, de Bohun, and Tregoz were ordered to perform military service in person. They did so, with the exception of de Riparia who was infirm. There is no record of any case referred at the 1282 eyre ever being brought before the king or parliament.

THE REGARD

The regard for the 1282 eyre (*Plate p 49*) was made by five knights and seven other men, all named in Appendix I. Its compilation took several months, but it is dated 11 February 1282.[19] There is no record of the days on which the justices considered this very long and comprehensive regard, and indeed by the time the eyre was prorogued, 12 April 1282, the only subjects upon which they had adjudicated were those of assarts, purprestures, forges, ports, boats, and the woods in one only (Abenhall) of the nine baili-wicks. There is no evidence of judgement relevant to other sub-jects reported upon by the regarders, such as honey, eyries of hawks, coal, iron ore, and dogs. Instead of enrolling the answers of the regarders one by one and chapter by chapter, the clerk of the justices drew up, as usually was the case, an abstract divided into paragraphs which between them contained all the information required. Each paragraph contained a series of for-mal entries, each of which related to a particular assart, purpre-sture, or act of waste, and was noted with the fine.

Under the heading 'Of old assarts' the justices dealt with the assarts made in the Forest since the last regard (1270). Some had been made in the king's woods, and others in granted woods with-in the metes and bounds of the Forest. The punishment for the wrong was a fine; but the person who held the assart was also obliged to pay an additional sum as acknowledgement for the crops sown and raised upon it. The regarders had viewed the assarts and estimated the acreage; and they reported of whose fee they were, who held them, and how many times they had been sown with winter corn (*iuernagium*) and with spring corn (*tramesium*). The sum for sowing winter corn was 1s (5p) an acre, and for spring corn 6d ($2\frac{1}{2}$p); if the land was fallow, no charge was made. All these charges were dependent upon the assarts not being enclosed; if enclosed the assart was clearly a purpresture and the levies were higher, and the dykes, fences or hedges were ordered to be thrown down. Usually the assarts seem to have been sown alternately with winter and spring corn, and to have remained fallow for a year after a certain number of crops had been raised. The tenant of an assart was usually allowed to retain the land (under the fee of his 'overlord') subject to his accounting for the crops at each eyre. Thus the new assarts of one eyre became the old assarts at the next and subsequent eyres.

Instances are given where assarts had not been presented at the previous eyre, and in these cases two sets of charges were levied. The usual size of the assarts was ½ to 2 acres, but there are examples of 18 acres and 20 acres. They had usually been cropped eight or nine times, and, allowing for fallowing, it confirms that no previous regard had been made for ten to twelve years. The assarts are set out in the regard by vills, and the amercements total £98 5s 9d (£98.29). The most serious case was that of Sir Henry of Dene a sergeant-of-fee who, with his father, had assarted for many years. He was fined £7 arrears, but was allowed to continue the cultivation of his assarts at an annual rent of £1 6s 6d (£1.32).

'Of new assarts' the amercements total £238 17s (£238.85). The fine for small assarts was 1s (5p) or 1s 8d (8½p) in addition to the usual charges for having sown the land with corn. Of the total fines, £45 was imposed upon the earl Marshal for sixty acres of assart held by him although within his fee. The person most heavily fined was the abbot of Tintern who had £168 6s (£168.30) levied upon him for various assarts totalling 352 acres made and occupied by his predecessor. The illegal assarts in all cases were taken into the king's hand, and any dykes, fences or hedges were ordered to be thrown down.

The next heading in the regard was 'Of new purprestures', ie illegal enclosures of or encroachments upon lands within the Forest, such as the enlarging of a curtilage; or the erecting of a mill; or again the making up of a fishpond within the covert. The purprestures in the regard included the making of a marlpit, the obstructing of a public way by a ditch, and the occupying of land; the fines respectively were 1s (5p), 2s (10p), and 6d (2½p). Two houses illegally built were ordered to be thrown down, as was also a grange. The abbot of Flaxley had made a new high hedge between his land and an adjoining wood; this was said to be against the assize of the forest because wild beasts could not enter and leave freely, but the only judgement was that 'it should be measured'. Furthermore, the abbot of Tintern had built a mill and a sheepfold; they were ordered to be thrown down, but a respite was given so that the abbot could appear before the king. The fines under this heading amounted to 19s 7d (98p), but some cases had not been concluded.

Under the heading 'Of the King's woods and the destructions

made in the same', the regarders had viewed the king's demesne woods and reported upon any destructions made therein. This was done for each of the nine bailiwicks, but by the time of the prorogation of the eyre only the woods in the bailiwick of Abenhall had been dealt with by the justices. The regarders reported that therein the king's wood of Oures had been wasted anew by the forester-of-fee, by his having taken trees to his own use. They had found 122 stumps of oaks felled since the last eyre, of which they valued 42 at 3s 6d ($17\frac{1}{2}$p) each, 40 at 2s 6d ($12\frac{1}{2}$p), and 40 at 1s 6d ($7\frac{1}{2}$p)—a total of £15 7s (£15.35). The custodian had also committed waste of the underwood to the extent of £5 by having had charcoal pits therein contrary to a prohibition made at the previous eyre. The same forester-of-fee had also wasted the king's wood of Haywood where 338 stumps of oaks had been found : 235 were oaks sold on the king's behalf which, added to 21 others accounted for, meant that 82 oaks had been taken by the forester-of-fee and his foresters, and which the regarders valued 42 at 3s (15p) each and 40 at 2s (10p). The underwood had also been wasted, there having been found 345 'hearths' where charcoal-burning had taken place since the last eyre, and for which fines totalling £10 were levied. Similar waste had been committed in the king's woods of Wydenhaye, Barndemore, Gardino and Chestnuts within the same bailiwick. The forester-of-fee challenged the accusations of the regarders, and attempted to excuse himself. Whether he would have won his case if the eyre had not been prorogued is doubtful : failure to have done so would have meant fines in the region of several hundred pounds. The fines for the whole Forest under this head might have exceeded £1,000 if the war in Wales had not caused the adjournment of the pleas.

The king's demesne formed but a portion of the land within his Forest of Dean. The residue included extensive woods outside the demesne, over which the owners enjoyed, by the king's grant, the ordinary rights of property except that they could do nothing by which the woods would cease to afford shelter for the beasts of the forest, nor could they take or harm venison. Thus the owners could not 'assart, encroach by purpresture, or enjoy waste' without the king's licence, but usually they could take wood for fuel and for repairs to their property. They were obliged to have a woodward to protect the king's venison as well as to protect the granted wood. Any abuse of their rights and privileges were recorded in the regard as 'waste'. When the grantee of a wood which he had wasted had made fine for his wrongdoing, and another fine for having his wood returned, he was still bound to pay ½ mark (33½p) at every eyre until the cover was rehabilitated. Under the heading 'Of old waste of woods outside the demesne', fines of ½ mark (33½p) each were made on five grantees of woods—Walter of Huntley in respect of his wood between Birdwood and Lawardok, the abbot of Tintern for Harthill near Hewelsfield, the prior of Newent for his wood, William of Aston for Aston Ingham, and Bogo de Knovile for Kilcot. The prior of Llanthony next to Gloucester paid 2 marks (£1.33) for the redemption of his wood of Aylburton, the regarders having testified that the part wasted had regrown. The abbot of Gloucester similarly redeemed his woods of Birdwood and Hopemansel, by payment of 40s (£2.00). Walter of Huntley and Cecilia de Muchegros paid likewise 20s (£1.00) and one mark (66½p) respectively for their woods of Huntley and Taynton. The amercements touching 'old waste' totalled 4½ marks (£3.00).

Under the heading 'Of new waste of woods' the abbot of Gloucester was presented for waste in his wood of Ruddle; and the abbot of Flaxley in his woods of Littledean, Castiard, Timberhugge, and Welshbury. Both abbots were quit by the king's charter. The bishop of Hereford was likewise presented for his woods of Ross and part of Penyard; they were ordered to be taken into the king's hands but were subsequently replevied until such time as the pleas were continued. A similar concession was made to Richard of Heydon in Notwood (near Little London) and to the earl of Warwick in his woods of Ascumbe and Lydney. Other offenders were not so fortunate: Richard Talbot's woods of Haygrove in Eccleswell, Longhope, and part of Penyard were taken into the king's hands; and the same was the case in regard to Ralph of Abenhall's wood of Blaisdon. A grove wasted anew by Simon de Ribbesford, rector of Huntley, was taken into the king's hands as well as a grove in Littledean similarly wasted by Henry of Dene. Three woodwards in charge of Taynton wood were ordered to appear to answer concerning the deterioration of the same by sale during the three last years to the extent of 2½ marks (£1.66). Walter of Huntley was granted permission to fell a certain part of the dead trees and undergrowth in his wood next to the highway because doing so would obviate 'a certain bad transit and a repair of robbers'. The amercements touching 'new waste' totalled £3 13s 4d (£3.66). The park of Ley, held jointly by three knights, had not been wasted; and the abbot of Gloucester received special licence to fell part of his wood of Hope Mansel. Offences of both vert and venison within granted woods were dealt with in the same way as those in the king's demesne woods.

The justices were concerned at the destruction of the Forest by the taking of wood for 'forges', which also implied bloomeries for smelting iron ore. The regarders pointed out under the heading 'Of forges in the forest' that many itinerant forges were, and had been in Dean and that those who owned them had committed much waste concerning the trees, underwood and branches, thereby causing much deterioration in the cover. The holders of fifty-nine are named; they had held them for periods ranging from three months to ten years. The fines imposed ranged from 2s (10p) to £1 6s 8d (£1.33), and totalled £34 4s (£34.20). In addition, the abbot of Gloucester had held one forge for two years in his wood of Hope Mansel by licence of the king, but no damage had thereby been done to the Forest; a licensee of the abbot held another forge for the same period. There was no fine in either case. The abbot of Flaxley held under grant a forge with as free liberty to work as any of the forges which the king himself held.

'Of ports and boats' the regarders stated that there was an 'old port' at Purton on the Severn in which boats plied with wood and timber stolen by malefactors to the loss of the king and the damage of his Forest; seven owners of boats were fined, the sums for damage amounting to £4 5s (£4.25) and of fines to 7s (35p). Owners of six boats at the 'old port' of Lydney on the same river were likewise presented and fined £3 3s 8d (£3.18). A boat owner at the 'old port' of Allaston (now inland due to silting of the Severn) was also accused; he appeared, and for many transgressions he was adjudged to prison. The prior of Llanthony had on the Wye boats at his weir of Hadnock, and a boat at Bishopsweir. His boatmen were accused of being privy to the malefactors of venison and of aiding them in transport; also of stealing wood for sustaining the prior's former weir to the damage of 40s (£2.00) and to the latter weir of 1 mark (66½p). The prior was

ordered to appear to answer on 14 April. Similarly, William de
Valence was ordered to appear on the same day because he had
a boat at his weir on the Wye under The Doward in which his
boatmen likewise carried venison. Nine people who owned a
boat at the 'old port' of Beachley were presented as carriers of
illegal venison, and ordered to appear. Likewise, were two owners
of a boat at the 'old port' at Striguil bridge (on the Wye above
Chepstow), as well as the boatman at Tintern ferry, and eight
boatmen who had between them a boat at Aust ferry, on the
east bank of the Severn. The amercements under this heading
total £10 9s (£10.45).

The whole of the amercements under the regard amounted to
at least £587 15s 4d (£587.76) made up of :

	£	s	d	
Old assarts	98	5	9	
New assarts	238	17	0	
New purprestures		19	7	
Damage in the King's woods	200	0	0	(Estimated)
New waste of woods		Nil		
Old waste of woods	5	0	0	
Forges	34	4	0	
Ports and boats	10	9	0	
	587	15	4	(£587.76)

How much of this sum was actually paid by the offenders is a
matter for conjecture. The income was substantial, and the royal
profit from the Forest much increased thereby .

ILLICIT TRADE IN VENISON AND VERT

The proximity of Dean to two navigable rivers, the Severn
and the Wye, provided facilities for a widely extended trade in
illicit venison and wood. The regard named owners of boats
employed for the purpose. Bristol was the main destination; and
the names are given of those of its citizens who were receivers
of stolen venison. The burgesses of Bristol had obtained a charter
from Henry III granting that none of them should be called in
question for venison found within their walls, but the charter,
produced as evidence in connection with a case concerning a

Page 67 (above) St Briavels Castle, built c 1130; *(below)* A hunting horn used in the Forest of Dean—one of the two owned by Dr Cyril Hart

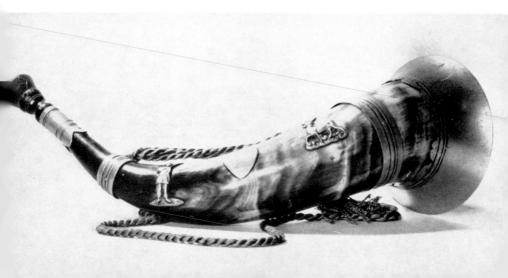

Page 68 Saxton's Map of the Forest of Dean, 1577

butcher in Bristol, bears no date, and was obviously regarded by the justices with suspicion. The citizens were ordered to delegate twelve good men to produce their charter *coram rege*, and proceedings were stayed pending the king's decision. Some illicit venison was secretly sold to a burgess of Bristol in exchange for green cloth of Ireland for summer tunics for foresters. Other illicit venison found its way to Monmouth, Goodrich Castle, and into Wales and Worcestershire.

THE CLERGY AS MALEFACTORS

'One of the worst evils of the later Middle Ages,' wrote Maitland,[20] 'was the benefit of clergy.' The section of the medieval church that was under least discipline was the numerous one of the unbeneficed priests, deacons, and clerks who were scattered about the country in many varieties of employment, often under no control beyond that of their lay employers. Sometimes they acted as private chaplains in castle or manor house, or as 'chantry priests' paid by laymen to say masses for the souls of departed relatives, and to perform other duties. Clerks, when they committed crimes of theft or murder, could plead benefit of clergy and thereby escape from the severe justice of the king to the lighter penances of the Spiritual Court. The Statute of Westminster the First (1275) provided that a prisoner 'clerk' must first be indicted before he could be claimed. However, there is no instance on the roll of benefit of clergy preventing justice being done by the forest officials, and there is no evidence that clemency of ecclesiastical courts tended to increase clerical criminality.

Generally, if a clerk accused of a forest trespass failed to make an appearance at the eyre the justices directed the bishop to cause the clerk to come; if he did not then appear the justices directed that he be exacted in the county court; and if he did not then come he was outlawed. If, however, the clerk duly appeared, the justices proceeded with his case just as if he were a layman—and could sentence him to prison—but if the bishop then claimed him as a clerk, the justices surrendered him as one convicted of an offence against forest law. He did not, however, escape punishment, but had to make fine just as if he were a layman. Frequently the forest records state that the clerk made fine, without noting that he had been delivered to the bishop.

E

Usually the clergy enjoyed immunity from the necessity of finding pledges for their appearance at the eyre when accused of offences against the venison, but they were liable to arrest when found in the act of trespassing in the forest.

One of the striking features of the forest pleas presented in the 1282 roll is the large number of clergy against whom charges were brought. It is not easy to explain this phenomenon. Usually their offence was against venison (but sometimes against vert) either by themselves taking or receiving venison in whole or part, or by aiding and abetting or sheltering malefactors. Almost all such clergy thus guilty were resident within the diocese of Hereford of which Dean at that time formed part. A rector, three vicars, two parsons, seven clerks, and six chaplains appear on the roll as malefactors of venison. The higher clergy were apparently well behaved, except in the management of the woods they held under grant, and in assarting. There is no mention on the roll of the case of Thomas bishop of Hereford who had taken in the Forest two wild boars and a wild sow without licence; the king had pardoned him in 1279.[21] Usually the clerics were fined in the normal way, but a clerk of Bristol was pardoned at the instance of the bishop of Bath because he was poor. Besides the foregoing clerical offenders there were the dean, precentor and a clerk of Hereford who were mainperned by a constable and a sergeant-of-fee to appear before the king or parliament regarding transgressions of venison whereof they were indicted in the previous eyre and for which they had not given satisfaction.

Instances of the mismanagement by clergy of woods held under grant are many. The prior of Llanthony had wasted his wood of Aylburton; he redeemed it by payment of 2 marks (£1.33). The prior of Newent and the abbot of Tintern had been accused in the previous eyre of wasting their respective woods of Newent and Harthill; they continued to pay $\frac{1}{2}$ mark ($33\frac{1}{2}$p) each until their woods became rehabilitated. The abbot of Flaxley had wasted his woods of Littledean, Chestnut, Timberhugge and Welshbury but was quit by charter. The abbot of Gloucester was likewise quit in respect of his wood of Ruddle. The bishop of Hereford had wasted his woods of Ross and Penyard but was excused until the eyre should be continued. The rector of Huntley had wasted his grove, and it was taken into the king's hands.

The clergy apparently had no qualms at making assarts. The

abbot of Tintern was fined £168 6s (£168.30) for 352 acres of various assarts. The Brothers of the House of the Infirm next to Striguil (St David's) were fined £1 15s (£1.75) for 12 acres. The rector of Huntley was in mercy for a purpresture, namely of occupying a parcel of land and wood, and building a house upon it. The abbot of Flaxley had raised a hedge around certain of his land; and it was ordered to be measured (under forest law, hedges, fences, and dykes were not to impede the movement of the king's beasts, and it was usual to supply leap-gates—a low gate which can be leaped by deer). The abbot of Tintern had erected a sheepfold and a mill on the boundary between the forest and the earl Marshal's Tidenham Chase; the case was ordered to go before the king. It would seem that the number of malefactions by clergy is not to be explained merely by the alleged large proportion of clergy to the lay population of medieval England.

THE EXTENT OF DEAN FOREST

The metes and bounds of Dean, as was the case in other forests, underwent many changes in the thirteenth century.[22] The Forest's extent was ascertained in preparation for the 1282 eyre, and the perambulation reads:

The limits of the Forest of Dean begin at Gloucester bridge and thus stretch by the main flow of the Severn going to as far as the place where the bank of the Wye falls into the Severn, and thus going up by the Wye as far as Striguil bridge. Going up thence by the Wye as far as Monmouth bridge, and going up thence by the Wye as far as the ford of Goodrich Castle, and thus as far as Dunnes Cross, and thus by a certain lane called Mersty as far as Alton, and thus by the stream of Alton as far as the public way coming from Ross as far as the oak outside Weston. And so by the King's highway beyond the bridge as far as a certain tree called Bolletree. And thus by the King's highway as far as the millpond of Buriton which is Richard Talbot's. And thus by the King's highway up to a certain cross called Luce Cross. And thus by the King's highway through the middle of Gorsley as far as Gorsley Ford. And thus going down by the brook as far as Oxenhall bridge. And thus by the King's highway as far as the prior of Newent's bridge. And by the same King's highway as far as Gloucester bridge.

A map showing the above limits of Dean Forest is given as *Fig 3*. It will be seen that the chase of Tidenham is included within the metes and bounds of the Forest; however, in the eyre roll a clear distinction was made between the Forest and the chase, when it was asserted that the latter was 'outside the county'. Nevertheless the justices ordered the chase to be taken into the king's hands on account of misdoings of the earl Marshal.

Although it is not clear from the above perambulation, the small park of Hadnock on the east bank of the Wye north of Monmouth was 'without the forest' (*extra forestam*); it had been granted by King John to John of Monmouth. Again, the chase of Penyard east of Ross-on-Wye, although included in the above perambulation, is stated in the roll to be 'without the forest' and 'deforested by the King, as it is said'. The vill of Huntsham in the loop of the Wye north of Symonds Yat is stated by the regarders as having 'been withdrawn from the Forest, and the men of that vill do not appear before the steward nor the verderers at the holding of inquisitions, and they have even failed to appear before the justices at their justice seat'. Many places are referred to in the roll as *in foresta*. It would seem from the absence of place-names that the central portion of the Forest was sparsely populated; it was most probably heavily wooded.

CHASES, PARKS, WARRENS AND GROVES

The intricacies of forest law as touching chases, parks and warrens have been noted elsewhere.[23] The 1282 roll throws little light on the matter. Deer started in Hadnock were not to be pursued into the Forest. The chase of Tidenham, belonging to Roger Bigod, earl of Norfolk and Suffolk, and earl Marshal, appears frequently in the roll, but its exact relation to the Forest is doubtful. It is included within the Forest in a perambulation of the regarders (*supra*) but on the roll it is stated that the riding forester of the earl Marshal in his chase of Tidenham is wont to come into the Forest with many others and take venison and return to the chase aforesaid, where he cannot be attached because it is 'outside the county'. The keeper (*parcarius*) of Tidenham was likewise indicted. The earl ignored the order of the justices to produce the malefactors under his protection or to appear in person, and in consequence directions were issued that his 'liberty' of Striguil (later, Chepstow), together with the lands of the earl in other counties, should be taken into the king's hands. The constable of St Briavels was ordered to cause Joan de Knovile to produce her warrant by which she claimed the liberty of the chase of Penyard, to the south-east of Ross-on-Wye. The references to parks at Hadnock, Ley, and Tidenham are the only ones in the roll. There are three records of grants of warren to the monks of St Peter's, Gloucester, and four instances of groves held under the king's licence, all subject to the usual restrictions concerning waste : two were taken into the king's hands on account of the bad custody of their holders.

GIFTS OF VENISON

The king's gifts of venison from his forests were numerous in the thirteenth century. For Dean the entries in the 1282 eyre roll do not fully cover the twelve year period since the 1270 eyre. For the second to ninth years of Edward I's reign the roll shows royal gifts chiefly to earls, bishops, and knights, totalling 79 bucks (10 alive), 20 does (10 alive), 3 hinds, and 22 harts. Authority for most of the gifts is recorded in the Close Rolls. The queen mother's hunters took, in the fifth year, 32 bucks, 2 harts and 4 roes : it was to be inquired whether or not she duly received the venison. Edmund the king's brother took during the first, sixth, seventh, eighth and ninth years 37 bucks, 2 does, 2 hinds, 2 harts, 3 roes, a fawn, 4 boars, and 3 sows, besides 50 other deer comprising bucks, does, and prickets of bucks (*prickettos damorum*). Most of the takings are noted as without warrant, but Edmund received the king's acquittance.[24] Nine bucks and does, and one hind were taken in the first year by William de Valence. In the same year two bucks and one hart were taken by Roger de Mortimer, one of the Keepers of England.

Edward I in the sixth year of his reign took 65 bucks by his hunters, of which 55 were delivered to his larderer, while six were delivered as tithe to the abbot of St Peter's, Gloucester. The remaining four, according to the constable, were eaten by the king's huntsmen and dogs. The total number of deer recorded in the roll as having been delivered as tithe to the abbot of St Peter's, Gloucester is thirteen. The justice of forest was apparently permitted to make gifts of venison : under 'prises and gifts of Sir Roger de Clifford' are noted 5 bucks, 13 does, and 2 roes, these being taken in the sixth, seventh and eighth years of the reign. Thus were accounted 357 deer, 4 boars and 3 sows. As to how far the justices were satisfied or otherwise with their investigations under this head the roll makes no comment except that attention was drawn to the fact that five beasts hunted by the household of the Lord Edmund were afterwards found torn in pieces by swine and that the household of William de Valence wounded nine beasts, but they survived. Perhaps where the king's near relations were concerned the justices felt it was unwise to go further, although no grounds can be discerned for doubting their impartiality.

RELIGIOUS HOUSES AS BENEFICIARIES

Several religious houses both within and around Dean received royal grants and privileges; and many of the charters are noted in the roll. Privileges enjoyed by the Cistercian monks of Flaxley Abbey, the only religious house fully established within Dean, included the land on which the abbey was built, 'quit of all regards and secular exactions', common of pasture, wood and timber for repairs and other necessaries, without liability of waste, and a forge without any restrictions. Two woods were among their gifts, as well as a tithe of chestnuts. Tintern Abbey, a Cistercian house just over the county boundary in Monmouthshire, enjoyed land at Hewelsfield and Aluredestone,[25] also the wood of Harthill. The Benedictine Abbey of St Peter's, Gloucester, had a tithe of all venison taken in Dean, besides the right of warren; and in addition it was granted the grove of Sudridge in the manor of Ruddle, and the woods of Birdwood and Hope Mansel. The priory of Newent, a Benedictine cell of Cormeilles (Normandy), had in the north of the Forest an extensive wood, now named Newent Wood. The Cistercian house of Grace Dieu in Monmouthshire was granted land named *La Paternoster* for the site of its small cell at Stowe north of St Briavels.

Other religious houses existed with known or probable interests in Dean, although no references to them are made in the roll. There was a small house, St Davids, belonging to The Brothers of the House of the Infirm next to Striguil, but it is not known what forest rights if any it enjoyed. There was a hospital of St Margaret at Briavelstow; Llanthony priory in Gloucester, had a grange at Alvington; and Bath priory had lands at Tidenham.

There were, too, the Hermitage of St Whites at Cinderford and the Grange at Littledean, both under the aegis of Flaxley Abbey.

MILITARY EQUIPMENT IN ST BRIAVELS CASTLE IN 1275

The roll included copies of two noteworthy documents. The first is a list of arms and equipment handed over from one deputy constable of St Briavels Castle to another. Unfortunately it has been tampered with and some of its problems remain unsolved, but the document has been transcribed as faithfully as possible so that its uncertainties may be compared with their like elsewhere :

> Chirograph of Richard de Muleford which they showed without a seal. These are the arms in the castle of St. Briavels delivered to Richard de Muleford by Philip Wyther on the morrow of the feast of St Mary Magdalene 3 Edward [23 July 1275], namely, a sleeveless hauberk coming from the heriot of Thomas of Blakeney with an old saddle and a bridle and lance and an iron suit quilted with camail [or an iron suit of chain-mail quilted], a pair of leggings with iron cuisses and a pair of plates and an iron gorge and a cross-bow with a screw and two crossbows for two feet and five crossbows for one foot, and six bawdrics belonging to the earl [of Warwick], and a chasuble of the castle chaplain, and 1,000 quarrels and two thick ropes and a pair of cartwheels bound with iron and a gridiron. These the aforesaid Philip Wyther received of Sir William le Blund and he delivered them to Richard de Muleford, and with them he delivered three nets and an old stew-pot. The said Philip Wyther also delivered to the said Richard three prisoners who were in the said castle-prison, of whom one was called Philip Tirry, and another Adam Chacegray, and the third Walter of Bicknor.

The second document, headed 'Chirograph between the earl of Warwick and Ralph of Sandwich', records that on Sunday in the feast of St Thomas the Martyr 4 Edward I [29 December 1275] there were in the chapel of St Briavels Castle a chasuble, an alb with apparels, a frontal, and an apparel for an amice. In addition there were 8 crossbows with 5 baldrics, a crossbow with a screw, 2 crossbows for two feet, 5 crossbows for one foot, besides 1,000 quarrels, two thick but weak ropes, and 12 pairs of iron fetters. There were also two prisoners: one was an offender against venison; the other had stolen a sheep.

THE PROROGATION OF THE EYRE

The eyre was suddenly prorogued 12 April 1282 due to the rebellion in Wales which led to Edward I's second Welsh War. The roll records that at Easter 1282 'the war in Wales unexpectedly occurred and the itinerant justices at the pleas of the Forest of Dean in Gloucestershire prorogued the same on the instruction of the King from the quindene of Easter [12 April 1282] until a time appointed by the King, on this wise, that there should come to Gloucester all the forest officials with all those indicted, attached or on bail who have not yet made fine, on a fixed day, by the foregoing summons of three days, for the ending of the pleas, under a heavy penalty of amercement'. Likewise thirty jurors were chosen, each under a penalty of £10, who duly carried out their assignment. The roll ends with a list of seven persons, with their mainpernors, 'attached for vert by grand inquisition', and of twenty-three persons, again with their mainpernors, indicted for venison, 'who were adjourned until the coming of the justices to determine the pleas on account of the prorogation of the eyre'.

The justices made other orders concerning the expected interim period before the next eyre. The constable of St Briavels together with all the foresters-of-fee and other officials were ordered 'to prohibit charcoal-burning with the King's vert in his woods, either using stumps or dead or dry wood, under the penalty of losing their bailiwicks and goods, except it be in outside woods for which there was the King's special leave'. The constable was also to ensure that offenders against the vert should be rightfully tried and pledges taken, and not imprisoned at St Briavels for offences triable before the justices. He was instructed to sell for the king's use the oaks which had been felled in the Forest during the winter snow for the sustenance of the deer. Together with the foresters and verderers, he was given directions relating to the procedure concerning attachments for vert and for maintenance of the Forest.

Four of the seven foresters-of-fee and the six sergeants-of-fee found pledges that they would faithfully keep their bailiwicks, and properly execute their forest duties. The constable of Striguil found pledges for himself and was instructed to produce 'on a certain day when the eyre shall be determined' three of his foresters who had not appeared. Orders to the constable of Goodrich Castle and to the sheriff of Hereford regarding the prior of Llanthony in Wales are not fully legible. Five named offenders against venison were ordered to be borne to prison 'for the coming of the justices of Gloucestershire on Tuesday next after the quindene'. Authority was given for one of the offenders to be delivered 'on the instruction of the justices if he found twelve good and safe mainpernors and for 5 marks for his release'.

In April, Edward I issued an Order in Council for a protection to those going to the war in Wales.[26] Almost all the nobles whose cases had been adjourned for trial before the king or parliament gave military service in person.[27] Tany was assigned the task of conquering Anglesey, and by September 1282 he had occupied it. However, on 6 November he and many of his soldiers were drowned in attempting to cross the Menai Straits near Bangor.

The prorogation of the eyre opened to many a welcome prospect of respite. To others it may have brought disappointment that the long-awaited judgement of their cases was again indefinitely postponed. But the eyre was never resumed, as explained under 'Conclusions' (infra), and all those who had not been punished or fined escaped scot-free.

THE FINANCIAL ASPECTS

The fines imposed at the eyre amounted to almost £900, and the details, so far as they can be ascertained with certainty from the roll, are :

	£	s	d
Concerning pledges	25	3	8
Pleas of vert	46	16	2
Pleas of venison	201	10	8
Concerning the Regard	587	15	4
	861	5	10 (£861.29)

The sum would have been much higher if the eyre had run its full course. No trace can be found on the Pipe Rolls of the fines being paid to the exchequer. The whole matter of accounting for the money was apparently upset by the Welsh War. From the outbreak of the rising Edward decided, so far as possible, to act with paid levies, not only of household troops, crossbowmen, archers, and paid companies raised by individual barons by agreement with the Crown, but also of the feudal host.[28] In the summons to 158 vassals issued 6 April 1282[29] the king used the words 'at our wages'. The financial aspect of the Welsh War has been dealt with elsewhere,[30] and it is clear that the proceeds of the Wardrobe played an important part. The financial account of William of Louth, Keeper of the Wardrobe from 20 November 1280 to 20 November 1290 confirms that £100[31] was received towards the cost of the war from Grimbald Pauncefot the constable-warden, and it seems possible that this sum may have been part of the issues of the eyre. Although Pauncefot held the Forest from 1281 to 1287 the exchequer officials do not appear to have discovered his existence until 1285;[32] even then, no account from him was forthcoming, though a payment of £30 towards his ferm is recorded that year.[33] As late as 1315 his brother and heir was trying to settle the financial account of Pauncefot with barons of the exchequer.[34] Every likely source at the Public Record Office has been consulted to try to discover what became of the remainder of the issues of the eyre, but without success. In the absence of any proof to the contrary it would seem that the issues were used for the king's expenses in Wales.

CONCLUSIONS

Tany died 6 November 1282,[35] and on 21 October 1283 the executors of his will were ordered to deliver to his successor the rolls, memoranda and other things touching the office of justice of forest south of Trent.[36] On 2 November 1283 an acquittance was given to the executors for the delivery into the treasury of thirty-four rolls of the eyre and the rolls of the regard and of the general inquisition made at Gloucester.[37] The rolls, contained in a box (loculo) signed with the seal of Adam Gurdon, one of the justices, are noted as 'still remaining to be pleaded'.[38] But the pleas were never resumed. The eyre of 1282 was the last under Edward I of which record remains. (The only certain subsequent eyre for Dean was that held in 1634[39].) However, there is a record of 'fines and amercements of divers men indicated for transgressions in the forest eyre before Roger Lestrange, justice of forest south of Trent', in Gloucestershire, between 21 and 25 Edward I, pending a new eyre.[40] Several fines in connection with Dean make their first appearance in the Pipe Rolls of 22 and 23 Edward I, but it has not been possible to identify them with those imposed by Lestrange.

There are no means of knowing what the proportion of malefactors was to the population of the vills in the Forest and on its confines, but it is clear that depredations of many kinds were a common feature of their life. The eyre roll tends to give the impression that forest law was not at this time so harsh as has been often represented. There are certainly many signs of mitigation : frequently offenders against vert and occasionally against venison were pardoned because they were poor (the usual rendering in the roll is *pro anima regis quia pauperes sunt*). The justices certainly took into consideration the time a prisoner had already spent in gaol; and they appear to have been prepared in deserving cases to use clemency in their administration. They realised that forest law was of the will of the king and that he too was by no means always ruthless. The clemency in any case was eleemosynary, and this conception of alms did much to soften the asperity of medieval life. Many of the malefactors in the roll escaped punishment because of the intervention of the war. The many cases which were referred by the justices to the king or to parliament were never adjudicated.

It is instructive to consider how far the Forest Charter of 1217 was being observed in 1282. Article 1 had offered great expectation—the deforestment of certain districts, a hope long deferred by royal reluctance. Other Articles (2 to 17) were meant to be of immediate practical value in checking abuses of officials within forest and safeguarding certain forestal privileges. By Article 1, Henry III had promised that 'all forest made by our grandfather King Henry shall be viewed by good and lawful men, and if he turned away any other than his own proper woods into forest, to the damage of him whose wood it was, it shall forthwith be deforested; and if he afforested his own proper woods they shall remain so'. Article 3 further promised that 'all woods which were afforested by King Richard our uncle, or by King John our father, until our own first Coronation, shall forthwith be deforested, unless they shall be our demesne woods'.

At the time of *Domesday*, Dean extended to only one-third to one-half of its wider later limits. Within a century and a half of *Domesday* forest law had been extended over practically the whole area between the angle formed by the rivers Severn and Wye and stretching northwards to Ross-on-Wye, Newent and Gloucester. Thus areas had been afforested which included many vills, particularly in the south, east and north. It is difficult to decide at what date this extension occurred and which king was responsible for it. One record[41] says the extension dated 'from ancient times, that is before the time of King Henry, grandfather of King Henry, son of King John'. This would mean before 1154. Opposed to this, a second record[42] asserts that the boundaries had not been extended by 1154 and that in fact the extension had not occurred until the reign of John (1199–1216). This assertion has been questioned[43] with reasons to suggest that at least some of the additions were made by John's predecessors, particularly Henry I and Henry II. Following the charter, a perambulation of Dean was ordered in 1219,[44] another in 1225[45] and a third in 1227.[46] Only the last, completed in 1228,[47] is recorded and this followed the boundaries already asserted to have been 'before 1154':

> From the bridge on the west of Gloucester, along the great road to Newent, thence by the same road to the stream of Gorsley, thence ascending that stream to its source, then by a road to Bromsash, thence descending by the same road to Alton, thence by the same road to the Wye, and thus between the Wye and Severn to the bridge of Striguil. [Chepstow].

Thus the perambulation of 1228 followed (except perhaps in the southern tip near Beachley) the widest boundaries of the Forest as enlarged between *Domesday* and 1216. No other perambulation of Dean appears to have been made until the preliminaries to the 1282 eyre. The boundaries as recorded by the regarders have been noted (*supra*) from which it will have been seen that the metes and bounds followed those of 1228 except that the Forest extended to the confluence of the rivers Severn and Wye at Beachley. It is clear therefore that Edward I had not deforested any substantial tracts of Dean.

At the 1282 eyre no man who lived outside the Forest was in-

cluded in the common summons to the eyre except those 'im-
pleaded there' or those who were pledges : thus Article 2 of the
Forest Charter was in that respect observed. Also the pleas were
held before the justices-in-eyre—the 'chief foresters' provided for
by Article 16—and not by the constable or anyone else. This
greatly curtailed the power of the constable-warden, which was
one of the objects of that article : it prevented him from being
judge in his own cause. The justices on behalf of the king certainly took advantage of Article 3, which made nobles and
others liable for waste and assarts made without licence in their
woods. Foresters-of-fee had vested interests which the Forest
Charter by Article 14 was careful to respect, and there is no
evidence in the roll of constraints on their legal interests, but
neither is there reference to their due of 'chiminage' ie toll for
wayfarage.

The duties of the verderers, referred to in Article 16 of the
charter, were apparently duly executed. They had helped in
inquiring, viewing and attaching. They had held their courts
of attachment where they had imposed fines up to 4d (1½p) for
vert, and obtained pledges; and they had forced offenders against
the venison to find pledges, and had ordered some to prison to
await judgement. The verderers had enrolled particulars of
offences and duly presented them to the itinerant justices. Only
occasionally had they lapsed in their duties (*supra*, page 53).

The making of a regard in readiness for the eyre complied
with Article 5 of the charter, but there is no evidence in the roll
or in contemporary documents that the investigation of the
'lawing' of dogs as provided for in Article 6 had been carried
out, ie the expeditation or hambling of hunting dogs by cutting off
three claws from the ball of the front feet. The charter had made
no change in the system of collective responsibility of vills after
the discovery of a dead beast or its remains : the roll confirms
that many townships were amerced. Previous to the charter the exactions of the foresters were mainly for their own personal profit,
and Article 7 had provided safeguards against their mis-
demeanours : there is no evidence in the roll of unlawful exactions by them.

The roll does not show whether certain general directives in
Article 7 had been complied with; or whether the courts of swanimote and attachment had been regularly held as provided for by

Article 8 : certainly some sessions of the courts had been held. Again, there is no evidence of failure to allow the privileges of commoning and pannage granted by Article 9. However, there is no evidence of the commoning of sheep; and goats were expressly prohibited.

The roll does not include references concerning the privileges granted in Articles 12, 13 and 14; for example certain privileges of free men in their own woods of making ponds and marlpits, and the taking of the fowl of the forest and wild honey : the absence of any relevant complaints would point to the assumption that the privileges had been enjoyed without hindrance. Article 10, granting freedom from the loss of life or limb for taking the king's venison was certainly observed, and in many cases the punishment of imprisonment and fine was leniently enforced. Certain nobles appeared in the roll as apparently having taken advantage of the concession of taking deer as granted by Article 11 : Edward I had allowed his relatives and nobles to partake of some of his hunting.

Thus, from what evidence is provided by the roll, it appears that, except for the question of deforestation there are more signs that in 1282 the Forest Charter was being observed than otherwise. The great expectation of some deforestment had not been fulfilled, but the many other concessions granted in the charter had gone a long way to in some measure off-set this by way of mitigating the incidence of forest law and the exactions of forest officials. Furthermore, the severity of restrictions and penalties was rarely as grievous and one-sided as has sometimes been asserted. The king knew that his subjects needed estovers, herbage, and pannage, as well as the privilege to mine and smelt; he was lenient so long as his beasts were secure in their covert— but his concern was more for his prestige, gifts, and larder than for the little hunting that he and his relatives enjoyed. Commoning and mining privileges were generously interpreted by the king and the inhabitants. The forest system, although it restricted and punished, recognised the inhabitants' needs and allowed the kind of husbandry suited to rough woodland and waste. The king was well satisfied with Dean, for he had abundant venison, iron, and timber, and his relatives, favourites and servants benefited from privileges and gifts. At his call, particularly in wartime, were men brought up as woodcutters, charcoal-burners, miners, and workers in iron; many were skilled in using bows and arrows, crossbows and quarrels, in tunnelling, and in making passages through woods. His manufactory and arsenal of quarrels for his armies and castles were at St Briavels. Revenue came from sales, assarts, fines, herbage, pannage, and mining dues. Well might the king be assured that depredations in Dean were compensated by issues in cash and kind, and that his prerogative was secure.

Forest Law after 1282

The war in Wales in 1282, which incidentally caused the prorogation of the Dean Forest eyre of that year, also for a while put in abeyance the struggle against the more severe aspects of the forest system, and for some deforestment. The struggle was renewed in 1297,[48] and in that year Edward I confirmed the Charter of the Forest. On 18 November 1300 he appointed a commission to investigate the misdeeds of his justices, foresters, verderers, and other officials. Because the territory under forest law contained many vills and hamlets, some distant from the woods and the haunts of the beasts, it is understandable that renewed pressure was brought upon the king by the barons and populace to reduce the limits of declared forest. In 1300[49] Edward strove to retain the widest limits, and the sheriff of Gloucestershire was ordered 'to cause proclamation to be made that all those who have lands within the bounds of the king's forest and who wish in any way to challenge its current perambulation, shall show any proofs and challenges that they may have'.[50] Perambulations of the widest limits quoted on behalf of the king,[51] were challenged by other perambulations reducing the limits considerably.[52] In 1301[53] Edward reluctantly and temporarily conceded the narrower limits which included only his demesne woods and lands, and vills and hamlets within or adjacent to them. In Dean, forest law was thereby restricted to not much more than the area covered by the nine bailiwicks. The various perambulations continued to be the subject of much argument,[54] and no conclusive action was taken to implement the Crown's ostensible concession. On 31 March 1305[55] proclamation was made :

> Whereas certain men are put out of the forest by the perambulation and by the King's grant have requested at this

parliament that they shall be quit of the puture and of the things that the foresters demand of them as they were wont to be before : the King answers after granting the perambulation that it well pleased him that it should be as he had granted it, notwithstanding that the business had been sued and demanded in an evil manner, but at least he intends and wills that all his demesne woods and all his demesne lands, in whatever part they may be, that have been anciently of the Crown, or that have reverted to the Crown by way of escheat or in any other way, shall have the estate of a free chace and of free warren, and shall be held and guarded in such manner for his use for all manner of beasts and for all manner of sport that shall please him.

And in regard to those whose lands and tenements are deforested by the said perambulation and who demand to have common within the bounds of forest, the King's intention and will is that, since they claim to be quit by the perambulation of the puture of foresters and in order that the King's beasts may not have their haunt or repair on the lands deforested, as they had it when the lands were within the forest, these men ought not to have common or other easement within the bounds of the woods or of the lands that remain in the forest.

But if any of those people who are deforested by the perambulation would rather be within the forest, as they were before, than outside as they are now, the King is well pleased that they shall be thus received, to the end that they may remain in their ancient estate and have common and other easements within the forest as they had before.

Wherefore the King wills and commands that his justices of the forest on both sides of Trent shall thus keep and guard and cause to be kept and guarded firmly the aforesaid points in their bailiwicks in the form aforesaid.

On 27 May of the following year, 1306, the perambulations delineating the narrower limits were annulled by Edward I under a dispensation from the Pope,[56] and the wider bounds were restored. The king thereby tightened his hand on Dean as on other parts of his forest. However he admitted that the misdeeds of the forest officials had not ceased, and that correct legal procedure was not observed—accusations were presented not by the 'good men' of the country but by one or two foresters or verderers, and the innocent were condemned. He commanded that the regular procedure should be followed; the jurors should not consist of officials; and oppressive and corrupt foresters should be punished. Edward had given little away. The struggle for deforestment continued without success against Edward II, but after his dethronement Isabella and Mortimer declared in 1327 that the Forest Charter was to be kept in all points and that the conciliatory perambulations of Dean, as of other forests, conceded and then withdrawn by Edward I, were to hold good.[57] Three years later, 12 July 1330,[58] Edward III warned the justice of forest south of Trent not to allow regarders and verderers to charge with offences against the vert and venison dwellers in deforested districts, some of which were now referred to as purlieus; the conciliatory perambulations were to be strictly observed. This proved almost the end of the long struggle for deforestation; there was at last for Dean a defined area, much reduced from that of earlier times, within which forest law was to be administered.[59]

In later times, notably in 1347 and during the first years of the reign of Richard II, the commons complained because the royal officers 'of their malice have afforested, and strive from day to day to afforest, what had been deforested'. The Crown countered that the Forest Charter should be respected. Throughout most of the fourteenth century, there is evidence of care of the woods in Dean, but there was little administration of forest law. Insignificant work was done by the justices. Only the efforts of the verderers and woodwards made for the preservation of the woods and the beasts, and regulated the customary privileges of the inhabitants. Deer were less abundant, and the pleasures and perquisites of hunting are rarely mentioned. From 1385 to 1435 most of the issues of the castle and Forest were granted to noblemen, but the Crown received a ferm, retained the venison, and benefited by forest fines and by sales of trees and underwood. No loss of royal prerogative resulted from the grants, and forest courts continued to be held (infra).

In the fifteenth century the policy of the Lancastrian kings, and the anarchy which almost threw forest law into desuetude, well-nigh wrecked the forest system.[60] In Dean the system was seriously discredited as early as the last quarter of the fourteenth century. Control by the constable and other officials became less effective as forest law became effete. Some courts of attachment

F

were held, but there is no evidence of an eyre. Not a single instance of royal sport or of a requisition or grant of venison is recorded from the accession of Henry IV to the end of the reign of Philip and Mary. Elections of verderers were infrequently held. The importance of the office of justice of forest had diminished and no longer struck terror into the hearts of those preying on Dean's woods, fast becoming free to all. Moreover, there is no indication that the office of surveyor-general of woods, in existence soon after 1544, had as yet any concern with Dean: persons holding the Forest under grant probably ensured that there was little intrusion. Parts of Dean had been sold, leased, or given away, becoming subjects' estates, chases, parks, woods, groves, and warrens. Assarted land had become private leasehold or freehold, and the occupiers, often without authority, enclosed the better areas by hedges and fences. The wellbeing of the population had gradually been set above the conservation of deer and their covert. But in the king's woods, trees suitable for ship-timber were becoming increasingly important; and from acorns falling in Dean during the sixteenth century were to grow oaks indispensable to England's sea-power, and to become of extreme utility at a time when timber was scarce in other parts of the country. Henceforth, what remained of forest law was meant not to maintain deer and their habitat, but to conserve timber for ships, and to produce underwood for charcoal and other uses.[61]

By the time of Elizabeth I's accession, 1558, the forest officials of the old tradition remained, but most of them were ineffective. The ancient but disintegrating forest organisation continued to be based upon the preservation of deer, despite the fact that the Crown took no interest in hunting, and beasts of the forest were disappearing. Elizabeth retained her forest for prestige and the royal prerogative, and for the conservation of ship-timber. A survey made in Dean in 1565 by Roger Taverner, her surveyor-general of woods, begins with a list of the forest officials: the constable's bow-bearer and nine rangers, a master or chief forester and his bow-bearer, nine foresters-of-fee, seven woodwards, a riding forester, two rangers, a bailiff-at-large, and a beadle. No verderers or regarders are mentioned; probably attachments were made by bow-bearers and rangers. The offices of forester-of-fee and woodward were by this time sinecures; their holders, being concerned only with ancient perquisites, exercised little restraint on the inhabitants. Many of Taverner's plans to effect improvements in Dean's administration were at first thwarted by ill-defined rights of the Guise family, farmers of the issues of St Briavels and some of those of the Forest, who much spoiled the queen's woods, made grants of assarts, and usurped the inhabitants' privileges of herbage, pannage, and estovers.[62] Eventually many fines were collected from the Guises and other offenders, and the court of attachment was duly held (infra). Nevertheless, when in 1598 John Manwood[63] published his 'Treatise and Discourse of the Lawes of the Forrest' it was in the hope of reviving laws of which 'very little or nothing' remained. James I tried to resuscitate them, but without success. Charles I was more successful in recalling forest law to life, and the famous Justice Finch even demanded that the reduced perambulations should be revoked, and the extent of forest enlarged—see Chapter 3.

The Verderers to 1633

The rôle of the verderers up to and during the eyre of 1282 has been related earlier in this chapter. Those named were Elias de Heydon, Philip of Hatherley, Robert de Ledene, Robert Malet, William de la Hythe, Roger le Bret, and Philip Wyther (deceased). One was still in office on 25 July 1287, namely Roger le Bret who, with two more recently elected verderers, Alexander of Bicknor and William le Fawkener, took part in an inquisition concerning a dispute relating to iron ore between the abbot of Flaxley and the warden of the Forest.[64] By 10 March 1291, the colleagues of Roger and Alexander were Ralph of Ruddle and Richard of Pulton, but all four were 'insufficiently qualified' and the sheriff was ordered to cause them to be replaced :[65]

Of Election of Verderers : And because Alexander of Bicknor, Ralph of Ruddle, Richard of Pulton, and Roger le Bret, verderers of the Forest of Dean, have insufficient means for fulfilling their office, the instruction is to the sheriff of Gloucestershire that in his full county with the assent of the same county, in place of the same Alexander, Ralph, Richard and Roger, he cause four verderers, to wit, two dwelling in the Forest and two in places contiguous to the Forest, who the better know and are able to give attention to that office, to be elected, who having taken their oath as the custom is, thenceforth do and preserve the things which belong to the office of verderer in the aforesaid Forest.

The sheriff met difficulties. Richard of Bisleigh, elected verderer that year, had to be removed because he could not attend to his duties, being in the service of Walter of Helyun. Alexander of Bicknor held to his office, and with three newly elected colleagues, Ralph Hathewy, Simon of Framilode, and Roger of Aldewick, assisted with a perambulation in 1300.[66] Alexander of Bicknor and Roger of Aldewick were still verderers in 1307 when they assisted in an inquisition relating to the Bleyth family.[67] On 25 August 1311[68] the sheriff was ordered to cause verderers to be elected in place of Roger of Aldewick who was not resident within the Forest, and of Richard White, insufficiently qualified and incapacitated by infirmity, both of whom the king had removed from their office. Ten years later William Holt of Boseleye was a verderer, and had therefore relinquished his appointment as a coroner because he could not attend to the duties of that office.[69] In 1326 Holt and another verderer, John of Box, assisted in a sale of underwood, but by 1327 they and two other verderers, Alexander of Bicknor and Walter Nasse, were deceased.[70] Orders to elect verderers in place of Holt and Elias of Aylburton, and in place of Richard Billing, William Lewelyn, William Gamage, and Henry of Chaxhill, were given to the sheriff in 1328, 1329, and 1331;[71] Elias and the two Williams had been removed because of insufficient qualifications, while Henry had no lands within the Forest, and Richard being a coroner was unable to attend to his duties of verderer. However, Henry and Billing were still in office in 1335 (*infra*).

Of the references to courts in Dean in the first third of the fourteenth century, one is an order in 1318[72] to the justice of forest south of Trent to deliver two inhabitants, in prison at St Briavels for trespass in the Forest, in bail to twelve mainpernors who were 'to have the offenders before the justices at their next coming'. On 10 March 1333[73] an impressive forest inquisition was held at Great Dean (Mitcheldean) before John de Loudham, deputy of Sir Robert de Ufford, justice of forest, assisted by the warden, Robert de Sapy, his deputy, John of Rustele, twelve sergeants-of-fee, four verderers, thirteen regarders, and as jurors twelve 'free and legal men' dwelling in the Forest. Its business was to consider the state of the Forest and to enquire into transgressions within it. Many cases related to vert offences, and others concerned the taking of venison in several places within the woodlands. No indication is given as to who attached or presented the offenders; no foresters or woodwards took part. The jurors set ther seal to the record but no subsequent action is apparent, and it is uncertain whether the offenders in St Briavels Castle in 1333, 1334, and 1336 for venison offences (they included the parson of Abenhall church) were ever indicted.[74]

For the period 1335–41 a roll records fifty-four sessions of the court of attachment in Dean,[75] patently effective and businesslike, and presided over by the deputy constable. The verderers attended but they appear in a somewhat subsidiary though still useful capacity. Two, three, or four were present at each session, namely John of Heydon, John of Box, Henry of Chaxhill, Richard Viel, Richard Billing, and John of Okle near Newent. On two occasions the fact was noted that a newly elected verderer was attending for the first time. The court met on Thursday of every sixth week with unfailing regularity throughout the period of the roll, and dealt with vert, not venison, offences. Most of the entries are simply records of oaks and beeches delivered *pro orbold*, a reference to the release of trees for timbering mines. Other entries relate to trees taken by writ of the king, the justice, or the constable; no charge was made for the trees, but they were enrolled by the verderers in the same way as attachments, and the trees had usually been taken by their view. The same court recorded trees sold to sundry persons, again by view of the verderers. There are many instances of persons attached for specified vert offences and imprisoned at St Briavels till they could obtain pledges to produce them at the next eyre. When the offenders were not taken to the castle their attachers, usually the woodwards, riding foresters, or sergeants-of-fee, were to answer. The names and offences of the malefactors were enrolled for the next eyre of the justices. However, no justices arrived, and it is doubtful whether any action was ever taken on the matters enrolled. Noteworthy in the roll of the foregoing sessions is the fact that on two occasions the venue of the court is given, once 'at the house of Kensley (*Kenesleie*)', and once 'at Kenesley (*Kenesleye*)'. This is the earliest mention of Kensley House in the centre of Dean on the site of which, or near to it, the King's Lodge or Speech House was built c 1676 to accommodate courts (see Chapters 3 and 4).

By 8 November 1336[76] a verderer was needed to replace John of Box because he was 'sick and broken by age'. In 1337[77] and 1338[78] the verderers were Heydon, Billing, Viel, and Henry of Chaxhill. By 27 April 1340,[79] the last named was deceased; so too by 15 September 1343[80] was Billing. In 1350[81] the constable was ordered to arrange for the payment of four foresters 'whom the King has newly ordered to be found for keeping the vert and venison, to stay in Dean at the King's wages'. Thereafter, many forest offices were granted to members of the king's retinue, yeomen of the Crown, clerks, grooms, pages, servants, and ushers, some of whom never had, or would, set eyes on the Forest; all that seemed to matter was that in some way money or perquisites attached to the office, or that the appointment saved the Exchequer a pension; even so, the appointments were some curb on any inhabitants of Dean who contemplated exceeding the customary privileges.[82]

On 20 October 1358[83] elections were commanded in order to replace as verderers John of Okle, Richard Viel, and John of Heydon; the last named was 'weak and aged', and the other two were deceased. On 12 December 1375[84] Walter of Aust was to be replaced 'if he be dead, as the King has learned'. The sheriff received similar orders 17 October 1386[85] and 6 November 1389[86] for Thomas Bray of Hurst, deceased; 23 October 1405[87] for Richard Longe, deceased; 27 November the same year[88] for Walter Milward of Longhope, sick and aged; 3 March 1410[89] and 6 February 1412[90] for Richard Foxley, also sick and aged; 8 November 1424[91] for Richard Grene of Westbury, insufficiently qualified, and John Shortgrove, deceased; 16 November 1424[92] for William Grey, insufficiently qualified; 26 October 1426[93] for Richard Penbrugge, also insufficiently qualified; and 5 November 1433[94] for John Box, deceased.

There are records of two courts held in Dean about this time. First a court held at Kensley about every forty days during part of 1435–6,[95] the verderers' court of attachment, by then sometimes known as 'the court on Speeches Day': two men owed 10s (50p) for charcoal for 'Speeches Day', obviously to heat the court-room at Kensley when inhabitants appeared before the verderers to speak of their requirements and privileges. (This is

important as explaining Speech
House, a derived designation, being
the name of the King's Lodge—later
the Speech House—built *c* 1676 in
the centre of Dean, on the site of, or
nearby Kensley House—see Chapters
3 and 4.) Eight courts in all were held,
the fines, dues and acknowledgments
totalling £18 6s 8d (£18.33). The
second court is by inference related to
that of the justices in eyre : no certain
record has been found of an eyre in
Dean after that of 1282 (*supra*), but
the following evidence suggests some
actions by the justices in 1407–8 and
in 1432–3. In 1434–5[96] the receiver of
the Forest accounted for £7 15s 4d
(£7.76) 'from the collector of fines
for indictments made before the justice of forest in 1407–8 of arrears not
paid'. The same receiver 'rendered
nothing of fines of divers transgressions made before the justice in the
sessions held in the Forest in 1432–3'.[97]
In 1436[98] £12 1s (£12.05) was received of 'perquisites of pleas of the
forest'.

A lapse in the appointment of verderers occurred in the 1450s. On 7
July 1461[99] the sheriff was commanded to arrange for 'the election of
as many verderers as there ought to be

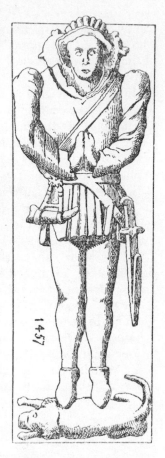

Fig 4. The tomb and
effigy of Jenkin Wyrral,
forester-of-fee, 1457, in
Newland Church

and used to be in the Forest of Dean, as no verderer is as yet elected
therein by command of the King'. Probably, because forest law was
falling into desuetude, few people would offer themselves for election to what could have been an unpopular, as well as unpaid,
office. For over one hundred years there is no record of a verderer. They are not included in a list of forest officials drawn
up by Taverner in 1565 (*supra*). None are mentioned in the
rolls of fifteen sessions of the court of attachment held at Kensley

every six weeks from 17 October 1566 to 19 August 1568.[100] The deputy constable, William Winter, presided, and the persons who attached are named but not their office. Fourteen sessions of the court were similarly held between 30 September 1568 and 3 August 1570.[101] None of the attachments concerned venison. In 1584[102] is a reference to money and timber allocated to repair 'the swanimote courthouse', that is, Kensley House.

The court of attachment was continued 1 October, 12 November, 24 December 1601, and 4 February 1602.[103] In attendance were three verderers—Thomas Bucke, Charles Jones, and William Brayne—but again the deputy constable presided. Between ten and fifteen vert attachments were dealt with at each session. Acknowledgments of 6d (2½p) were paid for using a bill and 1s (5p) for using an axe, when having taken estovers. This and the charges made 'for advising' (*pro consilio*) show that the court continued not only to fine offenders against the vert but also to regularise estovers. Inhabitants with such privileges, and others enjoying herbage and pannage, jealously guarded them: they continued to see some good in the remnant of forest law. The enforcement of the laws relating to deer was by now relatively mild.

Following James I's accession, the constable-warden, Sir Edward Winter, with the verderers, supervised from 29 September 1604 to 29 September 1609 the sessions of the court of attach-

Fig 5. A Bowbearer, from an ancient tomb in Newland Churchyard

ment, increasingly being called 'the speech court'. Fifteen sessions were held, one every six weeks in 1604–6,[104] usually at Kensley House but sometimes at *Kannope* (Cannop), which is a mile to the west (see Chapter 4): the fines for vert offences and acknowledgments amounted to £37 8s 4d (£37.41). The verderers were Charles Jones and James Banke; and their steward was William Carpenter. At nine similar sessions held from 29 September 1606 to 29 September 1608[105] the levies were in all £43 9s 4d (£43.46), and at sessions in 1609–10[106] £27 15s 4d (£27.76). No appointment of officials other than verderers and rangers have been found. Deputies of hereditary woodwards, who held token office in the nine woodwardships (previously called bailiwicks), assisted in attaching and presenting offenders.[107] A document of 1610[108] states that William Winter and Roger Myners, deputy constables, kept the court of attachment at the speech house; William Carpenter was the steward, Robert Bridgeman the bailiff, and James Yennys the deputy bailiff. Comprehensive claims in 1612–13[109] show how widely the inhabitants had come to interpret their privileges. Forest law had become desultory, had lost its terrors, and its objective had changed. Designed to establish and strengthen the exercise of the royal will it continued to safeguard the interests of the inhabitants, and also conserved ship-timber. Those inhabiting the Forest and compelled to endure its law came to regard the burden as beneficial: 'it was the Crown which might reasonably resist it as restrictive'.[110] However, ironmasters and their workmen made havoc of the underwood in order to fuel their voracious charcoal iron blast-furnaces.

The court of attachment punished minor offenders against the vert during sessions held in 1623–5.[111] The verderers who presided either at Kensley or at Cannop were William Brayne, James Banke, Charles Jones, Thomas Morgan, Warren Gough, John Berrow, and Anthony Wye. The offences with which they dealt were infinitesimal compared to the misappropriation by the ironmasters. The Forest's administration, and the large and often long-term contracts for cordwood, became more confused by the Crown's granting of a variety of minor concessions; and the duties of the verderers were partly supplanted by overseers. Woodwardships were held by persons who had little concern for the cover beyond the privileges enjoyed by themselves and others.

Many of the appointments made under Charles I were sinecures, to reward minor favourites, or servants, to save the payment of a pension, or the like. More energetic measures were needed towards conservation and replenishment of trees for ship-timber, but these measures could not be pursued without the co-operation of all interests in Dean—a Forest in turmoil, intensified by apathy, abuse, and mutual accusations.

References to Chapter 2

1 Hart, C. E., *The Extent and Boundaries of the Forest of Dean and Hundred of St Briavels*, 1947
2 Ibid *Royal Forest*, 9
3 C.66, 18 John, m.8. Turner (op cit, 3) found the first allusion to a verderer (not in Dean) in 1209
4 Ibid 8 Hen III, m.10
5 C.54, 7 Hen III, m.15; C.66, 40 Hen III, m.6, 15
6 C.66, 7 Hen III, m.6; C.62, IV, 38; 8 Apl 1252; ibid, 519, 19 May 1260
7 C.54, 15 Hen III, m.3
8 E32/30, m.9d
9 Ibid m.4
10 Maitland, F. W., ed *Pleas of the Crown for the County of Gloucester, 1221*, 47, 182, 392
11 Ibid 392
12 *Cal. Misc. Inquisitions*, 31 Hen III, 51; 93
13 E32/28
14 E32/29
15 E32/30; Hart, M.A. Thesis, University of Bristol.
16 C.66, 10 Edw I, m.8d
17 C.54, 1279–88, 177
18 C.66, 10 Edw I, m.19; 1281–92, 9
19 E32/31; Hart, M.A. Thesis, loc cit
20 Maitland, F. W., *Canon Law in the Church of England*
21 C.54, 1272–9, 528
22 Hart, *The Extent and Boundaries . . .*, op cit
23 Turner, Bazeley, and Petit-Dutaillis, op cit
24 C.54, 1279–82, 147, 4 Feb 1282
25 Hart, C. E., 'Aluredestone of *Domesday*', *Severn and Wye Review*, 1970, 1/2
26 C.49/1/21, 22

27 C.77, 10 Edw I, m.10d
28 Powicke, M., *The Thirteenth Century*, 422
29 *Foedera*, I, ii, 603–4
30 Tout, *Chapters in Mediaeval Administration*, II, 113–15; Morris, J. E., *The Welsh Wars of Edward I*, 1901
31 *Chronica Johannis de Oxendes*, 326
32 E372, 9 to 13 Edw I
33 *Exch of Receipt*, E.403, 63
34 C.54, 8 Edw II, m.19, 24 Jan 1315
35 Tout, op cit, 163
36 C.60, 1272–1307, 193; C.54, 1282–92, 84
37 C.54, 1281–92, 85
38 Ibid
39 Hart, C. E., *The Commoners of Dean Forest*, 1951, 29
40 *Exch K.R. Accts Forests*, bdl 535/2
41 C.54, 12 Hen III, m.10d
42 E32/255
43 Bazeley, op cit, 158–60
44 *Rot Litt Claus*, i, 434b
45 C.66, 9 Hen III, m.17d
46 C.54, 11 Hen III, m.5d
47 Ibid 12 Hen III, m.10
48 Petit-Dutaillis, op cit, 207–19
49 E32/255, m.2
50 C.54, 28 Edw I, m.3d
51 E32/255, fully given by Hart, *The Extent and Boundaries* . . . , op cit, 32
52 Ibid 42
53 Bazeley, op cit, 154; E32/255
54 C.47/12, No 45; E32/284; See Hart, *The Extent and Boundaries* . . . , op cit, 51, 53
55 C.54, 33 Edw I, m.18d
56 *Statutes of the Realm*, I, 149
57 Ibid 255
58 C.54, 1300–3, 147
59 Hart, *The Extent and Boundaries* . . . , op cit, 56
60 Petit-Dutaillis, op cit, 244
61 Hart, *Royal Forest*, 75
62 Ibid 79
63 Manwood, op cit
64 *Glos I.P.M.*, IV, 144; *Chanc I.P.M.*, 15 Edw I, 67
65 C.54 19 Edw I, m.8

66 *For Proc Anc Chanc*, 102
67 *Glos I.P.M.*, V, 95
68 C.54 5 Edw II, m.28
69 Ibid 14 Edw II, m.8
70 E101/140/18
71 Ibid 19; C.54 2 Edw III, m.12, 19, 8, and 5 Edw III, m.2
72 C.54, 11 Edw II, m.12
73 E32/258
74 Hart, op cit, 55, m.20
75 E32/33
76 C.54, 10 Edw III, m. 11
77 *Glos I.P.M.*, V, 267
78 Ibid 274
79 C.54, 14 Edw III, m.20
80 Ibid 17 Edw III, m.23; 20 Edw III, m.25
81 C.66, 1350–4, 5
82 Hart, *Royal Forest*, 54
83 C.54, 32 Edw III, m.3, 10
84 Ibid, 49 Edw III
85 Ibid 10 Rich II, m.31
86 Ibid 13 Rich II, m.6
87 Ibid 7 Hen IV, m.42
88 Ibid m.40
89 Ibid 11 Hen IV, m.18
90 Ibid 13 Hen IV, m.28
91 Ibid 3 Hen V, m.17
92 Ibid
93 Ibid 5 Hen VI, m.17
94 Ibid 12 Hen VI, m.22
95 S.C.6/858/15
96 E101/141/1
97 Ibid
98 S.C.6/858/15
99 C.54, 1 Edw IV, m.6
100 E146/1/31; Hart, *Royal Forest*, 80
101 Ibid 30; Hart, *Royal Forest*, 80, 81
102 L.R. 12/1126, Series III
103 E146/1/32; Hart, *Royal Forest*, 81, 82
104 E137/13/4, m.1
105 Ibid m.2
106 Ibid m.3
107 E178/3837, m.66

108   *B.M.*, Lansd. MSS 166, f.350
109   E112/82/300; Hart, *Royal Forest*, 93, 94
110   Hammersley, G., 'The Revival of the Forest Laws . . .', *History*, 45 (1960), 87
111   E137/13/4, m.5–8

Three: 1634 to 1808

The Justice Seat in Eyre of 1634 and the Verderers to 1667

The abuses in Dean and other Crown forests during the first three decades of the seventeenth century called for a new order to re-establish the royal prerogative and popular privilege. An attempt to this end was made in 1632 by a resuscitation of forest law with its eyres. The agents used by the Crown were the attorney-general, Sir William Noy, and the chief justice, Henry, earl of Holland,[1] who held their first eyre at Windsor and Bagshot in September 1632; this was mild in judgement but was a prelude to wider exertions in Dean, to which its disorders had drawn attention. The first move in regard to Dean was the appointment in December 1632[2] of Sir John Bridgman, chief justice of Chester and vice-president of the Council of Wales, as deputy constable of St Briavels. His protégé John Broughton became the first deputy surveyor of Dean in 1633, under Sir Charles Harbord, the surveyor-general of woods. Broughton related 15 April 1633[3] that he 'came to Gloucester Friday, which was the wettest day he had ever travelled. . . . The spoils in Dean are so great that he will undergo excessive toil to reform abuses'.

In April 1634[4] the king informed Bridgman that he had ordered the earl of Holland to hold a 'court of justice in eyre' within Dean 'for redressing the great abuses which through the discontinuance of the forest laws are there grown so high'. Bridgman was to assist the sheriff in choosing regarders and to instruct them in their duties. Hammersley[5] has discussed how far part of the policy pursued was an intrigue by Noy against Lord Treasurer Portland. At least part of Noy's policy against offenders was to base proceedings on a series of Exchequer enquiries into conditions in Dean which had already served in some inconclusive prosecutions of concessionaires, officials, and inhabitants, past and present.[6] But a fatal illness removed Noy from the preparations,

and his place was taken in April 1634 by Sir John Finch, who
took steps to dispute and then to widen the Forest's perambulation which had stood since the reign of Edward III. He collected
documents purporting to invalidate the then reduced bounds,
together with copies of those perambulations of Edward I within whose bounds were seventeen vills with their 'woods and plains'
long treated as deforested. He visited Gloucester and obtained
much evidence useful to his purpose from Sir Baynham Throckmorton Bt, and from woodwards and other officials.

The justice seat opened at Mitcheldean 10 July 1634 and was
adjourned to Gloucester Castle.[7] The judges were the earl of
Holland, baron Thomas Trevor, Bridgman, and justice William
Jones. Finch, as Crown counsel, had the ancient and wider
bounds of the Forest recited, and supported them with the fact
that some supposedly deforested villages had continued to claim
common within Dean. The jury of local men, under pressure,
found for the Crown, but Finch agreed not to proceed against
anyone outside the metes and bounds in use for the last three
centuries. Note was taken of 120 formal presentments of claims,
which ranged from privileges of common, pannage, and estovers
to offices within the Forest; extracts of all of the claims have been
published.[8] Three verderers, Charles Bridgman, Warren Gough
and John Berrow, each claimed by virtue of his office a buck in
summer and a doe in winter, also each year an oak and a beech
by warrant and allocation of the other verderers. Claims by other
persons were generally for 'housebote and heybote for repair and
rebuilding of messuages and buildings, by view and delivery of
the foresters and verderers at the speech court, and firebote of
dead and dry wood',[9] and for 'common in all open wastes and
places of the Forest', making a small payment for the same,
and pannage for which were paid a few pence called 'swine-
silver.' Hereditary holders of woodwardships further claimed by
ancient custom the lop and top of trees given by the king, and
all wind-thrown trees. The court did not pronounce judgement
on the claims.

Offences were next dealt with, on the basis of presentments
drawn up by a special swanimote court held in Dean 10 June
1634.[10] Of the eight hundred cases set forth, many concerned
more than one person; some related to events forty years earlier.
Cases concerning cutting, taking, or selling wood totalled 420, of

illegal enclosure or other encroachments 260, of poaching 80, of unauthorised building of ironworks 10, and of miscellaneous matters 30. About £130,000 in fines was endorsed against the presentments. The four main offenders, John Gibbons, Sir Basil Brooke, George Mynne, and Sir John Winter, were dealt with by way of special indictments and not upon presentments by the swanimote. Gibbons was fined £8,600, of which he paid £8,000,[11] for enclosing more land than he had been granted in and around Cannop, and for felling trees thereon. The swanimote presentment against him was 'for cutting 4,000 oaks and 200 beeches worth 20s each between 31 March 1629 and 30 April 1634, for spoiling certain coppices to the damage of the King £1,200, and for enclosing with a wall 940 acres valued at £113 13s 4d (£113.66) annually',[12] whereas the indictment by the jury was 'of cutting divers goodly timber-trees marked by the King's officers for shipping, and other uses of His Majesty'. King James had 'at his great charge enclosed with a pale two parcels of land for coppices of which Gibbons obtained a lease for 21 years of 574 acres at a rent of £28 14s (£28.70) yearly and a fine of £280'. Gibbons had 'joined the two enclosures and thereby increased the whole to 1,000 or 1,100 acres'. His sale of the lands to Sir Robert Bannister was allowed to stand.[13]

Brooke and Mynne were charged for 178,200 cords of wood at 6s 8d (33½p) each, ie £59,400, taken in the last six years.[14] Other accusations against them concerned irregularities of measurement in cords, and the taking of timber-trees.[15] Though the defendants asserted that they had paid for considerably more than 10,000 cords a year, they were fined £50,039 16s 8d (£50,039.83).[16]

Winter, advised by the recorder of Gloucester, withdrew his defence to a charge of taking 60,700 cords, and was fined £20,230.[17] He with Brooke and Mynne by June 1636 had their huge fines reduced, Brooke and partner to £12,000 and Winter to £4,000.[18] Fines on other offenders, about £55,000, included £17,000 on other ironmasters and magnates; the remainder ranged from a few shillings for minor vert offences to several pounds for illicit dwellings, and over £100 for trees or underwood. Many of the fines, on appeal, were much reduced. Hammersley[19] has estimated that of the £130,000 of fines imposed[20] only about one-fifth was collected. In the year following the eyre,

1635, the justices sent instructions to be carefully observed by the
'lieutenants' and deputy constables :[21]

That according to Letters of Privy Seal 8 November 1634
they restrain all foresters-of-fee, verderers, woodwards, and
all others that pretend to have right to have fee trees and fee
deer in the Forest from either, until they shall make their
rights appear in the Exchequer and obtain a judicial order
of the Court for the same by confession or consent of His
Majesty's attorney-general.

That the country who challenges common of estovers be
punctually tied to take no other fuel wood than such as only
their own plea and by their own consent is lately decreed
unto them in the Exchequer, being only dead and dry wood
as by the same decree made about 4 years since may appear.
That when any suit is made by any of the inhabitants at the
Speech Court for timber for repairing their ancient tenements, care be first taken to see that such tenements as are
pretended to be in decay are convenient and ought of right
to be repaired with the King's timber; next that they are
truly in decay; lastly that no more timber be granted or
more taken nor of better quality by colour of that grant
than the necessary use of those tenements require, for which
purpose some able and trusty persons are to be chosen and
appointed at the Speech Court before the delivery of such
timber, to view and certify at the next Court the decays as
also the quantity and quality of the timber which of right
for that present occasion ought to be granted, and that
within a convenient time after delivery of the timber, the
Court likewise authorise the same trusty persons to view the
reparations so made and see whether all the timber is be-
stowed thereon or not, and to certify the truth thereof at the
next Court.

And because the Forest for the most part lies within no
parish by means whereof there is neither constable or other
officer to suppress disorders or prevent bloodshedding which
within that desert place is likely often to happen, if any
victualling or alehouse is suffered there, these kind of houses
being great means of the unlawful waste and consumption
of the King's woods and the destruction of his game and the
rendezvous of all lawless and disordered persons; therefore
special care is to be had from time to time wholly to suppress
all alehouses within that part of the Forest and also the

G

multitude of alehouses in villages adjacent to the Forest.
That upon information made or given unto you of any
stealers of cordwood either before or after delivery thereof
to the King's farmers, you shall convent before you the persons accused and either bind them over with good sureties
to answer their offences in His Majesty's Court of Exchequer, or otherwise you shall give them corporal or other
punishment as you shall think meet. That you cause to be
pulled down and demolished all cabins within the Forest
except such as are inhabited by workmen ordinarily employed by the farmers in the King's works, and you shall also
punish such persons as have presumed (not being workmen
employed as aforesaid) to come and dwell there, and take
good security of them to depart without returning. You shall
also punish corporally by binding over as aforesaid all such
as carry wood or timber out of the Forest whether in wayne
or on horseback and those that set them on work, except
the same be first granted and appointed by the Speech Court
for repair of some ancient tenement in manner as aforesaid.
That you also punish all such as make any charcoal fire
within the Forest, together also with such as set them on
work, except the said charcoal be made for the King's
farmers and no others.

You shall carefully preserve such part of the woods where
the King's eirie of great hawks are wont and used to timber
and not suffer the same or any part to be cut down. You
shall not suffer any of the inhabitants or any others to
shred, shroud, lop or top any tree within the Forest for
browse for their cattle or otherwise, but shall take special
care to punish all such offenders from time to time with
severity.

You shall take special care that no sheep or goats to be
suffered to feed within the Forest contrary to the forest
laws. You shall not suffer any trencher-makers, cardboard
makers, shovel-makers, saddletree-makers, turners or any
other timber men whatsoever to dwell or harbour themselves within the Forest who do apparently supply themselves with timber for their several uses by stealth and
destruction of His Majesty's timber there which is to be
carefully prevented.

That special care be taken to prevent the keepers killing
any deer without lawful warrant nor take or cut down any
timber of browsewood without assignment and allowance

of some persons to be by you authorised from time to time
on that behalf. And that all stealers of deer, and other trespassers within the Forest be severely punished, and all other
abuses as well in vert as venison carefully reformed according to the best of your wisdoms and the course of justice.

The court of attachment, increasingly called the speech court
and usually held at Kensley, was still the means by which the
inhabitants could obtain estovers. Courts under the guise of
swanimotes had, as noted, been held in 1634 to prepare lists
of offences; and there was little distinction between the attachment court and the swanimote: in Dean they appear to have
merged. The records of a speech court held at Littledean 5
October 1637[22] were signed by two 'clerks of the court of the
swanimote'. The verderers were now the only class of ancient
official among several others of a new order which included two
deputy surveyors, concerned particularly in selling timber and
cordwood, and several new type regarders and woodwards.[23] In
addition there was Throckmorton, an important local person,
and his bowbearer, Richard Powell.[24]

A sign of the policy since the eyre of 1634 was the willingness
of the Crown to sell some concessions in Dean, where the newly
extended bounds included the estates of some men of substance,
many anxious to be 'out of the Forest'. Sir John Winter in 1637
compounded to deforest his lands in and around Lydney for
£1,000,[25] and lesser men paid a total of almost £600.[26] In the
same year,[27] Winter wrote to Secretary Windebank:

His Majesty having declared by you that he holds me not
unfit to serve him, I have been elected verderer by the freeholders on Wednesday last. And because there has been
great opposition made for the place by Sir Robert Cook
[of Highnam], assisted by many of this county that deny payment of ship-money, I beseech you to be the first that made
it known to the King for prevention of sinister information.

Concurrently, proposals for deforesting Dean were drawn up.[28]
The king did not as yet reveal his intentions, but he agreed for
£250 to deforest the lands of Richard Darling and others, and
to pardon them for offences committed against the forest laws.[29]
Concern was being shown not only for damage by charcoal iron

blast furnaces, but also for the effect of leases, commoners' privileges, and abuses in the Forest.[30] Efforts to 'settle the Forest'
were shattered in 1639 by an intention to grant to Winter almost
the whole of Dean.[31]

On 18 March 1640 Henry, earl of Holland, the chief justice
in eyre, constituted James Kyrle and William Guise his deputies
'to continue and adjourn all pleas to such a day and place as
they should determine, and to perform all duties this term'.[32]
However, two days later Charles I granted to Winter virtually
the whole of Dean.[33] The grant was enjoyed only for about
eighteen months. Litigation ensued in 1641 between the Crown
and Winter and the inhabitants who were fighting to preserve
their privileges of herbage and pannage, and their estovers—for
which they paid at the speech court 6d (2½p) for a bill-hewing
and 1s (5p) for an axe-hewing.[34]

Since the eyre of 1634, the administration of Dean had been
much as before, and was in fact threefold, under the surveillance
of the earl of Pembroke, at least until the grant to Winter. First,
the only remnants of the old régime, the verderers (and regarders
who by this time were permanent officials, not appointed for
special occasions only) trying, with the assistance of the deputy
constable, to punish offenders against the vert and venison, and
to allocate estovers fairly at the attachment or speech court, still
loosely called the swanimote. Second, an innovation, the deputy
surveyor and keepers, acting under the surveyor-general of woods.
Third, the few holders of hereditary offices: sinecure-wood-
wards and their deputies, one forester-of-fee, and a chief forester,
Throckmorton with his bowbearer. The heriditary officials were
concerned more with perquisites than with the well-being of the
Forest. The Long Parliament repudiated the forest eyres in
1640.[35] Bounds of Dean and other forests were henceforth to be
restricted to those at the end of James I's reign. Forest law restored in 1634 survived undiminished, at least in appearance, but
no law could compensate for the absence of competent staff and
effective policy, 'least of all an archaic code designed to uphold
chaos'.[36]

During the Civil War (1643–5) administration in Dean was
erratic, and its inhabitants suffered by the supporters of both
parties. The usual forest officials could not fully undertake their
duties; and 'preservators' were appointed.[37] However, in 1643,[38]

three verderers, Warren Gough, Anthony Wye and John Berrow, held six sessions of their court of attachment. By this time they were imposing fines of greater maximum than the 4d (1½p) of earlier years—for example : (a) cutting one oak, 30s (£1.50), one beech 7s 6d (37½p), one crabtree 5s (25p); (b) carrying away 10 horseloads of bark 20s (£1.00); and (c) having a brace of large dogs 6s 8d (33½p).

Government by a Council of State was begun 14 February 1649, after the execution of Charles I. Four newly appointed verderers, Thomas Berrow, Christopher Worgan, Andrew Horne, and Arthur Rowles,[39] were ordered to examine and report on offenders who had cut trees and underwood. But the administration was in chaos : the preservators 'overtopped' the deputy woodwards and keepers who 'scarce dare look into the woods'.[40] On 27 August 1653[41] Major John Wade of Littledean was appointed by the council as chief administrator in Dean, but the Forest was expressly excluded 22 November[42] from the provisions of 'An Act for the Deafforestation, Sale, and Improvement of the Forests, etc'. In December[43] the inhabitants petitioned for the appointment of a constable and verderers, and for their privileges of common and estovers to be safeguarded and allowed through the speech court. Wade, though occupied with iron-making for the Commonwealth, pressed for reforms :[44] 'A settlement of the government of the Forest is of no small moment for its preservation, as hundreds live upon the spoil thereof'; 'the spoil carried on daily in the Forest makes my blood boil.' However, he achieved success in organising ship-building, despatching ship-timber, producing iron, and enclosing and planting parts of the Forest. He paid six keepers, twelve regarders, one bowbearer and two rangers; also three verderers (he himself was one) at £10 a year.[45]

In 1655[46] the inhabitants again petitioned for the restoration of their privileges. The following year,[47] the government considered holding a new eyre for Dean, and the exchequer was asked to send down to the swanimote the reports of commissions of 1645 and 1649; they were too bulky to be copied, and the Keeper of the Tower Records wanted to deliver them personally, for which he would require £50 and three horses. However, 9 June 1657 the government passed 'An Act for the mitigation of the rigour of the forest laws within the Forest of Dean and for the preservation

of wood and timber in the said Forest'.[48] The Act granted many
powers to freeholders, tenants, and other inhabitants; never before had they legally had such freedom in the management of
their properties and in the exercise of their privileges. The Lord
Protector was empowered to enclose and encoppice up to one-
third of Dean at any one time; the enclosures were to be thrown
open within twelve years. But the Act did not bring full order
into the Forest : abuses continued; and much of the enclosing was
opposed by the inhabitants. Wade begged the Admiralty 8 April
1659 :[49]

> It were well if a Justice in Eyre were resolved upon and
> empowered : never more needed, when horrid offenders can
> so impudently appear with petitions in their hands, calling
> that to be right which is against all law and justice. One of
> those petitioners has come down, making great brags of what
> great favour their petitions receive, and that all the inclo-
> sures shall be put open, and the whole rabble put in their
> cattle of all sorts; there are boasts of what great promises
> some members of the House have made, that all things shall
> be granted that is desired; out of the encouragement they re-
> ceive by letters from London, they speak strangely, and act
> worse, for the Forest in the chief coppices has been set on
> fire in 20 places. The chief of these petitioners is named
> Stallard, and is now in London; he was heretofore a Cava-
> lier, and for offences done in the prime part of the Forest
> was fined at the last Justice Seat nearly £300, but it was
> mercifully mitigated to £20. Lord Desborow knows him well
> and so does Sergeant Siese. Some conference should be had
> about it. It were acting the part of a schoolboy to make
> complaints, but I have cause, as last Monday some of the
> officers were set upon in performance of their duty, one
> being knocked down; but the next day I sent some more,
> who met with no opposition.

Opposition from the inhabitants was too much for Wade, and he
again appealed for help : 'But if it be the Parliament's pleasure,
or any others, that the Forest shall be left at the pleasure of the
people, let me know it, and I shall willingly turn my back upon
it as ever I came from school.' On 11 May 1659[50] the Commons
heard that 'upon the third day of this instant month, divers
people in tumultuous way in Dean broke down the fences and

cut and carried away the gates of certain coppices enclosed for the preservation of timber, turned in their cattle, and set divers places of the Forest on fire, to the great destruction of the young growing wood'. The matter was ordered to be 'referred to the sheriff and the justices of the peace for Gloucestershire to take special care to suppress and prevent all tumults and riotous meetings', and a committee of twenty-two members of the House was appointed 'to take care of the preservation of the timber and woods of the Commonwealth'. The outrages are referred to in a letter of 4 June[51] which states : 'There were risen in Dean 800 men at the first meeting who declared for nothing but their forest privileges, which they say have been extremely violated.' Another letter of 24 August the same year[52] mentions that 'Colonel Okey was sent down to suppress those that met'. An Order in Parliament 9 July 1659[53] instructed the council 'to keep the peace of the Forest of Dean and preserve the woods there as they were enclosed 7 May last'. Wade found it impossible to obtain adequate help; by 13 April 1660[54] he could no longer stand the conditions, and he wrote to the Admiralty asking that his account should be taken and he discharged. He had been a commendable administrator and had done his best : he had superintended the ironworks, acted as both forest-manager and timber-merchant, and under great difficulties had accomplished much else. He will be remembered as the person responsible in Dean for the first sowing and planting. No longer was replenishment left wholly to nature, yet the inhabitants, finding their commoning and pannage reduced, frequently threw down enclosures and sometimes set fire to them.

From 24 April 1660 Wade's work was taken over by commissioners appointed by Charles II. The Acts of the Commonwealth were declared void, and in Dean men high and low petitioned for grants, leases, favours, and offices with perquisites. Henry Somerset, later third marquis of Worcester and first duke of Beaufort, was appointed constable of St Briavels Castle, and Throckmorton and others were ordered to preserve the vert and venison.[55] Winter and Throckmorton pressed claims to earlier grants, and in 1661 the inhabitants petitioned for the restitution of their privileges, yet sensibly offered to relinquish their claims to wood and timber for as long as the king would suspend the ironworks and the cutting of trees.[56] However, a second grant

of much of the Forest to Winter in 1662[57] upset many good
intentions; and a third grant to him of like nature in 1667[58] was
too much for the inhabitants to tolerate. On 8 August 1667[59]
the constable-warden was commanded to revive the forest courts,
and with renewed proposals from the inhabitants, by 17 December 1667[60] 'the whole business of the Forest of Dean' was before
parliament. The chief considerations were the unpopularity of
the grant to Winter, the need to replenish and conserve trees for
shiptimber, and the safeguarding of the inhabitants' customary
privileges. On 30 June 1668 Winter was relieved of both his
grant and his commission to 'improve the Forest'.

The Dean Forest (Reafforestation) Act 1667 and the Verderers to 1808

By 1667 the situation in Dean was 'a perpetual struggle of jarring
interests, in which no party [Crown, grantees, landlords, and
commoners] could improve his share without hurting that of
another'.[61] Dean's need of protection and 'settlement' was urgent.
With much goodwill, legislation was enacted 9 May for the
'settlement of the Forest', based partly upon the principles set
out by the inhabitants in their 'Proposals' of about 1665. The
Dean Forest (Reafforestation) Act 1667 (19 and 20 Chas II, c.8)
is given in Appendix II. Its preamble asserts that Dean's wood
and timber 'is become totally destroyed', except in the Lea Bailey,
'whereby there is an apparent scarcity of timber there'. The
Crown, through Inclosure Commissioners, was to enclose at any
one time, 11,000 of the 23,000 acres for the growth of timber.
The enclosures were discharged of all privileges of common and
pannage till thrown open, taking of estovers was no longer lawful,
and deer were not to exceed 800. Forest law was again to apply
to Dean, and verderers were to be elected, and regarders
appointed. At last there was legislation ostensibly acceptable to
most interests. Much would depend on the energy and integrity
of the officials. The marquis of Worcester, constable-warden, was
given the names of those who with him and Sir Baynham
Throckmorton, his deputy, were to be Inclosure Commissioners;[62]

and appointments were made of three verderers—Colonel William and Edward Cooke of Highnam, and Duncombe Colchester of Mitcheldean—and of twelve regarders.

Throckmorton took charge of the deer and attended to the keepers;[63] and on 23 July 1668[64] he was given £46 14s 3d (£46.71) to repair the court-house at Kensley and the prison in St Briavels Castle. The division between his duties and those of the marquis, John May, the supervisor, and Charles Harbord and Thomas Agar, the surveyors-general of woods, is not evident. May and the verderers were told in 1669[65] 'not to suffer any sheep to go into the Forest', and the treasury wrote to the verderers concerning 'the great spoils and destruction of young sprouts of oak and beech heretofore made contrary to law by sheep, hogs, and other uncommonable cattle, which have frustrated the King's intention of preserving a nursery of trees';[66] they were to 'proceed effectually against the like offenders in future'. The warden with Colonel Cooke, a verderer, attended before the treasury 13 December[67] and reported that the ground they had resolved to enclose 'is fit for wood, and agreed at a swanimote court'. Enclosure was begun, but this was abhorrent to some of the inhabitants, who frequently threw down fences and hedges. Opposition was rife for several years. The Crown's intention to halt abuse was shown by the dismantling of the ironworks (1674), the building (1676) of a new court-house—the Speech House at Kensley (see Chapter 4)—and five other lodges, and the appointment of six keepers.[68] Throckmorton was appointed conservator and supervisor, and the keepers were put in his charge. He was to 'stock the chase with deer in a limited time'; and he was 'entitled to fee deer—10 bucks in summer and 10 does in winter'.[69]

It is unknown how frequently courts of attachment were held at the time, but one swanimote took place each year, at least from 1673 to 1684,[70] usually at the Speech House, but sometimes at Mitcheldean or in St Briavels Castle, before three verderers in the presence of the deputy constable. The foresters, woodwards, and keepers attended, together with the reeve and four men from each township of the Forest. The rolls of the courts, which show the thorough way in which trespasses were inquired into, commence with the date and meeting-place of the swanimote and the names of the verderers—they being the chief officers of

the court. In addition there were twelve named jurors. The
number of officials and other people averaged about seventy-five
at each session. All presentments were by the foresters and the
twelve jurors; the conviction was by the verderers, whose seals
were appended. No records of the fines have been found. Extracts from the presentments in the rolls are given below :

Swanimote held at Mitcheldean
Tuesday 6 November 25 Chas II (1673)
before William Cooke, Edward Cooke and
Sir Duncombe Colchester, verderers.

(1) John Mutloe of Ruardean, nailer, 2 September 25 Chas
    II, was found in the Forest in the bailiwick of Abenhall
    with 2 lead bombards (in English 'slugs') to the harm of
    the deer.

(2) John Worgan of Clearwell, yeoman, 14 September 25
    Chas II, entered the Forest with a certain bombard and
    killed a dam.

(3) Christopher Webber of Mitcheldean, labourer, and
    George Martin jnr of Blaisdon with certain other male-
    factors unknown at the third hour 23 June 25 Chas II,
    entered the Forest with a certain bombard and grey-
    hound 'to the hurt and terror of the beasts of the Forest'.

(4) John Yerworth, of English Bicknor, yeoman, and 2 other
    persons unknown, about 10 pm 4 July 25 Chas II,
    entered the Forest carrying 3 bombards to the 'hurt of
    the beasts'; and when Richard Jelfe, one of the keepers,
    asked them to deliver up the bombards they abused
    him verbally and pushed the bombards into his face,
    against the peace of the Lord King.

(5) Philip Aston of Coleford, a glover, 18 August 26 Chas
    II, entered the Forest with a bombard and killed a
    dam; and when John Knight, one of the keepers,
    followed him he wounded him in the leg.

Swanimote held in the house commonly called the
King's Lodge 9 June 28 Chas II (1676)
before Duncombe Colchester and William Cooke, verderers.

(1) William Parlor of English Bicknor, yeoman, 20 Novem-
    ber 27 Chas II, entered a wood called Coverham and
    cut young beech trees to the value of 12d, and took
    away 6 loads with a horse and cart.

(*2*) William Powell of Llandilo, labourer, 5 April 28 Chas II, set fire to turf and heather in the bailiwick of Abenhall.

(*3*) To the same court came William Powell and acknowledged that he owed the King £10; William Fletcher of Flaxley and Henry Pyrke of Mitcheldean, yeoman, acknowledged that each owed the King £5 to be raised of their goods and chattels, lands and tenements. Under the condition however that if William Powell appeared before the justices at the next eyre for the Forest, doing there what the court enjoined and meanwhile being of good behaviour towards the vert and venison of the Lord King, then the same acknowledgement will be void.

(*4*) To the same court came William Parlor of English Bicknor who acknowledged he owed the King £20; and William Powell and David Powell of Llandilo acknowledged indebtedness of £10 each.

Swanimote held at St Briavels Castle
14 September 29 Chas II (1667)
before Duncombe Colchester, William Cooke and
Edward Cooke, verderers.

(*1*) John Mutloe jnr of Ruardean, blacksmith, and Richard Cooke and Thomas Prokett of the same, labourers, on the night of 4 July 20 Chas II, entered the Forest at Hawkwell Head with bombards and killed a dam and carried it away.

(*2*) The same 3 men on the night of 4 July 29 Chas II, entered the Forest near Bakers Damme with bombards, and killed a soare [deer].

(*3*) Edward Taynton of Ruardean, labourer made an encroachment on the waste of the King in the bailiwick of Ruardean namely enclosing with a hedge land 10 yards in length and 1½ yd in width.

(*4*) William Bonde of the parish of Awre, labourer, 11 June 29 Chas II, entered the Forest at Harebroke with 2 lead sclopos (called 'slugs') and 'virtrum' [powder].

(*5*) Thomas Roberts of Ruardean, farmer, 21 April 29 Chas II, agisted 5 beasts (in English 'rother beasts') of the price of 25s, in the Forest at Shuttersford, contrary to the 1667 Act.

(*6*) Thomas Knight of Ruardean, yeoman, on 24 May

29 Chas II, agisted 4 horses of the price of 13s 4d in a hay in the bailiwick of Ruardean, to the waste and destruction of the vert and contrary to the 1667 Act.

(7) John Davies of Ruardean, 14 May 29 Chas II, agisted 4 horses of the price of 13s 4d in a hay of the Lord King.

(8) Thomas Hayward of Lydbrook agisted within the bailiwick of Ruardean 4 horses of the price of 7s 6d during the defence month 29 Chas II.

(9) Thomas Churchman of English Bicknor, farmer, 10 July 29 Chas II, agisted 4 horses of the price of 20s in the bailiwick of Lea.

(10) John Wellington of Lea Bailey, 20 July 29 Chas II, agisted 4 horses of the price of 40s in a hay in the bailiwick of Lea.

(11) Thomas Matthews of Coleford and Martha his wife with Thomas Ellis jnr, miner, and William Rosser, mason, of the same place, 31 August 29 Chas II, entered at Birchill in the bailiwick of Staunton and with a gun and lead shot and dogs killed a dam and carried it away.

(12) William Milsam, Coleford, 12 August 29 Chas II, entered the Forest in the bailiwick of Staunton with a bombard, and although John Knight, one of the keepers, pursued him he escaped.

(13) To the same court came William Morwent of Newnham, and took oath to be of good behaviour towards the vert and venison.

(14) To the same court came Ketford Bonde of Littledean lime burner, and Thomas Hughes of Flaxley, labourer, and took oath to be of good behaviour towards the vert and venison.

(15) To the same court came William Milsam of Coleford, yeoman, and acknowledged a debt to the King of £20; and John Worgan, yeoman, of Coleford and Richard Wisham of Staunton, yeoman, each acknowledged that they owed the King £10.

(16) To the same court came Thomas Hugh alias Morgan of Flaxley, labourer, and acknowledged he owed £20 to the King and another Hugh, labourer, and John Adams of the same, labourer, acknowledged that they owed £10 each.

(17) To the same court came Richard Hooper of Coleford

and acknowledged that he owed £20 to the King and Stephen Cowles of the same, and William Vicke of the same, mason, acknowledged a debt of £10 each as a condition that they will all be of good behaviour to the vert and venison.

Swanimote held at the house of the King
commonly called the Speech-House
Monday 10 June 30 Chas II (1678),
before Duncombe Colchester and William Cooke, verderers.

(1) Thomas James of the parish of Newland, yeoman, 29 March 30 Chas II, 'beheaded and trimmed' an Oak in Lea Bailey value 12 pence.
(2) Eliza Parsons of the Speech-House on 8 June 30 Chas II, allowed her servant Thomas Awvett to cut down 20 'arbusonlies' [? saplings] to the value of 12 pence, in the bailiwick of Abenhall.
Four other minor presentments were made at this Court.

Swanimote held at Mitcheldean
10 June 31 Chas II (1679),
before Duncombe Colchester, William Cooke and
Edward Cooke, verderers.

(1) Charles James of Yorkley, quarryman, was found on 24 May 31 Chas II, in York Walk carrying a 'sclope' and lead shot.
(2) John Bennett of Ruardean, 18 April 31 Chas II, chased and killed a dam in Herbert Walk.
(3) On January 31 Chas II certain venison was found in the house of James Dyrb of the parish of Newland and the said James thereupon fled.
(4) William Weaber, an inhabitant within the county, erected a cottage at Soudley to the injury of the Forest.

Swanimote held at Mitcheldean
14 September 32 Chas II (1680),
before Duncombe Colchester and Edward Cooke, verderers.

(1) Evan Morgan alias Hugh late of Flaxley, labourer, 25 June 32 Chas II, was found at Flaxley with part of 2 dams and he with George Jordan and other common malefactors were receivers of illegal venison within the Forest.

Swanimote held at Mitcheldean
Friday 10 June 33 Chas II (1681),
before Duncombe Colchester, William Cooke and
Edward Cooke, verderers.

(*1*) William Hibbs of Coleford, 22 December 32 Chas II,
was found in the Forest at Barn Hill carrying part of a
beast which he had stalked.

(*2*) Abraham Hayward of the parish of Awre had stalked a
beast in the bailiwick of Blakeney, 27 December 32
Chas II.

Swanimote held 10 June 34 Chas II (1682),
before Duncombe Colchester and William Cooke, verderers.

(*1*) William Fletcher, labourer of Flaxley, 3 May 34 Chas
II, entered the Forest carrying a net and killed a damam
[ie a prickett] at Hall's Patch in the Chestnuts.

(*2*) Stephen Steele jnr, labourer, of Littledean, 17 May 34
Chas II, took a tree at Edge Hill value 12 pence.

(*3*) Thomas Stephens of Ruardean, labourer, 17 May 34
Chas II, entered the Forest at Great Kensley and killed
a fawn and carried it away.

(*4*) The same Thomas Stephens, 7 October 33 Chas II,
hunted with a dog and 'sclopum' and killed a doe; he
was caught by Giles Creed, a keeper, who took the
venison off him.

Swanimote held at the house of the Lord King
within the Forest of Dean commonly called the
Speech House, Monday 15 December 36 Chas II (1684)
before Duncombe Colchester, William Cooke and
William Wolesley, verderers.

(*1*) Andrew Vaughan, one of the keepers, 13 September 35
Chas II, hunted in the Forest with dogs and killed a
deer ('sorell') in the bailiwick of Lea.

(*2*) The same Andrew Vaughan, 18 October 35 Chas II,
killed a deer ('soare') in the bailiwick of Lea.

(*3*) William Blew of Weston-under-Penyard, 2 May 35 Chas
II, chased a dam with a dog near Lymecroft Hill.

(*4*) The same William Blew, 10 March 35 Chas II, erected
cots ('cotas') to the terrifying of the deer.

Efficient as verderer's courts (though termed swanimotes)
appear, there was need for additional action against offenders.

Specially appointed commissioners for Dean urged 23 April 1680 :[71]

We are humbly of the opinion that the most likely way to render the Forest Courts effectual and to compel the Officers of Inheritance to be diligent and faithful in the discharge of their several duties for the preservation of the Forest is to procure a Justice Seat once a year for 6 or 7 years to be held in the long vacation within the Forest and not remote from it, which might be so done at a small charge by a deputation from the Lord Chief Justice in Eyre and by adjournment thereof from time to time.

The commissioners also reported that 'Mr Rowles, steward of the Forest Courts, deposed that he had in his hands about £40 and no more, for amercements imposed at the said courts under the value of 4d upon trespass in vert'. In the same year, 1680, there seems to have been an intention of a visit by itinerant justices to Coleford : a treasury warrant was issued 21 July[72] to the surveyors-general to raise £40 by the sale of decaying oaks and beeches 'for completing and furnishing a courthouse over the market place in Coleford in which to hold a Justice Seat'. It is unknown whether the money was raised and whether it was expended, but in any case no Justice Seat in Eyre was held.

The same year, 11 March 1680[73] the treasury asked the attorney-general to submit his opinion whether it was incompatible for Sir Duncombe Colchester of Mitcheldean to hold the two offices of verderer for life and woodward-in-fee of the Forest of Dean. The last office was a remnant of that of the earlier foresters-of-fee. The verderers were by this time becoming increasingly important officials : they were always informed when purveyors intended to inspect and mark trees for the Navy.[74] They were unpaid, despite the fact that 30 November 1683 a warrant was issued by the treasury to sell £420 worth of decayed oaks and beeches in Dean for two years' salaries of 'the verderers, regarders, and other officers';[75] the earl of Chesterfield, chief justice in eyre south of Trent, was to be informed of the sale.

Meanwhile the commoners had again played havoc with many of the enclosures. In 1688 the lodges Worcester and York had been 'pulled down by the rabble', and the Speech House 'defaced and spoiled'.[76] The treasury were concerned at the conditions in Dean, and that only about 2,500 acres were enclosed

of 11,000 acres allowed by statute. The good intentions of the
Act of 1667 had been thwarted;[77] the attempts to overcome
opposition to enclosure proved inffective; and commoners extended their privileges almost everywhere. In 1692,[78] the warden,
Henry, duke of Beaufort, and ten other officials including the
verderers, reported on the state of the forest and gave recommendations particularly for the improvement of the oaks being
grown for the Navy. They further recommended the rebuilding
of the two lodges, and the repair of the Speech House. They
presented a list of recent offenders against the vert, and urged
that some of the principal malefactors should be prosecuted. The
miners should be allowed wood for their works by 'the order of
the verderers at the attachment or swanimote court and taken
by view of a woodward or keeper as formerly'. The report continued:

We have enquired how duly the Forest courts have been
kept, and certify the same are regularly held, but by reason
that the attachment and swanimote courts can only convict
but not punish, the proceedings in either of them are in-
effectual to the preservation of the Forest without a Justice
Seat. And the great negligence of several of the 'foresters and
woodwards-in-fee' contribute much to the spoils committed.
How far the lands which are held and enjoyed by the several
'foresters and woodwards-in-fee' for the exercise of those
offices are inseparable from them or forfeitable upon such
neglect of their duties is humbly submitted to your Lord-
ships.

We further certify that the most likely way to render the
Forest courts effective for the punishment of offenders,
which for want thereof have grown numerous and insolent,
and to oblige the 'officers of inheritance' to be diligent and
faithful in the discharge of their several duties for the
preservation of the Forest, is to procure a Justice Seat once a
year for 6 or 7 years to be held in the long vacation, or not
very far remote from it, which might be done by deputation
from the lord chief justice in eyre to some of Their Majesties'
justices of assize going in their ordinary circuits from Gloucester to Monmouth, by which means all the diligent officers
will be encouraged in their endeavours, the negligent re-
proved, the vain hopes that some persons have given the
many and daring offenders about this Forest that the same

shall be made a free chace and consequently destroyed and
they exempted from punishment, will be utterly defeated
and disappointed.

Little improvement is evident following the report. The constable-warden (the duke of Beaufort, followed by Charles, Viscount Dursley, and Charles earl of Berkeley) was unable on
account of other commitments to take an active share of re-
sponsibilities in Dean. His deputies, and the supervisor appointed
to look after the silviculture, made some attempts at improvements. The verderers' court, to which Nathaniel Pyrke was
elected in 1695,[79] certified to the treasury in 1698[80] that eight
regarders were required in place of those dead or unqualified.
The officials were still having trouble with some inhabitants;
each attempt to enclose was opposed by the commoners, and
many trees were stolen. In 1710, Francis Wyndham, a verderer
elected in 1703, persuaded the treasury to agree to his distribut-
ing to the 'under-keepers' the fines for offences.[81] However, the
management was inadequate to overcome opposition. The Crown
and the constable-warden were in part to blame : there was no
vigorous policy, courts were infrequent, and only a small proportion of money raised from wood sales was reinvested in Dean.
Officials' salaries were too low, and often in arrears, leading to
dishonest practices and reliance on perquisites and poundages.[82]

Thomas Pyrke was elected a verderer in 1715,[83] Richard
Machen in 1716[84] and Tomkins Machen in 1724.[85] By 15 September 1721[86] Viscount Gage of Highmeadow was a verderer—then
an office sought for local prestige and authority. Three verderers,
Thomas Pyrke, Roynon Jones and Richard Hackett, in 1730
supported the interests of George James, one of the keepers, who
had shot one Glassenburg, a deer poacher; they persuaded the
treasury to pay James £13 12s 6d (£13.62) law expenses and
£20 reward.[87] The following year a warrant was given for the
repair of the Speech House,[88] and in 1732 the verderers and the
justices of the peace received warrants for money with which
to repair roads.[89] Two years later,[90] the election of a verderer took
place at Mitcheldean :

Last Thursday, Benjamin Bathurst, Esquire, accompanied
by a great number of gentlemen and freeholders, came to

H

Mitcheldean, where he was elected verderer of His Majesty's
Forest of Dean, in the room of Roynon Jones, Esquire, deceased; after which he entertained the company at dinner
in a very elegant manner.

Despite verderers, a supervisor, and six keepers, depredations
continued. The treasury solicitor was instructed to prosecute
those who had stolen timber.[91] In 1735 there were renewed
outrages by some of the inhabitants when pounds were broken
into and lodges again despoiled :[92]

On 5 July 1735 a notorious and villainous gang of persons, after other rioting, adjourned to the Speech House
Lodge, which is in the possession of George James commonly called Captain Whithorne. Upon their coming they
immediately fell to work on the pound, but being desired
by the Captain, who rose to the window, to disperse themselves, they returned him for answer a brace of sluggs in at
the window. The Captain upon that ply'd them warmly with
small shot, who sent him in return a great quantity of sluggs
and balls, so that almost a continual fire lasted for nearly
half an hour.

The following day one of the gang was taken and committed
to Gloucester Castle. In 1736[93] the supervisor, Christopher Bond,
drew attention to abuses in a memorial to the treasury :

A great number of cottages were erected upon the borders
of the Forest, the inhabitants whereof lived by rapine and
theft. There were besides many other offences committed
such as intercommoning of foreigners, surcharges of commons, trespasses in the Fence month and Winter Haining,
and in the enclosures; keeping hogs, sheep, goats, and geese,
being uncommonable animals, in the Forest; cutting and
burning the nether-vert, furze, and fern; gathering and taking
away crab-apples, acorns, and mast; and other purprestures
and offences; carrying away such timber-trees as were
covertly cut down in the night; by which practices several
hundred fine oaks were yearly destroyed, and the growth
of others prevented.

Bond further asserted that 'within the last thirty years the
elections of officers had been neglected, the courts discontinued,

and offenders left unpunished'. Furthermore 'the officers of Inheritance, and others, were grown remiss and negligent; so that
a few enclosures, and those of a few acres only, of the 11,000
acres were kept up, and these not carefully repaired'. He feared
'that some of the inferior officers of the Forest, finding offenders
to go on with impunity, were not only grown negligent, but also
connived at, if not partook in, the spoil daily committed'. The
opinions of the solicitor-general and attorney-general were that
'the offences were chiefly due to the neglect of putting the Act
of 1667 into execution'.[94] They recommended that vacant offices
should be filled, that the courts should be regularly held, and that
the officials should be strictly enjoined to do their duty. The
treasury solicitor was given renewed orders to prosecute
offenders.[95]

There is no evidence of improvement. The verderers, local
country squires, were far too busy to give day to day attention
to offenders. They occasionally obtained warrants for road repairs,[96] and urged that timber should continue to be released to
miners,[97] but beyond this, and the occasional holding of their
court, they left the detailed guardianship of the vert and venison
to the keepers. Indeed, Viscount Gage, one of the verderers, was
himself accused of illegally appropriating trees,[98] and in 1743 he
relinquished his appointment in favour of John Probyn of Newland.[99] His chief accusers were two verderers, Maynard Colchester (elected in 1735) and Thomas Pyrke, the supervisor
William Jones (himself a verderer from 1752), and the deputy
surveyor Tomkins Machen.[100] In 1756 Thomas Crawley-Boevey
was elected a verderer (he held office until his death in 1770).[101]

John Pitt, surveyor-general of woods, tried to bring some order
to Dean from 1758.[102] Most of his efforts were unsuccessful:
from 1771 he made representations to the treasury regarding
abuses by miners, colliers, timber stealers, and others, and tried
means to prevent them, introducing checks on the delivery of
timber to mines, and paying rewards on the conviction of
offenders.[103] He was opposed by local officials, some of whom
by taking excessive perquisites were no better than those inhabitants who preyed upon the Forest. The small success following
Pitt's well-intended measures show how useless it was to attempt
improvement while resident officers gained by continuance of
abuses.[104] The two supervisors during much of Pitt's term of

office, Roynon Jones, senior and junior, were paid a salary of
£100 but are not recorded as forwarding the interests of Dean.
The constable-wardens, namely John, Lord Chedworth, Nor-
borne Berkeley, and Frederick Augustus, earl of Berkeley, and
many of the officials under them, and others over whom they had
no jurisdiction, appear to have been concerned more with perquisites than duties. The deputy surveyor and his assistant made
efforts to conserve the Forest and to prevent abuses, but they too
took many customary perquisites. A letter 15 May 1769 to the
Navy Board[105] said that the swanimote court 'ought to be held
by any two at least of the verderers annually on 25 September
where the keepers are to deliver an account upon oath of all the
timber delivered to the colliers within the past year, and of all
the deer killed that comes within their knowledge either by
warrant or otherwise; but their court I am told is not regularly
held, nor any proper register nor entry of the proceedings kept'.
Another letter, in 1744,[106] asserted that the abuses in Dean were
so great that the writer knew of no better preventative than 'a
troop or two of Light Horse to patrol the Forest day and night'.
Yet another writer, 30 April 1777,[107] asserted that Dean was
'going to wreck and ruin : the depredations made therein by the
colliers and country people are incredible'.

Despite the election of other verderers (Edmund Probyn in
1773, and Roynon Jones in 1776—whose election took place
at the Bear Inn, Newnham-on-Severn)[108] matters in Dean were
still the same in 1780 when 29 May[109] the treasury received from
their solicitor a report on the abuses, advising the offer of rewards
of £20 or £50 for information leading to the conviction of
offenders. Thereafter some action is apparent, for in the seven
years to Michaelmas 1787 no less than 247 persons were convicted of stealing timber, and of other offences, fines amounting
to £729 9s 6d (£729.47) were imposed, and £540 was paid out
as rewards by the deputy surveyor.[110] In 1786[111] warrants were
issued for raising £2,000 from timber sales in Dean towards the
cost of building a gaol and certain houses of correction at Gloucester, for which purpose Joseph Pyrke and Thomas Crawley-
Boevey, verderers, viewed and released 1,768 oaks and beeches.
At this time Thomas Blunt, who resided at Abenhall, was deputy
surveyor, and Miles Hartland was his assistant. By 1787 the four
verderers were Joseph Pyrke (who had been elected following the

death of Maynard Colchester), Sir John Guise, Bt, Edmund
Probyn, and Roynon Jones. Their steward was John Matthews.

Dean, in spite of being robbed, exploited, and largely
neglected, proved an immense national asset by supplying much
timber for shipping, mining, and other uses. During the seven
years to Michaelmas 1787 the combined court of attachment
and swanimote had issued to the miners 2,930 warrants for
timber.[112] The enclosing during the Commonwealth and following the Act of 1667, together with the encouragement of natural
regeneration and the sowing and planting of beech and oak had,
despite obstructions, been worthwhile.

The Report of 1788

In 1787 commissioners were appointed to 'inquire into the state
and condition of the woods, forests and land revenues of the
Crown', and to 'suggest plans for redressing any abuses in the
management of them, and for the protection, increase, and supply
of the Royal Navy'. The commissioners' third report, 7 June
1788, dealt with Dean,[113] wherein they state :[114]

We are induced to bring this Forest first under the public
attention because, in proportion to its extent, it is by far
the most valuable, and the most proper for a nursery of
Naval timber; because the rights of the Crown and of the
neighbouring inhabitants, and officers of the Forest, were
distinctly ascertained by an Act of Parliament in the 20th
of Charles II [1667], a period not too distant as to render
it difficult to support those rights against ill-founded claims
or usurped possessions; and because the encroachments there
are perhaps more numerous, the perquisites and undue
advantages taken by the officers more exorbitant and des-
tructive, and the waste and depredation more rapid, than
in any other forest belonging to the Crown.

They drew attention to the fact that 'from the relaxation in
the legal government of the Forest, and the neglect of those to
whom the care of this valuable property was intrusted, abuses
have crept in and have been suffered to increase to such a height
as sufficiently accounts for the unprofitable and wasted condi-

tion to which it is now reduced'.[115] The perquisites and emoluments of the officials in Dean under custom were many and varied. Perquisites had been taken openly by the surveyor-general of woods, John Pitt, the deputy surveyor, Thomas Blunt, and the six keepers.[116] The commissioners asserted that to attempt any improvement of the Forest 'while this absurd system remains must be uneffectual'. Furthermore, 'the gentlemen who held the ancient offices of verderers, foresters, and woodwards (the two last of which are hereditary) had gradually withdrawn their care of the Forest, which appeared to be no longer an object of the attention of government; the superintendance or co-operation of the surveyor-general of the Crown lands with the surveyor-general of woods, which had been attended with the best effect, seems to have been discontinued about the same time; and the deputy surveyor and keepers, finding no check from their superiors, appear very soon to have lost sight of the public interest in the Forest, which it was their duty to watch over and protect'. The commissioners added :[117]

> Most of the ancient forest offices are become merely nominal, and are bestowed rather as marks of favour and distinction on gentlemen of consideration in the neighbourhood, than as appointments of real use and responsibility; and the surveyor-general and his deputies, instead of coming in aid of the ancient system of management, have ingrossed the whole, and acquired the sole and almost uncontrolled management of this valuable and important part of the public property.

The officers of the Forest, according to a list drawn up at a 'court of swanimote' held at the Speech House 25 September 1787, were :[118]

Lord Warden and Constable of St Briavels Castle :	Frederick Augustus earl of Berkeley.
Deputy wardens :	Maynard Colchester, Sir John Guise, Bt, Thomas Crawley-Boevey, Roynon Jones, Edmund Probyn, and Joseph Pyrke.

Verderers :

Sir John Guise, Bt, Edmund Probyn, Roynon Jones, and Maynard Colchester (followed in 1788 by Joseph Pyrke). The steward of the 'swanimote court' was John Matthews.

Chief Forester-of-fee and
Bowbearer :

Charles Edwin.

Foresters-of-fee :

Mrs Clarkes of the Hill, Thomas Foley, The Mayor and Burgesses of the city of Gloucester, and the heirs of the following : Ralph Colster, Thomas Williams, John Ayres, Sir Robert Gunning and Henry Yearsley.

Woodwards :
  Staunton :   William Viscount Gage
  Bicknor :   William Viscount Gage
  Bearse :   Charles Edwin
  Mitcheldean :   Maynard Colchester
                                 (deputy : John Cooke)
  Lea Bailey :   Maynard Colchester
  Blakeney :   George Savage
  Ruardean :   Mrs Clarkes of the Hill
  Abenhall :   Edmund Probyn (deputy :
                                 Josiah Coleman)
  Bleyths Bailey :   John Beale (deputy : Walter Taylor)

Keepers :
  Speech House Walk :   Thomas Harvey (deputy :
                                 George Calaghan)
  Blakeney Walk :   William Stephens (deputy :
                                 John Phillips)
  Coleford Walk :   Richard Bennett (deputy :
                                 John Hampton)
  Littledean Walk :   John Brett (deputy :
                                 Thomas Hampton)
  Ruardean Walk :   Richard Bradley
  Parkend Walk :   Robert East (deputy :
                                 William Meredith)

In addition there was a comparatively ancient office of 'conservator' (Roynon Jones)—but no 'advantage to the Forest had
arisen from it of late years'—and a watchman (Thomas Wood)
who received £10 annually as well as a house built in 1782 and
perquisites arising from 'the fines and rewards on conviction of
timber stealers, of which he received a share in common with
others concerned with him in detecting and convicting offenders'.[119] Charles Edwin (*supra*) asserted that as bowbearer 'it was
his duty to attend His Majesty with a bow and arrow, and six
men clothed in green, whenever His Majesty shall be pleased to
hunt within the Forest'.

The court of attachment, usually called the swanimote court,
had been held only once in each year on 25 September, when
it was convened 'merely for the sake of form', and then chiefly to
certify warrants for timber to Free Miners, and to receive on oath
the returns of the keepers as to timber and deer delivered. The
four verderers informed the commissioners[120] that they had been
'elected by virtue of the King's writ, by the freeholders at large
in the county of Gloucester, which office is for life', and their only
emolument was 'a fee buck and doe in season, delivered by the
keeper under warrant from the verderer'. Their duty was 'to
preserve the vert and venison of the Forest, to preside as judge
of the courts of attachment and swanimote, to receive presentments from the keepers and other officers of all offences respect-
ing the timber and deer, to inquire into encroachments and into
the conduct of the keepers and the other officers of the Forest;
but with no power to punish abuses therein'. Conviction and
punishment were now in magistrates courts, by justices of the
peace. The commissioners recommended that an Act of Parliament should pass to appoint and empower a commission *inter
alia* to :[121]

(*1*) treat and agree with freeholders, commoners, and others
     as to their rights or claims,
(*2*) dispose of or destroy the deer,
(*3*) inquire into claims relating to mining-timber, and regu-
     larise cottages and other encroachments,
(*4*) ensure the prohibition of waste and destruction; and
     ensure the adoption of a new plan of payment of every
     efficient officer in the Forest,

(5) make six enclosures (18,000 acres) for the production of timber, excluding roads, mines, and 'open parts'.

Under proper management the Forest would be 'productive of the most solid national advantages, without hindering the rights of any individual'.[122] However, insufficient action was taken on the recommendations, other than some tightening of the administration as shown by notices announcing severe penalties for abuses displayed in the Forest in 1791,[123] and records of many prosecutions.[124] Nevertheless the luminating by the commissioners had done some good.

References to Chapter 3

1   Hammersley, G., 'The Revival of the Forest Laws under Charles I', *History*, XLV, 154, June 1960, 85–102
2   C.99/25
3   SP16/236, 20
4   Ibid 266, 576
5   Hammersley, 'The Revival of the Forest Laws . . .', op cit, 93
6   E178/3837, 5304
7   The proceedings of the Court are available at great length. Hammersley ('The Revival of the Forest Laws . . .', op cit, 93 sqq.) gives a résumé of them. Hart, *The Commoners of Dean Forest*, 29–32, has dealt with some of the detail. Additional information is available in C.99, X–XX; Gloucester Public Liby, Mss L.F.6.2; Bodl Mss Gough Glouc, 1; Bodl Mss Rawl D. 119; *H.M.C.*, 3rd Rep, App, 185, 211; 11th Rep, App pt vii, 250; *H.M.C.* Bath Mss 508/27, 185; Westminster Mss f.17/2, 211; f.6/193, 213; Phelips Mss 282/3; *Anc Kalendars* 3,437/8; B.M. Harl Mss 4840 and 738, ff.295–311; Lincolns Inn Liby, Hale Mss XLV (5) and Maynard Mss LIX (4)
8   Hart, *The Commoners* . . . , op cit, 29, 167
9   C.99, X
10   Bodl Gough Mss Glouc 1, ff.17–68d; *B.M.* Harl Mss 4850, ff.10–53d
11   E401/1924, 3 Jan 1637–8; SP16/402, 123
12   SP16/271, 143; *B.M.* Harl Mss 738, f.300
13   E112/181/131
14   *B.M.* Harl Mss 738, ff.303–5

15 Ibid 738, ff.306–8
16 SP16/293, 262
17 Ibid /289, 100
18 E401/1923, 9 and 19 Aug, 2 December 1636; E401/1924, 27 May 1637; c.66/2766; Bodl Bankes Mss 43/34
19 Hammersley, 'The Revival of the Forest Laws . . .', op cit, 100
20 SP16/273, 182 refers to £100,000
21 C.99/31, m.2
22 E146/3/29
23 E101/141/4, m.1–34
24 Hart, *Royal Forest*, 118
25 E401/1924
26 Ibid 1925
27 SP16/367, 412, No 52
28 Ibid/408, 276
29 Ibid /389, 400
30 Hart, *Royal Forest*, 123
31 Ibid 124
32 SP16/488, 560
33 Ibid /448, 560; Hart, *Royal Forest*, 125
34 Hart, *Royal Forest*, 127
35 *Lords' Journals*, IV, 349; Statute 16 Chas I, c.16
36 Hammersley, 'The Revival of the Forest Laws . . .', op cit, 102
37 Hart, *Royal Forest*, 131
38 E146/1/34
39 SP18/2, 176
40 Hart, *Royal Forest*, 138
41 SP18/39, 107
42 Firth and Rait, *Acts and Ordinances of the Interregnum*, 1911, II, 811
43 SP18/42, 326
44 Hart, *Royal Forest*, 141
45 Ibid 146, 147
46 SP18/102, 83
47 Ibid /129, 2; SP25/77, 246
48 Firth and Rait, op cit, II, 1114; Hart, *Royal Forest*, App. X
49 SP18/202, 328
50 *Glos Notes and Queries*, V, Pt III, new series
51 *H.M.C.* Bath Mss, I, 132
52 Ibid 136

53 SP18/203, 14
54 Ibid /220, 413
55 *H.M.C.*, VII, 85
56 Hart, *Royal Forest*, 157
57 Ibid 158
58 Ibid 161
59 SP29/212, 368
60 *Cal Tsy Bks*, II, 151
61 *Third Report of 1788*, 6
62 *Cal Tsy Bks*, II, 351, 382
63 Ibid 160
64 Ibid 584
65 Ibid III, Pt I, 112, 113, 262
66 Ibid
67 Ibid 170
68 Hart, *Royal Forest*, 173–6
69 Ibid 175
70 GRO, D36/Q2(09)
71 Ibid D23/31; Hart, *Royal Forest*, 300
72 *Cal Tsy Bks*, VI, 641
73 *Cal Tsy Bks*, VI, 470
74 Ibid VII, Pt I, 138
75 Ibid Pt II, 967
76 Ibid IX, 1495
77 Ibid, VIII, 1888
78 Ibid IX, 1495; printed in Hart, *Royal Forest*, App XV
79 Nicholls, H. G., *Personalities of the Forest of Dean*, 1863, 99
80 *Cal Tsy Bks*, XIV, 61, 284
81 *Cal Tsy Papers*, IV, 186
82 Hart, *Royal Forest*, 193
83 Nicholls, *Personalities* . . . , op cit, 99
84 Richard Machen died in 1735. A note made in 1860 by Edward Machen reads : 'There is a tradition in our family that in a fit of the gout the people carried him to a court at the Speech House on their backs.' (Mss *penes me*)
85 Nicholls, *Personalities* . . . , op cit, 88, 90
86 *Cal Tsy Papers*, VI, 81
87 *Cal Tsy Bks and Papers*, I, 355, 375
88 Ibid II, 138
89 Ibid 238, 258, 289, 302
90 *Gloucester Journal*, 4 Sept 1734
91 *Cal Tsy Bks and Papers*, II, 228

92   *Gloucester Journal*, 22 July 1735; *Glos Notes and Queries*, III, 372
93   *Third Report of 1788*, 22
94   *Cal Tsy Bks and Papers*, III, 159
95   Ibid II, 359
96   Ibid 298, 363, 532; V, 83
97   GRO, D23, 478
98   *Cal Tsy Bks and Papers*, IV, 338
99   In 1742 John Probyn had been appointed by the Justice in Eyre to the office of steward and registrar of the swanimote and court of attachment in Dean (GRO, D23, 664).
100   Hart, *Royal Forest*, 197
101   Nicholls, *Personalities* . . . , op cit, 44
102   *Third Report of 1788*, 23
103   Hart, *Royal Forest*, 198
104   *Third Report of 1788*, App 38
105   *Eighteenth Century Documents relating to the Royal Forests, &c* (selected from the Shelburne Mss in the William L. Clements Library), by A. L. Cross (Macmillan, New York, 1928), 103
106   Ibid 134
107   Ibid 141
108   Nicholls, *Personalities* . . . , op cit, 80
109   *Third Report of 1788*, App 37
110   Ibid App 38
111   Ibid App 35
112   Hart, *Royal Forest*, 200
113   *The Third Report of the Commissioners appointed to inquire into the State and Condition of Woods &c of the Crown*, referred to throughout this work as 'Third Report of 1788'
114   *Third Report of 1788*, 10
115   Ibid 20
116   Hart, *Royal Forest*, 203, 204
117   *Third Report of 1788*, 25
118   Ibid App 14
119   Ibid 30
120   Ibid App 16, 17, 18, 21
121   Ibid 41
122   Ibid 46
123   GRO, D23/X.4
124   L.R. 4/16/56–67; /17/108, 147–8; 18/166–9; /19/196

Four: The Speech Court and the Speech House

From as early as 1335[1] the verderers' court of attachment in Dean was held at Kensley House (*Kenesleie* or *Kenesleye*), which stood in the centre of the Forest alongside the track (in part it had been a Roman road) which ran westwards from Cinderford Bridge to Cannop Bridge. A hundred years later[2] the court was still held at Kensley House, but the court was sometimes called that held 'on Speeches Day'. Charcoal was used to heat the courtroom when Dean's inhabitants appeared before the verderers to speak of their forest privileges, and to pay an acknowledgement for having taken their necessary estovers. Fines continued to be levied for vert offences, and enrolments were made of cases concerning deer. During the sixteenth century Kensley House, then in use, was sometimes called 'the swanimote courthouse', for the repair of which the Crown in 1584[3] allocated money and timber. The same house was used for the court, increasingly called 'the speech court', during the first quarter of the seventeenth century.[4] Occasionally sessions were noted as being held at *Kannope* (Cannop) a mile to the west, where stood Cannop House.[5] The Free Miners found the speech court convenient and helpful: clause 26 of their 'Laws and Privileges', of which the earliest transcript is 1610,[6] reads:

> For the customs that the miners [have] done for the King, the constable that is for the time shall deliver [to] the miners in [every] six weeks at the Speech that is the court for the wood before the verderers, by the woodwards that keepeth the place (that is to say) sufficient of timber to maintain the King's advantages and profit, as also for the salvation of the miners as they did in time out of mind without hurt or attachment made of the King's officers (that is to say) free the Forest unto the miners.

The site of Kensley House was that where today stands the Speech House (an hotel with courtroom): this is evident because part of the present building was erected c 1676 'in the same place' as the earlier speech house.[7] (The name Kensley is retained by a keeper's lodge which stands about a quarter of a mile NNE of the Speech House; it was built on the site of an earlier lodge, part extant, of which one of the stones, referring to Kensley Enclosure, bears the date 1811.)

The intention to build the present Speech House (ie the oldest part of it) arose in 1669[8] when Sir Baynham Throckmorton of Clearwell, and other inhabitants of Dean represented to the treasury 'that the keeping and holding of forest courts for the preservation of vert and venison, in accordance with the laws of the Forest in pursuance of the Act of 1667 [noted in Chapter 3] draws together a great number of officers, gentlemen and free-holders, for whose reception there is no house within the liberty of the Forest'. They asserted that Coleford, in the west of Dean, was 'the most convenient place, being adjacent to the Forest and in the midst of the perambulation', and that the inhabitants of that town had offered 'at their own cost' to erect a 'speech-house' over their 'town house'. At a treasury meeting 21 July 1669[9] it was noted that John May, supervisor of the Forest, recommended the allowance of forty tons of timber to the town for this pur-pose. He was instructed 'to treat with the town about it', and 10 January 1670[10] he with Throckmorton attended the treasury; a minute of the meeting adds: 'The King to be moved in it.' Approval was obtained, and the treasury minuted 4 February:[11] 'The warrant for the Speech-House is to be sent up for the King's hand.' The warrant was signed 7 February, and forwarded 11 February to Thomas Agar, surveyor-general of woods.[12] How-ever, it soon appeared that the marquis of Worcester, warden of the Forest, and William Cooke one of the verderers, opposed the intention of siting the courtroom at Coleford. They attended the treasury 23 February and urged that the place where the old speech house stood was the most convenient for building a new one.[13] The treasury concurred, and the following day Agar was commanded to stop felling timber for Coleford.[14] On 7 March[15] the marquis and Agar attended another treasury meeting, at which it was decided to build the speech house 'in the old place, as, according to Mr Agar, it is the most convenient place, being in the middle of the Forest'. On 11 May it was reported[16] that Agar undertook to build the speech house 'for 40 tons of timber and £200', and a warrant was issued to him 10 August[17] to fell oaks for the purpose, but any fit for the Navy were not to be used.

There appears to have been a delay of three years in beginning the building. On 10 July 1673[18] a treasury warrant was issued to the two surveyors-general of woods and to the supervisor, to mark trees for 60 tons of timber for 'rebuilding the speech-house', and so many dotard (decaying) trees as will raise £200; the warrant was written over and redated 22 September 1673. The following year, 2 December,[19] the treasury agreed for £50 to be expended on the building of stables at the speech house, and 2 March 1675[20] a warrant was issued authorising the sale of dotard trees in order to raise the money. It seems probable that the building of the speech house and its stables was completed soon afterwards. The date 1676 is on a stone lintel (*Fig 6*), believed to have been originally over one of the doorways in the stables, transferred to the old northern entrance, but again removed when that entrance was blocked in about 1883. The lintel is now at the extreme east of the north elevation over the doorway leading to the saloon bar.

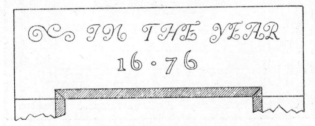

Fig 6.   Stone lintel (1676) on the north of the Speech House

The speech house was certainly substantially completed by 1676 because in that year it was possible to hold therein a swanimote attended by some 75 officials and offenders (see Chapter 3);[21] and another swanimote was held there in 1678. A treasury minute 15 March 1680[22] notes that 'the Speech House is to be repaired at the King's charge' : probably some building defects were patent. From about this time the house was often referred to as the King's Lodge and there is a tradition that Charles II visited it; the escutcheon dated 1680 and with the initials 'C.R.II' (*Fig 7*) may commemorate the visit: now much weathered, it is set above the west entrance to the court room. A session of the Mine Law Court was held in the Speech House 27 April 1680. Daniel Drake was the keeper of the Lodge and its 'walk' ie its large tract of woodland.[23]

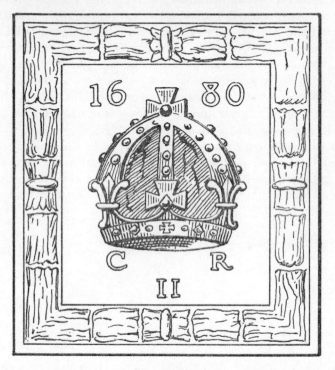

Fig 7.   Escutcheon (1680) on the west of the Speech House

At the time of the erection of the Speech House, five other lodges were built in Dean—those of 'York', 'Danby', 'Worcester', 'Latimer', and 'Herbert'—and the Forest was divided into six 'walks'.[24] The Crown's intention was to improve the management of the woodlands. In January 1688[25] the Speech House was seriously damaged during a riot by some of the inhabitants: it was 'much defaced and spoiled by the rabble'. At the same time, the lodges of Worcester and York had been 'pulled down by the rabble, and absolutely necessary to be rebuilt'. On 9 July 1689[26] Drake, keeper of the Speech House, was granted by the treasury £3 towards urgent repairs. On 21 April 1690[27] the surveyor-general obtained the treasury's agreement to repair the building 'at a cost of £200', but there was delay in proceeding: commissioners in 1692[28] pointed out that the cost 'over and above the moneys already laid out for the repairs of the roof will be

The Speech Houſe

Fig 8.   The Speech House in 1782 (after T. Pinnell)

£109 besides two tons of timber, and carriage £2 12s'. How much was eventually expended is unknown.

A sketch of the elevation of the Speech House in 1782 is extant (*Fig 8*)[29]. Information on the subsequent history of the building is given in Chapter 5.

References to Chapter 4

1   E32/33
2   S.C.6/858/15
3   L.R.12/1126, Series III
4   E137/13/4, m.1–8; E178/3837, m.66
5   Cannop House (which, according to remnants found by

I

the present writer, stood 100 yards west of the most southerly of the twentieth-century semi-detached houses built for Cannop Colliery) is mentioned in 1628 (E125/4/ 269), was owned in 1634 by Sir Robert Bannister (E112/ 181/131), in 1639 by John Mansell and Ambrose Bavin (BM Lansd Mss, 166), in 1660 by William, Lord Mainard (SP29/17, 295), and in 1667 by Banistree Mainard (Act 19 and 20 Chas II, c.8)

6   Knole-Sackville MSS (Cranfield Papers, 1444); Hart, C. E., *The Free Miners*, 1953, Chapter II
7   *Cal Tsy Bks, III*, Pt I; 372, 531
8   Ibid 112, 524
9   Ibid 112, 113
10 Ibid 342, 345
11 Ibid 358
12 Ibid 524
13 Ibid 372
14 Ibid 531
15 Ibid 380
16 Ibid 429
17 Ibid 648
18 Ibid IV, 369
19 Ibid 268
20 Ibid 689
21 GRO, D36
22 *Cal Tsy Bks*, VI, 482
23 Hart, *Royal Forest*, 177, n.198
24 Ibid 177
25 *Cal Tsy Bks*, IX, 1495; Hart, *Royal Forest*, 304
26 *Cal Tsy Bks*, IX, 40
27 Ibid 586
28 Ibid 1495; Hart, *Royal Forest*, 305
29 F17/4; Negative D2632A

Five: The Verderers of more recent times

The Napoleonic Wars had drawn attention to England's dire need of ship timber. Nelson visited Dean in 1802 and his memorandum[1] written in 1803 indicated deficiencies in its store of timber-trees and suggested remedies. That year, Lord Glenbervie became surveyor-general of woods; his deputy in Dean was James Davies. Both were anxious to replant the Forest. Davies was succeeded in February 1808 by his son Edward Tomkins Davies (later the surname was changed to Machen), of Eastbach Court and later of Whitemead Park, who had a great love for Dean and came from a family with deep roots in it. He was in time to undertake much work within the Dean Forest (Timber) Act, 1808,[2] given in Appendix III, which confirmed much of the Act of 1667 and provided the powers necessary for enclosure. Glenbervie and Machen encouraged an extensive programme of enclosure and planting. Messrs A. & W. Driver were given a contract to enclose, fence, drain, and plant 10,324 acres to complete the 11,000 acres. Their operations were in the hands of their agent Amos Sleed, and the work was supervised from 1810 by William Billington.[3]

In 1810 an Act[4] united the office of surveyor-general of land revenues with that of the surveyor-general of woods and forests, to form 'the Commissioners of Woods, Forests, and Land Revenues of the Crown'—thereafter referred to as 'the Office of Woods'. An Act of 1817[5] abolished the office of chief justice in eyre and wardens of the forest north and south of Trent. Henry Somerset, duke of Beaufort, now held the honourable but ineffective office of warden. The four verderers who were in office in 1788 were still holding office in 1810; but on 3 August 1819 Sir Thomas Crawley-Boevey of Flaxley was elected a verderer in place of Edmund Probyn.[6] Machen and his assistants, as well as looking after the Highmeadow Estate (lying to the north-west of Dean) repurchased by the Crown from Viscount Gage in 1817, tended Dean's 11,000 acres of plantations with wisdom and enthusiasm, and ensured that sheep and cattle were kept out of the enclosures. The inhabitants had given little opposition, and most of them looked upon Machen with mixed respect and awe. The Crown Lands Act 1829,[7] sections 100 to 105, authorised the verderers to inquire into 'unlawful inclosures, purprestures, encroachments, or trespasses' and to make fines 'not exceeding £20'; also to nominate and appoint an officer of the court to execute its judgements, and to inquire into the conduct of the officers of the Forest, and to impose on them fines up to £10. (The enacting part of section 100 was recited and repealed so far as regards purprestures only, by section 14 of the Dean Forest (Encroachments) Act 1838.[8] The verderers about this time were Sir Thomas Crawley-Boevey, Bt (elected in 1819), Sir Berkeley William Guise, Bt, Joseph Pyrke (elected in 1804), and Maynard Colchester junior (elected in 1817).

By 1831 the commoners were aggrieved that the enclosures were not thrown open; they deemed the trees to be now adequately established and of a size that would not be damaged by the grazing of animals (other than goats). In June a local anti-enclosure movement led by Warren James threw open most of the enclosures and drove sheep and cattle into them.[9] Some 2,000 people with pickaxes and spades left scarcely a mile of unbroken boundary. The Royal Monmouthshire Militia and Third Dragoons quelled the riot; James was apprehended, and the rioters had to remove the animals and repair the enclosures. It was necessary for the government to inquire into grievances, and this resulted in the passing of the Dean Forest Commission Act 1831.[10] The commission thereby appointed considered fully claims in the Forest, particularly those of commoning and free mining. The five reports rendered, and the consequent Acts, have been dealt with elsewhere.[11] Encroachments were compounded after the Dean Forest (Encroachments) Act 1838[12] whereunder the verderers were empowered to inquire into such encroachments (but not purprestures) at their court of attachment. The verderers were also given powers under the Dean Forest (Mines) Act 1838[13] to hear and determine appeals by Free Miners against decisions of the commissioners appointed under the Act.

By this time Charles Bathurst had been elected verderer (1835) in place of Sir Berkeley Guise, and in 1849 Sir Martin Hyde Crawley-Boevey, Bt took the place of Sir Thomas Crawley-Boevey, Bt, the election having been held at Newnham-on-Severn.

In 1835, following the death of the duke of Beaufort, the office of constable-warden was abolished[14] and the relevant duties and powers were merged into those of the commissioners of woods. The court of attachment was held infrequently from 1838 to 1848, chiefly dealing with encroachments; during the ten years there were about 50 convictions for vert offences. The verderers were given additional powers to inquire into encroachments by the Dean Forest (Encroachments) Act 1844.[15]

In 1849 a Select Committee ('The Duncan Committee') of the House of Commons reported on Dean and Highmeadow.[16] They published 'a Return of all verderers, and all officers acting under them, and their fees, perquisites, and emoluments'.[17] The verderers were Joseph Pyrke, Maynard Colchester, Charles Bathurst, and Sir Thomas Crawley-Boevey, Bt. Their only emoluments were one fee buck and one fee doe annually, for which they paid the keepers 21s (105p) and 10s 6d (52½p) respectively. Dates of courts are given as well as the names of the attending verderers. The encroachments and attachments presented are stated, with a note of the fines imposed. Most of the cases concerned encroachments, opening of quarries, carrying away of sand, building fern ricks, cutting turf, and erecting houses. Roynon Mason, appointed 6 October 1847, had the title of 'steward and registrar of all and every the swanimote and attachment courts of His Majesty's Forest of Dean'; his fees were:

Information : 1s (5p)
Summons : 1s (5p)
Conviction : 2s (10p)
Order to Abate, including copy for the keeper : 1s 6d (7½p)
Copy of proceedings : 6d (2½p) per 72-page folio.
Copy of any document : one-third the original.

John Clarke, appointed 28 October 1847, was the 'officer for exacting the judgements and orders of the court of attachment', for which he received the following fees :

Levying every distress : 7s 6d (37½p)
Keeping distress where the debt exceeds £1 a day : 1s (5p)
Attending at each Verderers' Court : 5s (25p)
Every other duty : 5s (25p) a day.

The committee commented :[18]

> The verderers' courts are held four times a year. En-
> croachments only are dealt with by the verderers. The com-
> plaints respecting their election will be found detailed in the
> evidence. The number of persons charged during the last
> ten years was about 50; the convictions were all of a sum-
> mary nature, and the fines and costs but trifling. Fresh
> attempts have been made to encroach, but these have always
> been defeated at the next court of attachment.
>   Most of the forest officers are become merely nominal
> since the forests have ceased to be places of royal sport and
> recreation, and are bestowed rather as marks of favour and
> distinction on gentlemen of consideration, resident in the
> neighbourhood of the forests, than as appointments of real
> use or responsibility. The salaries attached to these appoint-
> ments are generally inconsiderable in amount, the chief per-
> quisite being a supply of a certain number of bucks annually
> on which no fees are charged, though fees to the amount of
> £1 6s on bucks, and 13s for does, are charged on the war-
> rants of all other parties not even excepting Her Majesty
> and the other members of the Royal Family.

After the report of the Select Committee, matters in Dean went
on much as before, with one exception : in 1850 the fallow deer,
estimated to number 400 to 500 head, were almost wholly destroyed (see Chapter 7), chiefly on account of their 'tending to
foster bad and idle habits among the inhabitants'.

In 1851 Duncombe Pyrke was elected a verderer in place of
Joseph Pyrke, deceased. Machen resigned as deputy surveyor in
February 1854, to be followed by James Brown until 11 November, when Sir James Campbell, Bt, was appointed in charge of
the Forest. Machen had faithfully served Dean for forty-seven
years; and examples of his great efforts to prevent encroachments and other abuses are apparent in a note-book of William
Harvey, then keeper of Worcester Walk, which contains *inter
alia* presentments to the verderers' court from June 1836 to
November 1838. Machen was elected a verderer in 1860, and in
returning thanks for his election he said :[19]

> The office of verderer is one of great antiquity, and in
> former times of considerable importance, but by lapse of

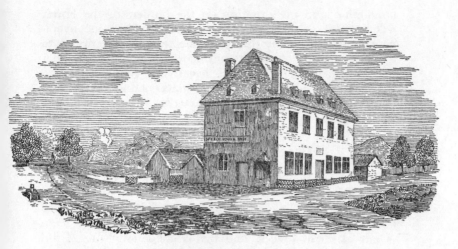

Fig 9. The Speech House from the north-west, c 1858 (from an old woodcut)

time and change of circumstances its duties are diminished and its privileges gone. The duty of a verderer as laid down in the old law books is to preserve the vert and the venison. The latter part of this duty has ceased by the destruction of the deer. For my own part I lament this—not because I should in this office have been entitled to a buck and a doe —but because they were an appropriate ornament of a Royal Forest, but the increase of population and works and public opinion, made it necessary.

The preservation of the vert still remains, and I trust I may do all in my power for that purpose having passed so many years of my life in the work of its production. Its purpose is no longer covert for the deer but the growth of Navy timber which when the planting began was thought a great national object, but really in these days so many changes take place that, before the timber is fit for the Navy, ships may be built of iron or gutta percha—yet the money value of the timber in this Forest will be great when fit for felling and will much exceed a million pounds.

I must now apologise for having offered myself at all to your notice at this very advanced age which it has pleased God to allow me to reach, but I assure you it was not my own seeking. I was asked to do so as a means of promoting unanimity, and my situation on the borders of the Forest will enable me to perform its duties without inconvenience. I beg also to say that your choice is very gratifying to me as it gives me an additional tie to the Forest to which I am so much attached, and because I have reason to believe that my election is not unacceptable to the verderers with whom I have before acted so long in a different office.

I am now going to take the oath of office which calls me to preserve the rights of the Crown and do equal justice to the poor and the rich. I will, as far as I can, keep both these objects in view, and not suffer encroachments on the rights and privileges of the people or the Crown. We have now a Sovereign we all love and who sets a bright example to all her subjects. The one great error I can find in the reign of our excellent Queen, and this is not a small one (I am not going to speak high treason), is that she has never visited her Forest of Dean. I hope she may still do so: she will find not only hills and vales unequalled in beauty for the eye, but stalwart arms and loyal hearts ready for her service.

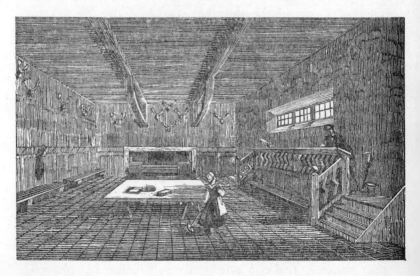

Fig 10. The Verderers' Courtroom in the Speech House, c 1858 (from an old lithograph)

Page 141 (above) The Speech House from the north (Frank H. Harris); (below)
The Speech House from the west (G. J. M. Smith)

Page 142 (above left) Sir Lance Crawley-Boevey, Bt (verderer); *(above right)* Sir Russell J. Kerr (verderer); *(below left)* Major Charles P. Ackers, OBE (verderer); *(below right)* J. W. Haines (steward)

Page 143 (above) The First Viscount Bledisloe, PC, GCMG, KBE, in his 90th year; *(below)* The stone outside the Speech House which traditionally marks the centre of Dean, renovated to honour Viscount Bledisloe's fifty years as Verderer, 21 September 1957. Left to right: A. H. Popert, Major Charles P. Ackers, OBE, Viscount Bledisloe, O. J. Sanger, and Dr Cyril Hart

Page 144 (above) HM Queen Elizabeth and HRH Prince Philip with the verderers and other officials at the Speech House 24 April 1957; (below) HM Queen Elizabeth planting an oak near the Speech House 24 April 1957 (see also Plate p 164)

In 1861 the Dean Forest (Amendment) Act[20] was passed, which in section 25, after referring to the Acts of 1829 and 1838, continued :

Whereas the verderers of the said Forest of Dean have powers to inquire into all unlawful inclosures, trespasses, and encroachments within the said Forest, and to proceed against persons guilty of the same, but doubts have been entertained as to the nature of the trespasses comprised within the said provisions : Be it enacted and declared, that the provisions now in force under and by virtue of the said Acts or either of them relating to trespasses within the said Forest of Dean, and the punishment thereof, did and shall extend to all cases of trespass by cutting, taking, or carrying away of turf, gravel, stone, sand, or other soil within the said Forest, in addition to all other trespasses within the purview of the said Acts or either of them.

On 6 July 1863 Edmund Probyn, Edward Owen Jones, and Charles Bathurst junior were elected verderers in place of Charles Bathurst senior, Edward Machen, and Sir Martin Hyde Crawley-Boevey, Bt. In January 1873 Sir Thomas Hyde Crawley-Boevey, Bt, was elected in the stead of Edward Owen Jones, deceased. On this occasion voting took place on three consecutive days, Alfred Goold being the defeated candidate; the state of the poll at the end of each day was :[21]

	1st day	2nd day	3rd day
Sir Thomas Hyde Crawley-Boevey, Bt	420	550	862
Alfred Goold	151	274	433
Majority	269	276	429

Evidence in regard to the verderers and their court was given to a Select Committee of the House of Commons in 1874,[22] to whom James Wintle of Newnham-on-Severn, steward to the verderers since 1863 (previous stewards had been Henry Smart and John Lucas) deposed :

It has fallen to my lot, within the last 10 years, to see three or four elections of verderers; it has caused a great disturbance in the county, unnecessarily I venture to think, though happily the elections ultimately quieted down, and I believe fit and proper gentlemen were elected. When you find an election resting with the whole of the freeholders of a large county like the county of Gloucester, and where there are no means of testing who are freeholders, I need not, I think, say more to show the unsatisfactory condition of the present state of things.

The duties now devolving upon the verderers are to hear any complaints that the Crown may bring against encroachers within the Forest, and to decide whether those complaints are well founded; and if the encroachments are proved, to inflict fines, and cause those encroachments to be abated.

The court, since I have been steward, has been held every 40 days [but often by adjournment]. There are three keepers of the Forest, whose duty it is to perambulate the Forest and watch any encroachment that may take place. If they observe any encroachment they report it at the court of the verderers, and the verderers decide whether or not summons shall issue, and if so the encroachers are served prior to the next court. They then appear, the Crown being represented by Sir James Campbell and the other local officers of the Crown. If it is proved to the satisfaction of the verderers that an encroachment has been made, they fine the parties for the encroachment, and direct the land encroached to be abated, the fence pulled down, and the land re-thrown open to the Forest, except in those cases where the encroachers elect to purchase the land encroached, provided it be approved and sanctioned by the officers of the Crown.

The verderers were Duncombe Pyrke, Edmund Probyn, Charles Bathurst, and Sir Thomas Hyde Crawley-Boevey, Bt. During the previous ten years, 63 courts had been held, 159 summonses had been issued, and there had been 99 convictions. The fines imposed totalled £60 7s (£60.35).

In 1858 Nicholls[23] commented that the courtroom in the Speech House retained 'its original character, only it has been floored with wood, and is no longer divided by rails into compartments for the jury and the accused'. He added: 'Stains of human blood once marked the ceiling over the north-east corner of the apartment, said to have been dropped down from the room above, where an unfortunate poacher, who had been much injured by a gun, was confined; it is asserted that for many years no water could remove nor whitewash hide the unsightly marks.' By this time the Speech House was let by the Crown as an inn, with the courtroom reserved for the verderers' use. From 25 March 1856 it was leased to John Coleman at £55 per annum;[24] from 3 November 1877 to J. W. J. Boyce at £200;[25] and from 25 September 1901 to George St John at £139.[26] The Speech House had been enlarged and improved in 1883.[27] About 1880[28] a board of the flooring of the daïs having perished, the then innkeeper, J. W. J. Boyce, descended through the opening and found that the space below had been used as a receptacle

Fig 11. The Verderers' Courtroom in the Speech House, c 1880 (from an old woodcut)

for rubbish of all kinds including old shoes, bones of deer, and a copper plate five inches long, with the inscription 'Sir Edmund Winnington, Bt, Bewdley', which had probably been fastened by rivets to the leather collar of a hound. The inn was the scene of many interesting episodes. One, recorded in 1886,[29] is of 'mine host' sitting with guests in the courtroom explaining the peculiarities of the Forest, its traditions, and so on :

'Why,' he says, 'in this very room we're now sitting talking in, the verderers still hold their court, and settle all that hap-

Fig 12. A gathering outside the Speech House, *c* 1880 (from a faded
photograph in the author's possession)

pens in the Forest hereabouts. And there's no appeal any-
where, not even to the Crown itself, for you see, gentlemen,
it really is the Crown; and no lawyer (saving your presence,
sir) can put in his nose here for many seconds without
having to put it out again, no matter how big a wig he may
wear in any other part of the country. Rare fun we have
sometimes along with lawyers who don't know the Forest
ways, or don't choose to own to them. I remember a big chap
from nigh Gloucester turning up one court-day, and calling
out grand-like to the verderers, "I appear for the Defendant." "You don't appear for anyone," says the Head Verderer, pulling him up rather short, "but you'll be good
enough to take yourself out of this room, sir. We don't hear
any lawyers in this court." "I'll see about that, by and bye,"
cries the lawyer, jumping up in a rage, "I'll let you know
whether I'm not to be heard in this court, or any other in
the kingdom," and with that out he went, for go he had to,
swearing that they should hear from him before he was
many months' older; but it's years ago now, and he's as
many years older, too, and they haven't had any news of
him so far.'

Philip Baylis, a barrister, succeeded Campbell as deputy-surveyor in 1893 and applied to his management much energy and wisdom. He had the full support of the verderers. On 13 September 1890 Maynard Willoughby Colchester-Wemyss had been elected a verderer in place of Edmund Probyn. Other elections followed: on 17 March 1894 Russell James Kerr replaced Duncombe Pyrke; 21 September 1907 Charles Bathurst (later the First Viscount Bledisloe, PC, GCMG, KBE), was elected in the stead of his father, deceased; 11 March 1911 Nigel Jones of Underdean, Newnham-on-Severn, in place of Russell James Kerr; June 1912 Sir Francis Brain in place of Sir Thomas Hyde Crawley-Boevey, Bt; and in 1916 Lt Col Sir Russell J. Kerr. Their court continued to deal chiefly with encroachments;[30] rarely were there any venison offences: only occasionally did a deer enter the Forest—usually from a private herd. The stewards of the court were successively John Guise, Reginald Phillip Sumner, and John W. Haines.

A statutory mention of the verderers is in section one of the Dean Forest Act 1906[31] which empowered the commissioners of woods with the consent of the treasury and the verderers to

Fig 13. A view to the north from the Speech House, c 1880 (from an old woodcut)

effect agreements whereby parcels of 'the waste of the Forest' not exceeding £1,000 in value could be freed from rights of common in exchange for other parts of the Forest (not part of the waste) which should be made subject to rights of common. The Forestry Commission took over from the commissioners of woods in 1919. Their powers to make byelaws were contained in the Forestry Act 1927 wherein the verderers are mentioned thus:

S.2(1): No byelaw shall be made under this section with respect to the Forest of Dean except after consultation with the verderers of that Forest.

S.2(5): Without prejudice to the power of any other court in relation to any offence against this Act, the verderers of the Forest of Dean may, in their courts, inquire into offences against this Act alleged to have been committed within that Forest, and may punish such offences so committed, and those courts shall, as respects their jurisdiction under this Act, be deemed to be courts of summary jurisdiction, and the provisions of the Summary Jurisdiction Acts, including the provisions as to the recovery of fines and as to appeals, and the provisions of any rules made under those Acts, shall apply accordingly.

S.3(3): Any byelaws made by the Commissioners under this Act shall be without prejudice to any byelaws made under any other Act by the verderers of the Forest of Dean as respects that Forest, and the powers conferred by this Act upon the said verderers shall be in addition to and not in derogation of any other power exerciseable by them at the commencement of this Act.

Following publication of the Act (which is now repealed by the Forestry Act 1967, c.10) the verderers at a court held 14 November 1927 carefully considered draft byelaws prepared by the Forestry Commissioners and certainly helped to ensure that the byelaws were more consistent with the privileges of the inhabitants of the Forest than they otherwise might have been.[32] The minutes of a court held 6 July 1929 include:

The verderers desired that it should be recorded that in accepting such byelaws they do not divest themselves of any

of their rights and duties nor to their jurisdiction as verderers being in any way ruled out. Mr D. W. Young, the
deputy surveyor, stated that although it was intended that
ordinary cases under the byelaws should be taken up to the
ordinary Petty Sessions, he would take care that all cases
which ought properly to be considered by the verderers were
duly brought before them.

The present byelaws of the Forest include the following clause :

Nothing in these byelaws shall take away, abridge or limit
any remedy now existing by way of indictment or otherwise,
or shall interfere with or prejudice the powers of the
Forestry Commissioners, the Court of Verderers or of any
Authority legally existing for preventing or punishing any
offences whether specified in these byelaws or not, or the
rights and powers of the Forestry Commissioners over the
Forest of Dean.

Since 1902, cases concerning vert offences and encroachments
have been dealt with in local courts of the magistrates, with the
following exception. On 30 July 1924 William Watson, a keeper,
presented Arthur Charles Load for 'having without authority
erected a hut on Crown waste of His Majesty's Forest of Dean
near Crumpmeadow Colliery'. The Minute Book of the court
reads : 'A summons directed to be issued for the next court.' The
encroached land was later vacated.

Sir Charles Fortescue-Brickdale of Newland was elected a
verderer in 1929. The following year, 3 November, at a con-
tested election when over 200 people attended at the Shire Hall
in Gloucester, Major Charles Penrhyn Ackers, OBE, was successful, defeating Evan A. Jones, then secretary of the Forest of Dean
Commoners' Association. Sir Lance Crawley-Boevey, Bt, of Flaxley Abbey was elected 17 December 1945 (his father, Sir Francis
Crawley-Boevey, had been a verderer for about seven years).[33] Dr
Cyril Hart was appointed a verderer 18 November 1952 in succession to Lt Col Sir Russell James Kerr (see Chapter 6).

Much of the court's endeavours during the first half of the
present century were under the guidance of Charles Bathurst,
the first Viscount Bledisloe, PC, GCMG, KBE, (*Plate p 143*). By
1957, the year of his ninetieth birthday, he had been a verderer

for fifty years—in honour of which, HM Queen Elizabeth II and HRH Prince Philip, Duke of Edinburgh, visited the forest 24 April 1957 (*Plate p 144*). Her Majesty graciously accepted a specially bound copy of Dr Cyril Hart's book *The Verderers and Speech-Court of the Forest of Dean*. She then planted an oak to the west of the Speech House (*Plate p 144*). The progeny of the tree is noteworthy : from an acorn of a tree in Panshanger Park planted by Queen Elizabeth I, an oak had been raised, and planted at the Speech House in 1861 by the Prince Consort (*Plate p 164*) : the oak planted by Queen Elizabeth II was from an acorn of the Prince Consort's oak—thus was established a silvicultural link between the two queens. The spade used by Her Majesty, and a similar one used by Prince Philip to plant an oak nearby, were afterwards suitably inscribed and presented by Viscount Bledisloe to be hung permanently in the verderer's courtroom.

The Forestry Commission, too, honoured the occasion of Viscount Bledisloe's ninetieth birthday and his fifty years of service as a verderer. On 21 September 1957 (*Plate p 143*) the Commission's chairman, Lord Radnor, unveiled opposite the main entrance to the Speech House a stone pillar which traditionally marked the centre of the Forest, and which had been recovered from where it had lain for several years in the undergrowth. The inscription reads :

This stone
which by tradition
marks the centre of the Forest
was replaced to mark
the 90th birthday
of Viscount Bledisloe, PC, GCMG, KBE
and his 50th year
as a Verderer
September 21st, 1957

Lord Radnor in congratulating his lordship added : 'Some people might feel that the office did not now entail many duties—that was probably true, but it did entail a lot of unofficial work, in particular for the senior verderer, who was a person to whom the Forest looked for guidance in many matters outside his official duties. Lord Bledisloe had dealt with such matters with a skill and understanding which had endeared him to everyone. Behind

all his actions had been love and understanding of the countryside and in particular of the beautiful Forest of Dean and his
own estate.'[34] This well-loved senior verderer passed away on
3 July of the following year.

The Forest of Dean Committee (the 'Creed Committee') which
reported in 1958 made the following recommendations in regard
to the verderers and their court :

(*1*) The administrative functions of the verderers should be
    extended particularly with regard to the control of graz-
    ing in the Forest and the management of the proposed
    Sheep Reserves.

(*2*) The verderers should take the initiative in making
    recommendations regarding the maintenance and im-
    provement of the amenities of the Forest.

(*3*) The duties and functions of the Forest of Dean Inclosure
    Commissioners should be vested in the verderers.

(*4*) The court of verderers should be reconstituted to con-
    sist of a chief verderer and seven other members. The
    chief verderer should be appointed by the Lord Chan-
    cellor to be *ex officio* chairman of the court of verderers.
    The seven other members of the court should be chosen
    as follows :

    The present four elected verderers who hold office for
    life should be confirmed in their appointments. As and
    when vacancies occur, due to death or retirement, these
    should be successively filled by two appointments made
    by the Gloucestershire County Council, and one each
    by the East Dean Rural District Council and the West
    Dean Rural District Council.

    In choosing a verderer the appointing Council should
    be required to select only a person who has knowledge
    or practical experience of agriculture, forestry or estate
    management, and should not be restricted to choosing
    one of their own members. The verderers appointed by
    the Councils should hold office for four years and on
    completion of the term of office be eligible for re-
    appointment. One verderer should be appointed by the
    Minister of Agriculture, Fisheries and Food, one by the
    Forestry Commissioners, and one by such a body of per-
    sons as may be designated by the Minister as being
    specially concerned with the amenities of the country-
    side.

K

None of the foregoing recommendations have been implemented. The Forestry Act 1967 (c.10) simply consolidated the Forestry Acts 1919 to 1963; and section 47 refers to the Dean verderers thus :

> 47 (1) Byelaws made by the [Forestry] Commissioners under section 46 with respect to . . . the Forest of Dean shall be without prejudice to any byelaws made under any other Act by the verderers . . . , but before making any such byelaws the Commissioners shall consult with the verderers.
>
> (3) The verderers . . . may in their courts inquire into any offence consisting in a failure to comply with, or a contravention of, byelaws made by the Commissioners under section 46, being an offence alleged to have been committed within the Forest, and may punish any such offence so committed.
>
> (4) As respects their jurisdiction under this section, the verderers' courts shall be deemed to be magistrates' courts, and the provisions of the Magistrates' Courts Acts 1952 and 1957, including provisions as to the recovery of fines and as to appeals, and the provisions of any rules made under those Acts, shall apply accordingly.
>
> (5) The powers conferred by this section on the verderers . . . of the Forest of Dean shall be in addition to, and not in derogation of, any other powers exerciseable by them, and shall be without prejudice to the power of any other court in relation to offences under section 46.

Further changes in législation relevant to the verderers are explained in Chapter 8.

References to Chapter 5

1 *30th Report of Commissioners of Woods &c*, 1852, App 16, 223; Nelson's Memorandum of 1803 is printed in Hart, *Royal Forest*, App XVII
2 48 Geo III, c.72
3 Hart, *Royal Forest*, 209
4 49 Geo III, c.159

5   57 Geo III, c.61
6   GRO, D33
7   10 Geo IV, c.50
8   1 and 2 Vict, c.42
9   *The Life of Warren James, the Reputed Champion of the Forest of Dean, Descriptive of the Forest Riots*, by a Resident Forester (Heath, Monmouth, 1831)
10 1 and 2 Will IV, c.12
11 As regards commoning : Hart, C. E., *The Commoners of Dean Forest*, 1951, 92; as regards free mining : Hart, C. E., *The Free Miners*, 1953, 254
12 1 and 2 Vict, c.42
13 1 and 2 Vict, c.43
14 6 Will IV, c.3
15 7 Vict, c.13
16 *Report of Select Committee of the House of Commons on the Woods &c of the Crown*, 1849
17 Ibid GG35, 610–20
18 Ibid 8, 9, 32, 33
19 Edward Machen's note of his speech, 1860, *penes me*
20 24 and 25 Vict, c.40
21 Gloucester Public Liby, L.10.3
22 *Report of Select Committee of the House of Commons*, 10 July 1874
23 Nicholls, H. G., *The Forest of Dean*, 1858, 64, 65
24 *34th Rpt of Commissioners of Woods*, 130
25 Ibid 66th, 12
26 Ibid 81st, 14
27 F17/143 : Plan, N and W elevations of the Speech House, 1854, G. Atkinson, MS coloured, 4 sheets, various scales and sizes; F17/144 : Roof plan, sections and elevations showing proposed additions; and plans, sections, and elevations of proposed alterations to stabling, with plan of premises showing drainage, G. Pearson of Ross-on-Wye, 1881, MS coloured, 8 sheets, various sizes, 16ft and 8ft to an inch.
28 Bellows, John, *Guide to the Forest of Dean*, 1880, 17, 18
29 Grindrod, Charles, *Tales in the Speech-House*, 1886, 306, 307
30 Records of the Verderers' Court 1829–77 are in F3/145–6, from 1837 to 1907 in F16/20–22, 1863–74 in F3/879, 880, from 1878 to 1905 in F3/474, and 1905–10 in F3/930

31 6 Edw VII, c.119
32 Haines, J. W., *Gloucestershire Countryside*, 4(3) 1941, 60, 61
33 Records of the Verderers' Court 1911–41 are in F3/1212
34 *Forest Newspapers*, 4 Oct 1957

Six: The Election of a Verderer and Today's Verderers' Court

Today the method of election of a verderer is the same as that used for about eight centuries. Following the death of a verderer, his burial[1] is notified to the Crown by the steward of the verderers' court. A writ *de viridario eligendo* tested at the Royal Courts of Justice, London, is then sent to the high sheriff of Gloucestershire, commanded by the sovereign to arrange for the election of another verderer :

> . . . , by the Grace of God, of the United Kingdom of Great Britain and Ireland, and of the British Dominions beyond the Seas, Queen, Defender of the Faith, to the sheriff of our county of Gloucester, Greeting. Forasmuch as . . . of . . . in the county of Gloucester, late one of our verderers of our Forest of Dean in your county as we are informed is deceased, We command you that if it be so, then in your full county by the assent of the same county you cause another verderer for our said Forest of Dean to be chosen in the place of the said . . . who having taken his oath in the usual manner may thereupon do and keep those things which concern the office of a verderer in the said Forest of Dean.
>
> And you shall cause such an one to be chosen as best knoweth and can intend that office, and certify unto us his name at the Royal Courts of Justice, London, then returning to us this our writ.
>
> Witness ourself at . . . , the . . . day of . . . and . . . year of our reign.

The high sheriff then fixes the date of the election and, after giving notice by advertisement and poster (*Fig 14*), supervises it at the Shire Hall in Gloucester. The present under sheriff of the county, Anthony A. Scott, TD, made a comprehensive note of the proceedings at an election held 18 November 1952 :[2]

> Lt-Col Sir Russell James Kerr, who was elected a verderer 8 April 1916, died 13 May 1952, aged 89 years, and his burial (not his death) having been notified, by the steward,

GLOUCESTERSHIRE TO WIT.

ELECTION OF A VERDERER

FOR HER MAJESTY'S

FOREST OF DEAN.

I, THE HONOURABLE WILLIAM RALPH SEYMOUR BATHURST, T.D., Sheriff of the County of Gloucester having received a writ of our Sovereign Lady the Queen, *de viridario eligendo,* commanding me in my full County by the assent of the same County to cause a VERDERER for Her Majesty's FOREST OF DEAN in the said County to be chosen in the place of Lieutenant-Colonel Russell James Kerr, Knight, late one of Her Majesty's Verderers of the said Forest of Dean in the said County, deceased, do HEREBY GIVE NOTICE that I shall at a COUNTY COURT to be holden at the SHIRE HALL, GLOUCESTER, in and for the said County, on TUESDAY, the EIGHTEENTH day of NOVEMBER, 1952, at TWELVE o'clock noon, proceed to the Election of a VERDERER for the said Forest of Dean, in the place of the said Lieutenant-Colonel Russell James Kerr, Knight, of which all persons concerned are required to take notice.

AND I FURTHER GIVE NOTICE that in the event of a Poll being demanded at the said election, the Polling will commence and the votes of the Freeholders will be taken on the said TUESDAY, the EIGHTEENTH day of NOVEMBER, 1952 at the Building known as the SHIRE HALL, at GLOUCESTER aforesaid, as soon as practicable after the nomination on that day.

N.B.—No person will be entitled to vote in respect of a Freehold situate in the City of Gloucester, or in the City of Bristol.

Dated this Sixteenth day of October, 1952.

THE HONOURABLE WILLIAM RALPH SEYMOUR BATHURST, T.D.

SHERIFF.

County Sheriff's Office,
    Berkeley Chambers, Berkeley Street,
                Gloucester.

Printed by Henry Osborne. St. Mary's Square, Gloucester.
Published by the said Sheriff.

Fig 14.   Poster notifying the forthcoming election of a Verderer

to the Crown a writ *de viridario eligendo* tested at the Royal Courts of Justice, London, 30 September 1952 was received by the high sheriff of the county of Gloucester (The Honourable William Ralph Seymour Bathurst, TD) 3 October 1952. By this writ the high sheriff was commanded by Her Majesty the Queen in his full county by the assent of the same county to cause another verderer to be chosen.

Notice was then given that the high sheriff would at a County Court to be holden at the Shire Hall, Gloucester, on Tuesday 18 November 1952 proceed to the election of a verderer [*Fig 14*] and that in the event of a poll being demanded the polling would commence and the votes of the freeholders would be taken as soon as practicable after the nomination. All freeholders of the county of Gloucester [except those of Gloucester and Bristol] are entitled to vote, and the election is decided by a show of hands, unless a poll is demanded : such a poll is a rarity, and there has not been one for many years past, for it may go on for several days, and the expense has to be borne by the candidates.

The County Court was duly held 18 November 1952 in the Crown Court at the Shire Hall, and considerably over 400 persons were present, the Court being packed to capacity. Even the dock was occupied by freeholders, and the number present was certainly the largest for very many years. The high sheriff took his seat on the bench at twelve noon, being supported by (among others) the Lord Bishop of Gloucester, Viscount Bledisloe, Major C. P. Ackers, OBE, and Sir Lance Crawley-Boevey, Bt (the three surviving verderers), J. R. Haines (deputy steward), and the under sheriff. The county bailiff then made proclamation :

> Oyez ! Oyez ! Oyez ! All manner of persons who have anything to do at this special County Court of William Ralph Seymour Bathurst, high sheriff of the county of Gloucester, may now draw near and give their attendance, when the said sheriff will proceed to the election of a verderer for Her Majesty's Forest of Dean in the county of Gloucester, in the place of Lt-Col Sir Russell James Kerr, late one of Her Majesty's verderers of the said Forest, in the said county, deceased. All persons are required to keep silence while Her Majesty's writ for the election of a verderer for Her Majesty's Forest of Dean is being read, and other proceedings incident to such election are being had, on pain of imprisonment.

Her Majesty's writ was read by the under sheriff, and the high sheriff addressed the freeholders :

The sheriff having long ago lost the power of compelling the freemen of the shire to do service at this Court, it behoves me, in the first place, to thank you, Ladies and Gentlemen, for your presence. As this Court, which necessarily meets at most infrequent intervals, is the only occasion on which the high sheriff makes any official utterance, it is naturally gratifying to him to be attended by so respectable an audience. As it is only on such occasions as these—and they are extremely rare—that the true nature of the sheriff's office becomes apparent, it is not to be wondered at that its significance is sometimes overlooked. Election of chieftains or magistrates is a common feature of peoples at a certain stage of their development. It is a system which can only have worked well while the number of freemen was small and it has generally been discarded when personal liberty became more widespread. Edward I conceded to the County Court the right of electing the sheriff. This seems to have been a revival of the ancient Saxon procedure. It was not successful and was shortly afterwards abolished. Two classes of judicial officers in each Shire have, however, constantly been elected in the County Court—the coroners and the verderers. The election of coroners continued until the nineteenth century, and verderers, wherever the office survives, still are or ought to be appointed in this manner. The verderer seems to have been regarded as a special variety of coroner, seeing that his principal duty was to hold inquest upon the King's deer if unlawfully slain. He is appointed for life, but one authority states that a coroner automatically vacates his office if chosen sheriff or verderer : in my opinion, a verderer would, in like manner, forfeit his post should he become coroner or high sheriff. Another authority asserts that both coroners and verderers should be knights, but adds 'or be possessed of lands worth £20 per annum'. The verderer receives no salary, but in most forests was entitled to one buck and one doe a year for his fee. Forest law, which reserved to the King alone the right of deer hunting, was detested by rich and poor alike, and the office of verderer was then highly unpopular. With the effluxion of time, however, the deer have disappeared, and with them the distasteful duties of

Page 161 (above) The verderers in session 16 December 1949. Left to right: Major Charles P. Ackers, OBE, the First Viscount Bledisloe, Sir Lance Crawley-Boevey, Bt, and J. R. Haines (deputy steward); (below) The verderers' courtroom (from a painting by H. M. Crowther, commissioned in 1953 by Dr Cyril Hart)

Page 162 The election of a verderer at the Shire Hall, Gloucester 18 November 1952: I: *(above)* Freeholders voting for Dr Cyril Hart; *(below)* The high sheriff, the Hon W. R. S. Bathurst, TD, FSA counting the votes

Page 163 The election of a verderer at the Shire Hall, Gloucester 18 November 1952: II: *(above)* The high sheriff, the Hon W. R. S. Bathurst, TD, FSA recording the votes; *(below)* The elected verderer, Dr Cyril Hart, swearing the oath of office

Page 164 (above) The Verderers and the 'Prince Consort Oak' at the Speech House 4 September 1961: The oak was planted in 1861 by Albert, Prince Consort, from an acorn off a tree planted by Queen Elizabeth I; the oak planted in 1957 by Queen Elizabeth II (see also Plate p 144) was from an acorn of the Prince Consort's oak. Thus is established a silvicultural link between the two Queens; (below) The Verderers in session 21 December 1964. Left to right: R. E. Crowther (district officer), John H. Watts (verderer), Dr Cyril Hart (senior verderer), R. G. Sanzen-Baker (deputy surveyor), and J. R. Haines (steward)

this office. The approaching Coronation reminds us of our peculiar genius, as a Nation, for retaining such picturesque shadows of a bygone age long after their often irksome substance has vanished away. In other countries, where the holders of antique privileges have used less restraint in exercising them, these interesting relics have been all too often swept clean away by revolution and the countries concerned have, I feel, been the poorer for their loss. I would not like to give the impression, however, that the office you will to-day confer by your election is a mere empty honour. It is still possible for the verderers to meet as a tribunal at the Speech House and you are in effect electing a judicial officer. The gentleman whom you elect must not be incapacitated through deafness or other infirmity. Most important of all, he must be of that high personal character which is so necessary to the proper administration of justice.

The high sheriff concluded by inquiring whom the freeholders proposed 'as a candidate for the Office of Verderer of Her Majesty's Forest of Dean in the County of Gloucester in the place of Lieutenant-Colonel Russell James Kerr, Knight, late one of Her Majesty's Verderers for the said Forest in the said County deceased'. Dr Cyril Hart, of Chenies, Coleford, was thereupon nominated by Alderman Charles W. Luker and seconded by Alderman Sydney J. Hawkins; and Alderman James Leonard Jones of Cinderford was nominated by Mr Evan Arthur Jones and seconded by Mr Harold Arthur Harris. The high sheriff then called for a show of hands (*Plate p 162*) in favour of each candidate and declared : 'It appearing to me on the view now taken that the majority of the freeholders would have Dr Cyril Hart to be returned, he is duly elected a verderer of Her Majesty's Forest of Dean in the county of Gloucester and I shall return him accordingly.' The majority in favour of Dr Hart being very large, a poll was not demanded, and the high sheriff thereupon administered to him the oath of office (*Plate p 163*) as follows :

'I swear by Almighty God that I will truly serve our Sovereign Lady the Queen in the office of a verderer in the Forest of Dean, I will to the uttermost of my power and knowledge do for the profit of the Queen so far as it doth appertain unto me to do, I will preserve and maintain the ancient rights and franchises of Her Crown, I will not conceal from Her Majesty any rights or privileges nor any offence either in vert or venison nor any other thing, I will not withdraw or abridge any defaults but will endeavour myself to manifest and redress the same, and if I cannot do that of myself I will give knowledge thereof unto the Queen or unto Her justice of the forest, I will deal indifferently with all the Queen's liege people, I will execute the laws of the Forest and do equal right and justice as well unto the poor as unto the rich in that appertaineth unto my Office, I will not oppress any person by colour thereof for any reward, favour or malice. All these things I will to the uttermost of my power observe and keep.'

Dr Cyril Hart, having now become a verderer of the Forest of Dean for life, thanked the meeting for his election, and Alderman Jones, the defeated candidate, addressed the meeting. A vote of thanks to the high sheriff proposed by Lord Bledisloe, the senior verderer, closed the proceedings, and all that remained was for the high sheriff to make his return to the writ certifying that by the assent of his full county he had caused Dr Hart to be chosen a verderer and that Dr Hart had taken his corporal oath in the usual manner to do and keep those things which concern the office of a verderer of the Forest of Dean in the said county.

Subsequent elections, all unopposed, have been those of the second Viscount Bledisloe (6 January 1959), John H. Watts (29 June 1961), and Alderman F. G. Little (12 June 1969). The present steward is J. R. Haines, appointed 3 July 1961, thus:

By virtue of the power vested in him the Minister of Agriculture, Fisheries and Food hereby appoints John Robert Haines, solicitor, of Bastion House, Brunswick Road in the City of Gloucester, to be steward and registrar of each and every court of swanimote and the court of attachment of the Forest of Dean, to have and enjoy the said customary offices which shall be executed by himself or his deputy during the pleasure of the Minister of Agriculture, Fisheries and Food for the time being. Full power, licence and authority is hereby granted to the said John Robert Haines to keep the said swanimote and attachment courts at the usual and legal times and to perform and execute all lawful acts and things to the said offices belonging.

The present verderers are Dr Cyril Hart, the second Viscount Bledisloe, QC, John H. Watts, and Alderman F. G. Little. The office is a cherished one and any vacancy in the court is soon taken up. It is satisfactory and appropriate that the three rural districts of East Dean, West Dean, and Lydney are represented on the court. Today the work and duties of the verderers continue ostensibly to be the 'guarding of the vert and the venison'. They are elected for life and hold office according to ancient custom. Consequently they are elected by authority of a writ of the Crown under the supervision of the high sheriff by the freeholders of Gloucestershire : but the elected verderer now pays the main expenses of the election, although the high sheriff is also put to some expense. Under the custom of their office, the verderers convene their courts every forty days (see their calendar, *Fig 15*); usually the court is adjourned until a time when there is sufficient business to justify a full session : then the courtroom is cleared (in the interim the room is used for dining). The deputy surveyor and two of his officers usually attend the court, where the subjects discussed range from commoners' privileges, and proposals for opencast mining, to the flora and fauna of the Forest. Commoners occasionally consult the verderers as to the current acreage of statutory enclosures. Individuals and bodies seek the verderers' views on the silviculture of the Forest and the method of management and policy followed or proposed by the Forestry Commission. The ever present problems of conifers versus hardwoods, and whether decaying, though attractive, oaks should be felled, are constantly before the verderers, who realise the difficulties of the Forestry Commission in trying to keep a correct balance between people advocating economics and those urging considerations of amenity and recreation. The verderers are also among the Inclosure Commissioners (Appendix V) appointed to authorise the enclosing of areas for planting or replanting—within the constraint that the Forestry Commission do not at any time have enclosed more than the statutory 11,000 acres.

The spacious courtroom (*Plate p 161*) and the pleasure of dining within it are among the many attractions of the Speech House. Its traditions and interest are 'ornaments' of the Forest. A wide and open hearth faces the western wall, at the south end extends a low raised gallery or daïs of oak, and on the walls hang a pair of huge dark oil paintings as well as several antlers which replace the time-worn ones of earlier centuries. On the east wall lie the two royal spades used in 1957 by HM Queen Elizabeth

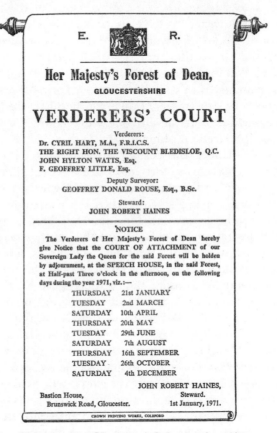

E.   R.

Her Majesty's Forest of Dean,
GLOUCESTERSHIRE

VERDERERS' COURT

Verderers:
Dr. CYRIL HART, M.A., F.R.I.C.S.
THE RIGHT HON. THE VISCOUNT BLEDISLOE, Q.C.
JOHN HYLTON WATTS, Esq.
F. GEOFFREY LITTLE, Esq.

Deputy Surveyor:
GEOFFREY DONALD ROUSE, Esq., B.Sc.

Steward:
JOHN ROBERT HAINES

NOTICE

The Verderers of Her Majesty's Forest of Dean hereby give Notice that the COURT OF ATTACHMENT of our Sovereign Lady the Queen for the said Forest will be holden by adjournment, at the SPEECH HOUSE, in the said Forest, at Half-past Three o'clock in the afternoon, on the following days during the year 1971, viz.:—

THURSDAY	21st JANUARY
TUESDAY	2nd MARCH
SATURDAY	10th APRIL
THURSDAY	20th MAY
TUESDAY	29th JUNE
SATURDAY	7th AUGUST
THURSDAY	16th SEPTEMBER
TUESDAY	26th OCTOBER
SATURDAY	4th DECEMBER

JOHN ROBERT HAINES,
Bastion House,   Steward.
Brunswick Road, Gloucester.   1st January, 1971.

CROWN PRINTING WORKS, COLEFORD

Fig 15.   The Verderers' Calendar for 1971

and HRH Prince Philip, and on the west wall hang etchings of trees, in frames made of the wood of the species depicted. The ancient roof beams were replaced in 1956 during extensive renovations and improvements of the interior; the new beams came from oaks well over 200 years old in the Highmeadow woods; each beam was 28 feet in length and weighed about two tons.[3]

The Speech House is an attractive hotel leased by the Crown to Trust Houses Limited. It stands at about 600ft elevation in isolation in the centre of the Forest, and is a substantial building of the grey sandstone of the neighbourhood. It commands a fine view to the north, and is close to other views and vistas of great beauty; and nearby are an arboretum and several oaks planted in and subsequent to the reign of Charles II. The west front of the building is practically in its original state, also two small rooms facing north—the bay window in one of which still bears its ancient roof of stone. Beyond the slight recess in the north wall all is of comparatively modern date, having been built about 1883. Not only was the ancient line of roof, with boldly curved and overhanging eaves, followed in the new additions, but the original stones of the demolished sides were preserved and placed in the front of the house. The lintel of 1676 (*Fig 6*) and the stone escutcheon of 1680 (*Fig 7*) are extant.

Besides the connection which the Speech House has with the Forest's laws, its grounds and outbuildings were in past years used for the annual meeting of those Free Miners and their beneficiaries who held shares in the six main groups of deep gales, where the gale-money was distributed by their trustees. There too, Free Miners' gales were sometimes 'auctioned'. The Miners' annual 'Demonstration' or fair was for many years held in the field at the rear of the Speech House.

References to Chapter 6

1   This requirement is confirmed by GRO, BRA 301
2   Scott, Anthony A., 'The Election of a Verderer for Her Majesty's Forest of Dean, held at the Shire Hall, Gloucester, 18 November 1952', *BGAS* 72, 1953, 144–9
3   *Forest Newspapers*, 30 Dec 1955; *Gloucester Citizen* (photograph), 3 Feb 1956

Seven: The Deer

There were deer in Dean from prehistoric times, and the fallow were probably introduced from the Mediterranean by the Romans. In Saxon times deer were abundant, and furnished kings and their relatives, favourites, and some churches with either the pleasure of hunting or the benefits of venison. The Norman and Angevin kings may occasionally have hunted the deer in Dean (see page 37) and certainly had from the Forest considerable supplies of venison. The abbey of St Peter's, Gloucester, received a grant of the tithe of all venison taken in the Forest.[1]

During the twelfth and thirteenth centuries, fallow deer were the most numerous, followed by red deer and roe (see Chapter 1, page 36). Care for them was the chief reason for forest law; their shelter and natural food were safeguarded, trees, shrubs, and branches were felled for them in hard winters, and their natural enemies, wolves, were kept in bounds. Offenders against the deer were usually heavily punished by fine or imprisonment, or both. Poachers used various types of dog, hound, and mastiff; some used bows and arrows, crossbows, nets, snares, and 'other engines' (see Chapter 2). There was almost as profound an inquiry on the death of a deer as there was on the death of a human, as explained in earlier chapters—and another example is available in 1286 :[2]

Be it remembered that when the Lord Bishop was at Ross on Monday next before St Matthew the Apostle, his huntsman with some of his men coursed in his Chace of Penyard and caught a young stag, and there arose a dispute between the huntsman and the foresters of the King about that stag as to the place wherein it was caught; and after the departure of the bishop an inquiry was held at Hull Cnole [Howle Hill near Walford] on Thursday before the feast of St Matthew 14 Ed I, 12 men out of Walford, Coughton, Bicknor, Ruardean, Hope Mansell, Longhope, Eccleswell and Dene being jurors. The witnesses, keepers and other servants were examined on oath by Grimbald Pauncefot [constable-warden] and the verderers, whether the stag was killed within the Forest or not. All the men examined declared that the stag was caught without the Forest where the Chace of the Lord Bishop was wont to be; and the villagers and the jurors agreed in all things. When Grimbald Pauncefot inquired of whom the hunting party consisted the villagers pleaded ignorance, but the foresters asserted that William de Clevering the huntsman, N. the Carter, and John de Herley were the persons.

Poaching of deer continued in Dean throughout the fourteenth century, but their numbers were dwindling, and the perquisites and pleasures of hunting are rarely mentioned.[3] The same was the situation during the fifteenth and sixteenth centuries: deer were scarce—there were only remnants of herds of previous centuries, and not a single instance of royal sport or of a grant of venison is recorded from the accession of Henry IV to the end of the reign of Philip and Mary.[4] Some fee deer were taken by the hereditary officials, and forest law certainly continued to safeguard a few herds and their habitat, the covert, and to the nation's future benefit incidentally conserved trees and underwood. During the reign of Elizabeth I (1558–1603) the same ancient but disintegrating forest organisation was still in part based upon the preservation of deer, despite the fact that the queen took little interest in hunting. Her silvicultural policy, based on the conservation of ship-timber, concurrently enabled the deer to increase. By about 1630 there were 'some 3,000 fallow deer, but no red deer except some strayed from others parts'.[5]

Eighty cases of poaching were dealt with at the forest eyre in 1634, and the following year the 'lieutenants' and deputy constables were commanded by the itinerant justices[6] 'to take special care to prevent the keepers killing any deer without lawful warrant, nor to cut down any browsewood without assignment and allowance of some persons to be by them authorised from time to time on that behalf; and to severely punish all stealers of deer'. In 1641[7] witnesses for the Crown were asked by the attorney-general whether it was true that 'since James I the Forest was stored with red and fallow deer'; also whether certain inhabitants had 'hunted or killed the King's deer', and whether 'the game and deer there were now utterly disposed'. Richard Powell, bowbearer, answered that during his sixteen years in office there had

been about 3,000 fallow deer, but they were now almost destroyed. Some fallow deer survived during the Civil War and the
Commonwealth; and the Council of State gave Colonel Edward
Cooke a warrant 8 September 1659[8] for 'a brace of fat bucks
of the season'. In 1662 the keepers estimated the number of deer
at 300.[9] Three years later the 'freeholders, inhabitants and commoners' urged that the deer should not exceed 800 at any one
time, and affirmed that they had no objection to fee deer being
taken by officials: their recommendations were embodied in the
Dean Forest (Reafforestation) Act 1667 (see Chapter 3). On 7
September 1666, Sir Christopher Guise of Brockworth had
written to the editor of the *Gazette* saying that he 'hears that the
King is resolved to destroy the deer in Dean' and begging some
breeding for his park.[10] After the 1667 Act, Sir Baynham Throckmorton, deputy constable-warden, took charge of the deer and
controlled the keepers.[11] On 17 November 1669 the treasury
agreed to insert in his 'constat that the King have liberty to
charge the warrants for five brace of bucks and as many does
each year, so as he charge none the first three years'. Also,
Throckmorton was to 'stock the chase with deer in a limited
time';[12] and on 14 March 1676 it was confirmed that he 'is entitled to fee deer—10 bucks in summer and 10 does in winter'.[13]
In 1680 commissioners reported that the keepers needed very
little browse, chiefly holly, to feed the deer.[14]

The records of swanimote courts held in 1673–84 (see Chapter
3)[15] show that much poaching prevailed during the period:
offenders had killed deer with guns and shot of various types.
In 1702 the keepers were commanded to permit John Howe to
take three brace of bucks.[16] Poaching was an ever present prob-
lem: in 1730, George James, a keeper, shot one Glassenburg, a
deer poacher; the verderers persuaded the treasury to pay James
£13 12s 6d (£13.62) for his law expenses and £20 as a reward.[17] In 1737, under Augustus earl of Berkeley, constable-
warden, his gamekeeper (Thomas James of Lydney) and his
steward (William James of Soilwell) were to have 'the sole rights
over the game'.[18]

In 1787[19] commissioners questioned the verderers about the
deer. Edmund Probyn deposed that the number could not be
ascertained, 'but the Forest is much understocked'; Maynard Colchester asserted that 'the deer, now almost all destroyed, were

Page 173 (above) An old fallow buck in Kensley Enclosure, 1971 (L. Starling); *(below)* Edgar Gwilliam, senior ranger, with a buck which he had to destroy following its being injured by a lorry at Symonds Yat East, October 1969

Page 174 A Dean buck, from a painting by Hubert Pepper, presented by him to Edgar Gwilliam, senior ranger

formerly the ornament and pleasure of the Forest'. The keepers
estimated that there were about 500 deer 'of all sorts'; and the
number of warrants for killing deer could be ascertained from
the steward of the swanimote court, 'into whose office the same
were annually returned', and for which they received a fee of
£1 1s (105p) for each buck and 10s 6d (52½p) for each doe.[20]
The verderers received annually a buck and a doe. Joseph Pyrke,
one of the deputy wardens, deposed that 'the bucks which ever
came to my share, had been three or four, by warrant under the
hand of Lord Berkeley [constable-warden]; for each of which I
paid one guinea to the keeper; hay or corn being purchased for
the deer, is what never came to my knowledge, and I may safely
say never was'.[21] Charles Edwin, chief forester-of-fee, claimed
to be entitled to 'the right shoulder of all bucks and does killed
within the Forest, and also to 10 fee bucks and 10 fee does,
annually, to be there killed and taken at his own free will and
pleasure'.[22] The same commissioners in 1788 recommended:[23]

> The deer should be disposed of or destroyed; from which
> no great inconvenience can arise to the Crown, as this Forest
> has supplied only four bucks and four does annually for the
> last seven years, to the orders of the cofferer or clerk of the
> venison warrants; and as it is proposed to make a recom-
> pence to the forest officers for the loss of their [fee] deer, no
> injury will be done to them. It will also take away from the
> deer stealers, and other disorderly people, a great tempta-
> tion for breaking into the inclosures; and prevent the des-
> truction of the young timber by the browse of the deer.

However, the deer were not destroyed. Edward Machen[24] remembered that in about 1790 'the deer were very numerous':
he recollected his father taking him 'up to the Buckholt in an
evening for the purpose of showing them, and they never failed
of seeing several'; but for some twenty years thereafter 'in consequence of the decrease of the covert and the increase of
poachers, they rapidly diminished'. In 1803[25] Nelson complained
that in Dean 'nothing can grow self-sown, for the deer, of which
only a few remained, bark all the young trees'. By 1810 there
were less than ten deer in the Forest, but at this time enclosures
to promote tree growth were begun in Dean; the few deer were
protected and when their covert improved 'they rapidly in-

L

creased, and in thirty years, *viz* in 1840, there were not less than
800 or 1,000 deer'. Red deer were introduced in 1842 by a Mr
Herring who 24 February brought two stags and four hinds
from Woburn. The cost delivered was £8 each. They were 'in
fine condition, and were turned loose in Russell's Enclosure, one
mile south-west of the Speech House'. Of these red deer, Machen
noted :[26]

October 1842 :	Two of the hinds have calves with them.
20 October 1842 :	One of the stags was hunted from Trippenkennet, in Herefordshire, and swam the Wye three times; the hounds brought him into Nag's Head Enclosure, and could not have killed him—they were so tired.
July 1844 :	Two stags, three hinds, and a calf are now in Park Hill Enclosure, and are frequently seen in the meadow in front of Whitemead. One old stag is at Edge Hills. A hind is sometimes seen in the Highmeadow Woods, and it is known that one was killed there.
October 1844 :	A young hind was sent down, and turned out in Haywood Enclosure.
October 1845 :	The two old stags are wandering about, and are seldom in the Forest.
1 October 1845 :	Tried to find that stag near Littledean, and failed.
4 October 1845 :	Hunted the stag near Park End; ran four hours, but lost him, night coming on.
20 November 1845 :	The stag seen at Newland.

On 28 March 1846 the Office of Woods wrote to Machen :[27]

The Queen having been graciously pleased to signify to
the Commissioners of Her Majesty's Woods &c, Her

Majesty's acceptance of a herd of deer from the Earl of
Ducie's park at Woodchester in the county of Gloucester;
I am on the part of this Board to acquaint you that they
have instructed Mr Herring of the New Road, London, to
convey 20 of the said deer to the Highmeadow Woods; and
I am to request that the proper keepers may be instructed
to receive them and to give Mr Herring an acknowledgement of the number delivered.

No mention is made by Machen as to the species of the deer
or whether they were received in Dean. He continued to note
the following regarding the red deer :[28]

28 September 1846 :   The stag that was about Staunton
and Newland was killed this day,
after a run of three hours. He was
found on the old hills near Newland,
and killed in Coleford. This was a
four years old deer, calved in the
Forest; the hind and calf went to
Staunton &c, and never returned :
the hind was killed but we do not
know by whom. The venison of the
stag was excellent : the haunches
were 45lb each.

October 1847 :   Another stag was killed after a good
run. Two were found, and ran some
time together before the hounds in
Park Hill.

6 October 1848 :   The last stag returned to the Forest,
after having been in the woods &c
near Chepstow almost a year. He
was found in Oaken Hill and killed,
after a run of three hours, in Sal-
low Vallets. His haunches weighed
51lb, and the whole weight 307lb.

Thereafter, only fallow deer remained in the Forest. On 8 May
1848[29] Machen was commanded by the Office of Woods to make
a return for each of the ten years ended 5 April 1848 of 'the
numbers of deer in Dean, as nearly as the same can be ascer-

tained, both male and female; and the expenses of maintenance;
the number supplied and the parties to whom supplied under
warrant in each season; the numbers supplied and the parties
to whom supplied in composition for trespass [by the deer], on
the surrender of rights, or otherwise; the number appropriated
as presents; and the estimated annual loss from death or other
causes'. Machen replied 12 May 1848 :[30]

After speaking to the keepers on the subject I find that
from the nature of this Forest and the wild habits of the
fallow deer, it is quite impossible to give precise and accurate
answers to the questions proposed, and I can only state
generally as near an approximation to the facts as I can and
which in substance may I hope give the information desired.

The numbers of deer at present in the Forest are supposed to be between 5 and 600. The number on 5 April
1838 might have been 800. There was a hard winter in
1840–1 which destroyed numbers and reduced them, but
they increased again to about 800 in 1843–4, and since that
time have been somewhat decreasing annually. (By the Act
of 20 Charles II, c.3 [1667] for the increase and preservation
of timber in this Forest the deer were not to exceed 800,
and I think they never have done so.)

There has been no expense of maintenance except, occasionally in very severe weather, 3 or 4 labourers have been
allowed to assist the keepers in cutting holly for them; no hay
has ever been given. The proportion of male and female deer
is thought to be one-third of the former and two-thirds of the
latter.

The four verderers are entitled to a buck and a doe by
virtue of their office : they have had a buck each year and
three of them a doe each in the last three years. Lord Dun-
raven [of Clearwell Castle] claimed in virtue of an old office
of bowbearer ten bucks and ten does a year : he has had
one buck in each year. The other bucks have all been killed
by warrants from the Commissioners and have not exceeded
thirty or have been under twenty in each year. In 1845–6
twelve inferior deer were given to the owners and managers
of coal and mine [iron ore] works in the Forest. In 1846–7
sixty does were killed and distributed amongst the poor
inhabitants.

I cannot state the numbers of deaths, but great numbers
are annually killed by poachers.

Summary:

To 5 April	Total	By Warrant	
		To Verderers	To others
1839	800	4	30
1840	700	4	28
1841	600	4	33
1842	750	4	30
1843	800	4	20
1844	700	4	19
1845	650	4	24
1846	600	7	23 and 10 to mines.
1847	600	7	23 and 50 to the poor.
1848	600	7	22

Machen added that prosecutions of offenders against the deer had cost £190 12s 8d (£190.635) in the ten years. The foregoing information was presented by the Office of Woods to a Select Committee who reported 1849 :[31]

The number of deer is limited by the Act 20 Chas II [1667] to 800. It is at present supposed to be about 500, but the number is not accurately known. No expense is incurred in their winter keep.

The number of prosecutions is heavy; independently of which numerous cases are alleged to occur in which the parties are not prosecuted. The number of persons charged with offences against the deer has been about 94 during the last ten years, of which about 36 were convicted and fined from £9 to £50 each; and in default of payment, the offenders have in some cases been imprisoned for various periods, with hard labour. The remainder were fined in small sums, with hard labour, or were imprisoned for different periods, occasionally without hard labour. The total amount of costs during the ten years was £68 13s, of which the parties offending had paid only £1 4s 6d, the Crown having paid £19 5s 10d for expenses in three of the cases, to witnesses.

According to Edward Machen, the deputy surveyor, the presence of the deer tends to foster bad and idle habits amongst the people. Complaints have been made about the deer by the owners of several of the collieries and other works, and (none of the fences in Dean Forest being deer-

proof) they commit damage in the young plantations: this
is confirmed by Mr Langham, the assistant deputy surveyor,
who has the immediate charge of the woods. Mr Nicholson,
who manages the Park End Colliery, and very extensive
works in the Forest, states that 'if once men absent themselves from the collieries to poach, he can never reckon upon
their working afterwards; that the nature of the work is
such, that if one man absents himself it sometimes causes the
whole of a company to cease work; and that his works have
often been hindered in that way'.

Following the Duncan Committee Report of 1849 (*supra*) and
the Deer Removal Act, 1850, almost all the deer in Dean were
killed. Machen[32] later noted that 'the fallow deer were reduced
in number by killing a large number of does: they were all fine
animals, and when the enclosures protected them they got very
fat, and the venison of fine flavour; and they were generally
hunted'. On 27 September 1850 Machen wrote to the Office
of Woods:[33]

In consequence of the demoralising effects produced by
poaching, and the damage done to the young plantations, I
was directed verbally by Lord Carlisle and Mr Milne to
destroy the deer in Dean Forest and the Highmeadow
Woods, and the keepers have proceeded in carrying this
order into effect so that there are now very few male deer
left, and those few are young and small. In the course of the
winter the does also will be destroyed if the same course is
pursued, but I have thought it right to bring the subject
under your notice now as in case of a desire that at some
future period the deer should still be kept here it would be
more difficult to get them if the whole are destroyed.

Many of the gentlemen have expressed their regret that
such an ornament to the Forest should cease to exist, and
the injury to the plantations may be said no longer to remain for they are now so few that before any increase would
take place all the plantations would be so advanced as to
be out of any danger to them.

The evil of poaching is very serious, and the mining population in spite of the bad state of the coal trade continues
to increase and may be thought incompatible with keeping
deer in such a locality. Some of the magistrates, however,

are of opinion that the evil will not be cured by the destruction of the deer, but will only take a different direction. The Highmeadow Woods, lying together and not being intruded into by the mine works, might afford protection for some deer if it was thought desirable to retain any in this particular spot.

I have thought it right to bring the subject under your notice at this time, but without recommending the course to be followed. If the destruction of them continues it will require the whole of the winter, as it has now become very difficult.

No reply is evident, but Machen wrote another letter mentioning that the keepers 'wished for some additional remuneration', to which Lord Seymour of the Office of Woods answered bluntly 26 November 1850.[34] 'It appears to me that they have situations which I could easily find other persons to take. If therefore they are not satisfied, it will be best that they should be replaced by new men. I should object to giving them any deer which you have hitherto given to the poor. I should wish a list to be sent here of the way in which the deer have been disposed of.' Machen answered in December[35] that 'there were perhaps 70 or 80 deer left', and that those disposed of during 1850 were as shown in the list on page 182.

Machen and many other residents in Dean were unable to halt the unfortunate slaughter of the deer, and it was probably with a heavy heart that he (having resigned as deputy surveyor in February 1854) noted in 1855 that 'there is not now a deer left in the Forest, and only a few stragglers in the Highmeadow Woods'. Nicholls[36] in 1858 wrote of the deer poachers of the Forest :

The remarks 'Going after the deer', or 'You don't, maybe, want to buy some meat?' are no doubt fresh in the recollection of many. Going about with guns, in numbers too formidable for the keepers to interfere, shooting the deer by day, and carrying them off at night, were by no means uncommon. Poachers of a poorer and more primitive stamp are said to have resorted to the expedient of dropping a heavy iron bar from where they had secreted themselves on the projecting branch of an oak, so that it might fall across

the neck of the deer which had come to browse under-
neath. Or they baited a large hook with an apple and sus-
pended it at a proper height by a stout cord over a path
which the deer were observed to frequent. They also were
known to set a number of nooses of iron wire in a row, skil-
fully fastened to a rope secured to a couple of trees, into
which, aided by dogs, they drove the deer.

	Males	Does	Fawns
By Robert Witts, keeper:	20	26	12
By John Gaudern, keeper:	30	19	9
	50	45	21

Disposed of thus:

Sir Martin Crawley	
Mr Mason	
Mr Jelfe	
Mr Pyrke	
Mr Colchester	9
Mr Bathurst	
Lord Dunraven	
Mr Crawshay	
Mr Machen	

The Speech House: for Gale dinner and Sale	2
Persons connected with the Forest	15
Distributed to the poor at Whitemead, about 3 in each week	65
Left with the keepers	4
	95 and 21 fawns

In view of such evil practices, ornamental to a forest as deer
undoubtedly are, it was perhaps well that these delightful animals
were carefully removed by the keepers, until such times as the
inhabitants became more enlightened and humane. As late as
1889,[37] the then deputy surveyor, Sir James Campbell, Bt, in-

formed a Select Committee that there was very little game in the Forest, adding :

It is not the slightest use to preserve it, because I should think that every born forester is a poacher by nature; therefore we think it far better not to encourage it, because even since I have been at Dean Forest, keepers and others have been absolutely killed by poachers. One man certainly was killed since I went there; that was a policeman. They took to shooting the keepers when they were not allowed to shoot the deer, and it was thought better to give the deer up.

However, there were some deer in the western part of the Forest, more particularly in the Highmeadow Woods. A journalist writing in 1914 on 'Deer Driving in Dean Forest' recorded : [38]

It does not appear to be generally known that there is quite a number of deer [fallow] running wild and breeding in their natural state and habits within the precincts of the Royal Forest of Dean. It is generally accepted that they have been for a number of years exterminated, save for private preserves, and that for a good wild deer hunt or drive it was necessary to travel to the bracing Scotch highlands. Such, however is not the case, for there are still a large number in the spacious woods on the extreme western side of the Forest which furnish splendid sport for privileged gentlemen amongst whom are the Crown keepers and those fortunate enough to possess shooting rights. Previous to the year 1850, it is stated, deer were to some extent preserved, but after which date, chiefly owing to the ravages of poachers, they were allowed to be killed, all the year round, irrespective of any 'close season', though at that time the most important drives took place in the early portion of the year.

The origin of the Forest deer appears to be somewhat obscure, there being put forth several opinions. Some say they escaped from various private parks that adjoin the Forest, which opinion in some measure appears correct. It will be interesting to note that in the coat of arms of the town of Coleford the deer figures. Let the origin of the present deer be what it may, there is still a fair number of fallow deer remaining at the present time.

The writer, on the occasion of a recent visit to Braceland Park, to the north of Coleford, was interested, and not less astonished, to learn of the many recent deer hunts which had taken place near there, and we took a photo of the 'bag' after a recent 'deer drive' at the above place. The occupiers of Braceland Park (which by the way, is the home of the 'Rhode Island Reds', a noted breed of fowls) possess the shooting rights over 200 acres of Forest land, stretching from Staunton to Symonds Yat, and down to the river Wye. The wood is situated in one of the most lovely portions of the Forest, far removed from any busy centre, and makes convenient breeding ground for deer second to none in the Royal Forest.

The herds are, of course, continually on the move, and one might be frequently in the Forest for months at a time and happen to see a single head. Their tracks, however, are everywhere to be seen, and their runs are innumerable. Occasionally a deer drive is organised and planned in advance, especially in the early part of the year, but in most cases they are very hurried, informal affairs. One of the Crown keepers may happen to catch sight of a buck and two does outside his cottage. Immediately all is confusion. He telephones to the next man, telling him to pass the word on, and runs out to spread the news to all those on the 'wire'. In half an hour from 10 to 20 men are on the spot with guns and dogs, and the drive commences. Each man is allotted a station (and woe betide him if he leaves it), and the line of beaters and dogs slowly advances, the dogs scouring the bush for the scent. Suddenly a dog catches the scent, and, with a high-pitched whine, is off, ventre-a-terre on the trail, the others following him. We wait impatiently, and presently—'Look out! here they come!' Crash! Flying through the thick undergrowth comes perhaps a fine buck and a doe or two. Bang! Bang! Bang! Perhaps the does are dropped and the buck wounded. It gives a mighty jump in the air and is off like an arrow, dogs and men after him helter skelter. Should there be any water about he is sure to be into it and, unless he is turned off or caught up previous to taking the water, he escapes. Our correspondent's informant says that a wounded doe has been followed miles by the blood trail, and has been known to clear a five-feet fence, apparently with little effort, and then swim through the swift-running Wye. A frightened doe is no easy thing to stop.

The 'guns' generally aim at behind the shoulders, as a wound in the back means 'hors de combat'. With a shot gun the head and neck are aimed at. Shot guns are generally used in woods, being regarded as safer among the beaters, the rifle carrying much farther. This present year, at the place named, there has been some capital sport, 15 to 20 having been bagged, in four or five drives. Of course it occasionally happens that a day's sport ends up with nil to the 'guns' credit, but not often, and sometimes the 'guns' are out all day and see not the sign of a deer from 'morn till dewey eve'. Oftentimes some of the men desert their post and thus miss the chance of a lifetime, to the mental fatigue of the other members, but it can safely be taken for granted that all the 'guns' equally share the unique and exciting sport of hunting 'big game' in Dean Forest.

Fig 16.   Fallow buck with three does (line drawing by Hubert Pepper, commissioned in 1970 by Dr Cyril Hart)

There have always been some fallow deer in or near the Highmeadow woods; and during the second world war they increased to some 400 to 450. From 1946 to 1958 deer shoots were organised by the Forestry Commission two or three times each year. The shooting was not selective but was chiefly to keep the numbers in bounds. Today the number of fallow in Highmeadow is about 105—perhaps 30 mature bucks, 40 does, and

35 yearlings and fawns. Some of the bucks often cross and re-
cross the Wye; they, and some of the does, frequently stray and
a few are killed or injured on roads or by unauthorised persons. In the vicinity of the Speech House are about 40 fallow—
perhaps 15 mature bucks, 13 does and 12 yearlings and fawns.
The does are usually found in the centre of the forest around
Beechenhurst and Serridge; the bucks wander as far as Stapledge
and Blakeney Hill. The Speech House deer are chiefly black;
only a few are of lighter colour. Their heads are of better shape
and higher quality than those of the bucks in Highmeadow, but
the weights are about equal in both herds.

Most people in Dean have never seen its deer. A few have
seen the imprints of their hooves, their droppings, shoots browsed
by does, and small trees frayed by bucks. These graceful
creatures may sometimes be found early in the morning on the
edge of a grassy ride, but any sudden movement will arouse
their suspicion and will result in the deer quietly moving off,
their colouring merging into the hues and irregular outlines of
the trees. Any motorist in the Forest may in the half light or
in the dimmed light of his car, observe a handsome buck or a
timid doe break cover to slowly move across the road and glide
gracefully again into the woods. Such a sight is both interesting
and pleasurable.

The Forestry Commission have to consider how many deer
can be permitted in the woodlands without the trees suffering
too much damage—which consists of browsing shoots and
foliage; stripping bark with teeth; and fraying saplings with the
antlers to remove velvet or to define rutting stands. The obvia-
tion of unacceptable damage depends on a sound knowledge of
the biology of the species, their habits, food, seasonal activities,
and haunts. In Dean, fencing would be uneconomic, except of
small areas such as the aboretum east of the Speech House.
Selective culling is necessary to ensure a healthy herd and a
tolerable number, carried out humanely within the regulations
of the Deer Act 1963. Deer have a high rate of increase, about
30 per cent each year. Sex ratios must be maintained at the
right proportion; and the age class is another important factor.[39]
No one can be held responsible for the damage done by the deer or
for any motor accident which they may cause.

In Dean and the Highmeadow woods the conservation and

Fig 17. Fallow deer crossing a Forest track (line drawing by
Hubert Pepper, commissioned in 1970 by Dr Cyril Hart)

culling of the deer are in the capable and experienced hands of
Edgar Gwilliam[40] (*Plate p 173*), the Forestry Commission's senior
ranger (from 1959) and his assistant Aubrey Neale. Edgar, who
has worked for the Commission since 1946, is a highly accurate
shot, with a powerful .270 telescopic rifle to ensure that the
culled deer do not suffer. He culls with great care about thirty
annually; some of the venison is sold to local hotels, and the remainder to game dealers.

Watching and studying the local deer will become an increasing pastime : already there are a few local enthusiasts, eg Hubert
Pepper, an internationally well-known wildlife artist (see *Figs 16
and 17, and Plate p 174*). It is to be hoped that in the Forest there
will be neither amateur nor professional stalkers (who regard
deer as sporting quarry for their rifle), nor recrimination between
over-zealous conservationists and agriculturists or silviculturists
who might suspect the presence of too many deer to be detri-
mental to economics. In and around Dean, all should appreciate
each other's point of view. All must protect and appreciate
these pleasurable creatures which once again adorn the Forest as
they have done throughout almost two millennia. Meanwhile,

the deer in Dean could not have better friends than Edgar Gwilliam and his colleagues in the Forestry Commission.

References to Chapter 7

1   *Hist et Cart Mon S Pet Glouc*, II, 177; E32/30, m.32
2   *Register of Bishop Swinfield of Hereford*, 1286; *BGAS*, XXIX, 302
3   Hart, *Royal Forest*, 55, 56, 57, 67
4   Ibid 71
5   E134, 16 Chas I, Mich Glouc 36
6   C.99/31, m.2
7   E134, 16 Chas I, Mich Glouc 36
8   SP18/223, 567
9   BM, Harl Mss 6839, f.332
10 *Cal Tsy Bks*, II, 160
11 SP29/170, 106
12 *Cal Tsy Bks*, II, 160
13 SP29/1676–7, 27, 28
14 GRO, D23/31
15 Ibid D36/Q2(09)
16 SP34, 1702–3, 503
17 *Cal Tsy Bks and Papers*, I, 355, 375
18 Mss *penes me*. The Deed of Appointment is dated 8 Jan 1738
19 *Third Report of 1788*, op cit
20 Ibid App 24
21 Ibid App 20
22 Ibid App 22
23 Ibid 41, 42
24 GRO, D33
25 *30th Rep of Coms of Woods*, 1852, App 16, 223
26 GRO, D33
27 F16/52
28 GRO, D33
29 F16/52
30 Ibid
31 *Report of Select Committee of the House of Commons on the Woods &c of the Crown*, 1849
32 GRO, D33
33 F16/52
34 Ibid

35 Ibid
36 Nicholls, H. G., *The Forest of Dean*, 1858, 203
37 *Report of Select Committee of the House of Commons*, 1889, Minutes of Evidence, 31
38 *The Lydney Observer*, 8 May 1914
39 For detailed information on fallow deer, see *The Fallow Deer*, Forestry Commission Leaflet No 52 by W. A. Cadman; *Fallow Deer*, British Deer Society Publication No 1. by N. and D. Chapman
40 *Cotswold Life*, 2(6) March 1970

Eight: Changes in Forest Law

The Wild Creatures and Forest Laws Act, 1971 (see Appendix VI) advanced the process of statute law revision by repealing a number of enactments relating to forest and forest law. In order to found the repeal of many of the enactments it was necessary to include a provision abolishing forest law itself and any royal prerogative right to wild creatures. Thus section 1(1)(a) abolished any prerogative right of Her Majesty to wild creatures (except royal fish and swans), and was the foundation for the repeal of the scheduled enactments relating to forest which regulated the exercise of some of the prerogative rights. Section 1(1)(b) formally abolished any franchise granted by the Crown of forest, free chase, park, or free warren. Subsection (2) of the same section abrogated forest law except in so far as it related to the appointment and functions of verderers. The abolition of forest law automatically deforested all surviving ancient forests, namely Windsor, the New Forest, and the Forest of Dean. Windsor Forest is now the only forest which remains part of the land revenues of the Crown.

The only part of the old forest administration which now survives with any active existence consists of the verderers in the New Forest and the Forest of Dean. These verderers are the one group of forest officials to have kept both their titles and some of their functions from the earliest times until the present day. The verderers of Epping Forest are not part of the old forest organisation but have a statutory office provided for by section 30 of the Epping Forest Act 1878 (c.208). In the case of the New Forest, the constitution and election of the verderers are governed by the New Forest Act 1877 (c.121) and the New Forest Act 1949 (c.69): section 22(1) of the 1877 Act provides that the verderers shall be a body corporate by the name of The Verderers of the New Forest, with perpetual succession and a common seal. The Dean verderers have not been incorporated and there is no statute or other instrument governing their appointment: this is regulated by custom. Section 1(6) of the 1971 Act provides that the Dean verderers shall continue to be elected and hold office as at the passing of the Act. The jurisdic-

Page 191 Commoners' Privileges: *(above)* Pannage of pigs (G. J. M. Smith); *(below)* Sheep—sometimes a menace on roads (G. J. M. Smith)

Page 192 James G. Wood, MA, LLB (1843–1928), author in 1878 of 'The Laws of the Dean Forest and Hundred of St Briavels, in the County of Gloucester'

tion of their court of attachment was extended by section 100 to 105 of the Crown Lands Act 1829 (c.50) and sections 14 to 17 of the Dean Forest (Encroachments) Act 1838 (c. 42), but all these sections are now repealed by the 1971 Act. Much relating to their election, duties and powers is under custom, and the only remaining enactments in which the Dean verderers are mentioned are in sections 19 and 20 of the Dean Forest (Mines) Act 1838 (c.43) and the Forestry Act 1967 (c.10).

The first limb of section 1(3) of the 1971 Act provides that any right of common originating in forest law shall be free of

Fig 18. Map of the present Forest of Dean and its neighbourhood

restriction by reason of the Fence Month or the Winter Heyning
or any payment in place of it. These terms have been explained
in Chapter 1. Section 1(5) of the same Act provides that except
for the abolition of the foregoing close seasons, no existing right
of common or pannage originating in forest law shall be affected
by the abrogation of forest law or by the repeal of any enactment giving or confirming that right.

Section 1(4) of the 1971 Act repealed many scheduled enactments to the extent specified in the schedule to the Act. All these
enactments fall into one or other of three broad categories. First,
those whose repeal was consequential on the abolition of the
prerogative right to wild creatures and of forest law; these include
enactments designed to regulate or mitigate the severity of forest
law which in early times was oppressive. Second, enactments
which are no longer of practical utility or are spent in their
operation. Third, enactments which in consequence of other repeals are no longer necessary. Repealed enactments relating to
forest law in general are chiefly those of the Charter of the
Forest (1297), an Ordinance of the Forest (1305, and another
in 1306) and the Delimitation of Forests Act 1640.

Repealed enactments relating specifically to the Forest of Dean
include the Dean Forest (Reafforestation) Act 1667 (see Appendix II). This Act recited the scarcity of timber and made provision
for the increase and preservation of timber within Dean; sections
1 to 4 provided for the inclosure of 11,000 acres in Dean for
the growing of timber, and for throwing the inclosures open when
the trees were sufficiently large, and inclosing an equivalent
acreage. The forest organisation has atrophied except for the verderers; and section 1(6) of the 1971 Act provides that the Dean
verderers shall continue to be elected and hold office as at the
passing of the Act. They may exercise jurisdiction in relation to
any alleged offence against a byelaw, and for this purpose their
court is deemed to be a court of summary jurisdiction (section 47
of the Forestry Act 1967); but the verderers have not functioned
as a judicial body since 1902, and there is no intention to revive
magisterial powers so long in abeyance. Section 6 of the 1667
Act was repealed by the Crown Estate Act 1961 (c.55). Section
7 provided that the Crown may restore up to 800 deer, but
the management by the Forestry Commission and the byelaw-
making power conferred by section 46 of the Forestry Act 1967

made the retention of the section unnecessary. Although no large
number of deer has been purposefully restored to Dean, there
are about forty in the centre of Dean and about 105 in the
adjoining Highmeadow Woods; these are merely wild deer and
not venison subject to the special protection of forest law. Sections 9 and 11 to 16 of the 1667 Act were either spent or obsolete. Privileges of common and pannage (section 10) are saved
by the 1971 Act (section 1(6)) and are also freed of restriction
by reason of the Fence Month or the Winter Heyning or any
payment in place of it. The references in section 11 of the 1667
Act to the rights of the Free Miners outside the inclosures are
covered by section 64 of the Dean Forest (Mines) Act 1838 (c.43);
section 17 is impliedly repealed by section 23 of the same act. In
view of the foregoing explanation the repeal of the 1667 Act
(while saving provisions regarding verderers and commoning)
was sensible.

Another enactment of which parts are repealed by the 1971
Act is the Dean Forest (Timber) Act 1808 (c.72)—see Appendix
III—which deals with the increase of timber in Dean (as well as
in the New Forest). As regards Dean the Act remains the operative text for making, planting, and throwing open of inclosures
(not to exceed 11,000 acres in total). Only the preamble, sections
1, 2, 5 and 7, and parts of sections 3 and 4 are repealed. The
preamble and sections 1 and 2 are spent. Section 3 is the operative provision for making inclosures, and because the procedure
for inclosure is still necessary the relevant parts of this section are
not repealed; it is necessary to prove to persons exercising privileges of common that only lawful inclosures have been made.
Parts of the section which are repealed as spent, and being mainly
references to the New Forest, are the words :

(a) from the beginning to 'be it enacted that';
(b) 'and New Forest respectively';
(c) 'in the said forests respectively' in both places;
(d) 'and six thousand acres in the New Forest' in both places;
(e) from 'and the quantities, butts and boundaries' to 'of
    record for ever';
(f) 'the said recited Acts and,' in both places.

Consequently on the preceding repeals, also repealed were
the words 'the said recited Acts or' near the end of section 4. The

words from 'the lord high treasurer' to the words 'shall determine that' near the beginning of section 4 were also repealed as no longer apposite. It is now the Forestry Commission who decide when the inclosures are past danger from animals. Section 5 was repealed as obsolete (this provided that the commissioners making the inclosure, with the assistance of one of the purveyors of the Navy, should 'set out' decayed trees in the Forest to finance the making and maintaining of the inclosure; this provision perhaps operated by way of exception from the requirement of section 4 of the 1667 Act that trees should only be felled on the allowance of two justices). Section 7, repealed, imposed a penalty for destroying any fences or inclosure (this is now left to the general law, and in particular section 25 of the Malicious Damage Act 1861 (c.97)). The unrepealed sections of the 1808 Act remained as noted above the operative text for regulating inclosures in Dean, and Inclosure Commissioners (see Appendix V), among whom are the four verderers, still act in conjunction with the regulations.

The Crown Lands Act 1829 (c.50), was repealed by The Crown Estate Act 1961 (c.55) except sections 100 to 105 (which relate to the powers of verderers) so far as they remained applicable to Dean. The 1971 Act repealed sections 100 to 105. Section 100 had authorised the verderers to inquire into 'unlawful inclosures, purprestures, encroachments and trespasses'; to fine the offenders; and to abate the inclosure, purpresture, encroachment, or trespass. (As regards purprestures, section 100 was repealed by section 14 of the Dean Forest (Encroachments) Act 1838 (c.42).) Section 15 of the 1838 Act then went on to allow the verderers to exercise the powers of section 100 as regards inclosures, trespasses, and encroachments either at the court of attachment or not. The explanation of this procedure seemed to lie in section 8 of the 1667 Act, whereunder the owner of lands in the Forest could, without committing any breach of forest law, inclose the lands and build on them as he wished. Accordingly there could not in Dean, unlike in other forests, be any purprestures otherwise than by encroachment or trespass on Crown land—inclosure on a person's own land which would otherwise be a purpresture being no offence but inclosures on Crown land amounting to an encroachment or trespass. The result is that references in section 100 of the 1829 Act to unlawful inclosures and purprestures are now repealed, though they will also cease to be offences with the abolition of forest law unless they amounted to encroachments or trespass on Crown land. Thus the repeal of section 100 was on the ground that in present circumstances an encroachment or trespass on Crown land in the Forest ought not to be dealt with as a criminal offence, and it was not considered desirable to revive the verderers' powers under the section—the cases can be more expeditiously determined by the local bench of magistrates. Section 101 allowed the verderers to appoint officers to carry out orders of their court of attachment; but the verderers now have only a steward of the court (appointed and paid an honorarium by the Forestry Commission through the Minister of Agriculture, Fisheries and Food) and no funds. This section is repealed, along with section 102 (court of attachment empowered to inquire into the conduct of the regarders and other officers of the Forest and to fine them for neglect of duty), section 103 (saving for the Crown right to proceed by information in the Court of Exchequer or under other existing laws for the punishment of the offences referred to in section 100), and sections 104 and 105 (the recovery and application of penalties under the Act).

Another enactment repealed by the 1971 Act is an Act for vesting the office of constable of the castle of St Briavels in the First Commissioner of His Majesty's Woods, Forests, Land Revenues, Works and Buildings; and for vesting the office of keeper of the Forest of Dean in the county of Gloucester in the Commissioners of His Majesty's Woods, Forests, Land Revenues, Works and Buildings, 1836 (6 and 7 Will IV, c.3). This Act contained two sections neither of which was wanted any longer. Section 1 vested the office of constable of St Briavel's castle in the First Commissioner of Woods : the object of this was to continue St Briavel's court which was held in the castle before the deputy constable; this court was, however, abolished in 1842 (by 5 and 6 Vict, c.83). Section 2 vested in the Commissioners of Woods the office of keeper of His Majesty's deer in Dean. Even if forest law had not been abolished the office could by now be regarded as obsolete in view of the lapse of time since there was a purposeful 'game of deer' in the Forest.

The 1971 Act also repealed, so far as previously unrepealed, the Dean Forest (Encroachments) Act 1838 (1 and 2 Vict, c.42), of which sections 5 and 13 had been repealed by the Crown

Estate Act 1961 (c.55). This was one of two Acts which resulted from the reports of the Commissioners appointed under an Act of 1831 (1 and 2 Will IV, c. 12) now repealed. The other Act was the Dean Forest (Mines) Act 1838 (c.43), parts of which were repealed by the Statute Law (Repeals) Act 1969. The Act now repealed by the 1971 Act began with a recital of the Acts of 1667 and 1831, and of encroachments in the Forest. Sections 1 and 2 provided for the relevant report of the 1831 Commissioners to be put on record among the land revenue records and the quarter sessions records in Gloucester and in the Speech House, and to be open to inspection. The copy put among the land revenue records is in the Public Record Office, and is evidence accordingly. Sections 3 to 13 dealt with the then existing encroachments in the Forest and provided for the possessors to have in some cases a fee simple title and in others the grant of a lease. As stated above, sections 5 and 13 had already been repealed. The rest, though in some cases forming the basis of existing titles, were clearly spent as enactments, and were repealed. Sections 14 to 17 operated on sections 100 to 105 of the Crown Lands Act 1829 (c.50) which were repealed by the 1971 Act. Section 14 repealed section 100 of the 1829 Act so far as related to purprestures, but not as regards encroachments and trespasses. Section 15 provided that the powers of the verderers under section 100 of the 1829 Act might be exercised by any two verderers either at their court of attachment or not, and went on to provide forms of information and of conviction. Section 16 provided for the recovery and application of fines in accordance with sections 104 and 105 of the 1829 Act. Section 17 required the verderers to transmit their proceedings to the Commissioners of Woods every three months, and the proceedings were to be enrolled in the Office of Land Revenue Records and Inrolments. In practice the records of the proceedings of the verderers are kept in a minute book and are eventually sent to the Public Record Office; copies are not normally sent to the Forestry Commissioners. Section 18 was a general saving of the 1667 Act, repealed, for the rights of the Crown and of the Free Miners. With the repeal of sections 3 to 12, section 18 was no longer required.

The foregoing are the more important Acts relating to Dean repealed in part or whole by the 1971 Act. Other Acts wholly repealed were the Dean Forest Act 1842 (5 and 6 Vict, c.65), which divided the Forest of Dean into ecclesiastical districts; an Act of 1844 (7 and 8 Vict, c.13) which extended the time limit under the Dean Forest (Encroachments) Act 1838, now repealed, for making leases or conveyances of encroachments on the Forest, and with referring to the verderers disputes as to the right to a lease or conveyance; and the East Dean and West Dean (Highways) Act 1883 (46 and 47 Vict, c.87). Other enactments repealed only in part by the 1971 Act, include an Act of 1861 (24 and 25 Vict, c.40) of which section 25 is repealed (it declared that the verderers' power to punish trespassers in Dean extended to trespasses of cutting, taking, or carrying away, of turf, gravel, stone, sand, or other soil); parts of this Act had been repealed by the Statute Law (Repeals) Act 1969. Other repeals were of an Act of 1866 (29 and 30 Vict, c.70) relating to Walmore Common and Bearce Common; and an Act of 1870 (33 and 34 Vict, c.8) which dealt with the title to Abbotswood (section 9 is saved). Furthermore, as regards Dean, the 1971 Act repealed section 1 of the Dean Forest Act 1906 (6 Edw VII, c.119) which had authorised the making of agreements between the Commissioners of Woods (with treasury consent) and the verderers for exchanging parcels of so-called waste not exceeding £1,000 in value for other land in the Forest forming part of the possessions and land revenues of the Crown and not being a part of the waste, so as to free the former from rights of common and incorporate the latter into the waste subject to the like rights of common. Finally, the 1971 Act repealed paragraph 2(a) of Schedule 2 to the Crown Estate Act 1961 (9 and 10 Eliz II, c.55) which provided for the continuance in force of sections 100 to 105 of the Crown Lands Act 1829 so far as they remained applicable to Dean : this repeal was consequential on the repeal of what remained of the 1829 Act.

In consequence of the foregoing repeal of enactments, it is instructive to set down, albeit briefly, the now much simplified laws which still relate specially to Dean—its 24,000 acres being managed by the Forestry Commission under the Minister of Agriculture, Fisheries and Food, as authorised by the Forestry Act 1967. In charge is the deputy surveyor who is also Conservator of Forests for South West England (Flowers Hill, Brislington, Bristol, BS4 5JY). Under him in Dean are a district officer and supporting staff (Crown Offices, Coleford, Gloucestershire, GL16 8BA).

As to the verderers, their election and holding of office are by custom: '. . . verderers in the Forest of Dean shall continue to be elected and hold office as at the passing of this Act [of 1971]'.[1]

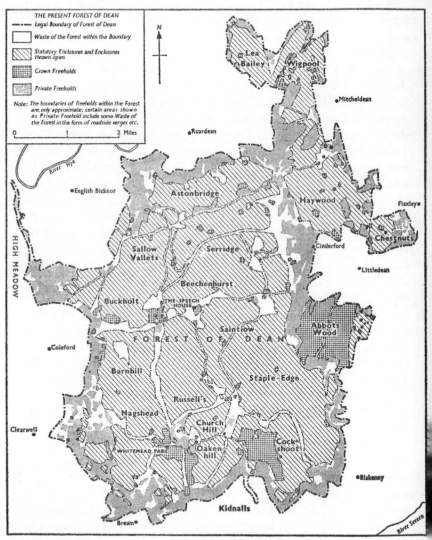

THE PRESENT FOREST OF DEAN
— ·— Legal Boundary of Forest of Dean

Waste of the Forest within the Boundary

Statutory Enclosures and Enclosures thrown open

Crown Freeholds

Private Freeholds

Note: The boundaries of freeholds within the Forest are only approximate; certain areas shown as Private Freehold include some Waste of the Forest in the form of roadside verges etc.

0   1   2 Miles

Fig 19.   Map of the present Forest of Dean. The Highmeadow Woods
lie to the north-west

Therefore, until legislation alters the procedure, verderers will continue to be elected by authority of a writ of the Crown, under the supervision of the high sheriff by the freeholders of Gloucestershire (except those of Gloucester and Bristol). Furthermore, they will continue to hold office according to custom. The only remaining enactments in which they are mentioned are the Dean Forest (Mines) Act 1838 (c.43), the Forestry Act 1967 (c.10), and the Wild Creatures and Forest Laws Act 1971.

As to privileges of common and pannage, these continue under custom, but are ill-defined and only partly regulated. Perusal of the book *The Commoners of Dean Forest*[2] and the treatise of James G. Wood (*Plate p 192*)[3] will indicate the difficulties which anyone exercising the privileges would experience in attempting to prove them as rights. Recourse would also have to be made to many acts and ordinances (chiefly repealed), decrees, and other judgements : then there would be the vexed question as to whether sheep are commonable animals in forest. However, the 1971 Act section 1(5) states that 'no existing common or pannage originating in the forest law shall be affected by the abrogation of the forest law or by the repeal by this section of any enactment giving or confirming that right'. Furthermore, the same Act by section 1(3), has lifted the restriction of the two close seasons for commoning : 'Any right of common originating in the forest law shall be free of restriction by reason of the Fence Month or the Winter Heyning or any payment in place of it.' The time of pannage, ie the period when pigs are allowed to feed on acorns and beech mast, is from 25 September to 22 November,[4] but neither pannage nor grazing are exercisable in enclosures. Nowadays only sheep and to a limited extent pigs are to be seen in the unenclosed parts of the Forest. The exercise of the privileges has been custom for many centuries, but now the wandering sheep are a menace on the roads and in private gardens; and the average annual cost to the Forestry Commission of fencing against them is some £5,000. The Forest of Dean Committee (the 'Creed Committee') which reported in 1958 made recommendations for dealing with this unrestricted free grazing—ostensibly available to persons who do not of necessity own any land. Because legislation would be necessary no action has as yet been taken. The first need in regulating the situation is a register of those persons claiming privileges of common and pannage. As to estovers or botes, there are no longer any recognised rights or privileges in Dean.

The official boundaries of the Forest are shown in *Fig 19*; and their origin has been discussed elsewhere.[5] Regulation of the statutory 11,000 acres by the Forestry Commission is through Inclosure Commissioners (see Appendix V). Byelaws of the Forest issued in 1929 (Appendix IV) are outdated; a new set approved by the verderers is awaiting publication by the Forestry Commission.

The rights of the Free Miners to mine coal, iron ore and stone are well defined by statute.[6] Briefly, any male person born and abiding in the Hundred of St Briavels[7] (which includes Dean), aged 21 years or more, who has worked for a year and a day in a mine, may register as a Free Miner. This does not mean that he can now search for minerals and stone at will, but he has the chance of being granted a concession (a 'gale') should one become available. The rights and 'gales' are dealt with by the Forestry Commission through a deputy gaveller (Crown Offices, Coleford, Gloucester, GL16 8BA).

References to Chapter 8

1   The Wild Creatures and Forest Laws Act 1971
2   Hart, C. E., *The Commoners of Dean Forest*, 1951
3   Wood, James G., *The Laws of the Dean Forest and Hundred of St Briavels, in the County of Gloucester*, 1878; Hart, C. E., *Laws of Dean*, 1952
4   Section 7 of the New Forest Act 1964 (c.83) provides that the time of pannage in that Forest shall cease to be the period from 25 September to 22 November inclusive in such year but shall be such period not being less than 60 consecutive days as may be fixed by the Forestry Commissioners annually after consultation with the verderers of the New Forest.
5   Hart, C. E., *The Extent and Boundaries of the Forest of Dean and Hundred of St Briavels*, 1947; Ibid *Royal Forest*, op cit
6   Ibid *The Free Miners*, 1953
7   A map of the Hundred of St Briavels is included in Hart, *The Free Miners, The Industrial History of Dean*, and *The Extent and Boundaries of the Hundred of St Briavels*, op cit

Appendix I Forest Officials in Dean in 1282

Justice of forest south of Trent
Luke de Tany, appointed 10 June 1281

Justices in Eyre appointed 18 January 1282
Luke de Tany, Adam Gurdon, Peter de Lenche, Richard de Crepping

Constable-wardens and their deputies

	Appointed	*Deputy*
William Beauchamp, earl of Warwick	25 January 1271*	Osbert de Berford William le Blund Philip Wyther Richard de Muleford
Ralph of Sandwich	29 September 1276†	Walter de Snappe
Grimbald Pauncefot	16 November 1281‡	Alexander of Bicknor

Verderers
Elias de Heydon
Philip of Hatherley
Philip Wyther
Roger le Bret
Robert de Ledene
Robert Malet
William de la Hulle

Foresters-of-fee
Bailiwick
Abenhall : Ralph of Abenhall
Berse : William Joce
Bicknor : Cecily de Mucegros
Blakeney : Walter of Aston

* Succeeded by Ralph of Sandwich 29 Sept 1276
† Succeeded by Grimbald Pauncefot 16 Nov 1281
‡ Died in office 1287. Succeeded by William Hathewy 15 April 1287

Bleyth (Blaize) : Ralph Hathewy, guardian of the heir of Bleyth
Staunton : Richard de la More
The Lea : Nicholas of The Lea

Sergeants-of-fee
  Henry of Dene, Kt
  Robert of Awre
  Thomas Warin
  William Boter
  William Hathewy
  William of Stears

Foresters
  John of Penyard, Forester to Ralph of Abenhall
  John the Porter of Hauekesbery
  Nicholas le Bret, forester of Lydney
  Robert of Wynterburn
  Walter de Riseleye

Regarders
  '*Regarders newly elected in the last eyre of the regard*'
  John de la Mare, Kt
  Maurice of Saltmarsh, Kt
  Milo de Langetot
  Nicholas de Gamages, Kt
  Peter of Stinchcombe
  Robert of Coaley
  Robert of Draycot
  Robert of Purton
  Walter Haket
  William de Burk
  William de Derneford, Kt
  William Maunsel, Kt

  '*Regarders in the other regard made earlier*'
  Hamo de Bisare
  Henry Cadel
  Henry of Walford
  Ralph of Rodley
  Richard of Pulton
  Robert le lung of Newland
  Robert Schort
  Stephen Malemort

Walter of Ketford
Walter Wytking
William Hyreby

Foot-Sergeant

John son of Hugo de Asshe under Henry of Dene, sergeant-of-fee

Riding-Foresters

John of Elbridge, to the earl Marshal in Tidenham Chase

Hugo Quatre Homes ⎫
Walter le Lou   ⎬ Under the earl of Warwick
                      ⎭

Richard le Venur
Philip Sawary
Adam le hultere

Sub-Foresters

John Crek   ⎫
John Gifford   ⎬ to Walter of Aston, forester-of-fee
               ⎭

Woodwards

Adam of Abergavenny, under the Bishop of Hereford at Bishopswood
Adam, woodward of Lydney
Geoffrey of Walmore
John de Lancumbe, under the abbot of Flaxley
John of Etloe
John Schort of Coughton, under Richard Talbot
Nicholas son of Isabel of The Lea, under John of The Lea
Robert Jonet of Coughton, under Richard Talbot
Robert Kroc of Kilcot, under the prior of Newent
Seysel de la Regge, under John of The Lea
Walter, under the abbot of Flaxley at Littledean
William, under Lord William de Valence

Appendix II The Dean Forest (Reafforestation) Act 1667*

19 and 20 Chas II, c. 8

An Act for the Increase and Preservation of Timber within the Forest of Dean. [9 May, 1667]

Forasmuch as the wood and timber of the Crown which of late years was of very great quantity and value, within the Forest or late Forest of Dean, in the county of Gloucester, is become totally destroyed, excepting what is standing within the woodwardship of the Lea Baily whereby there is an apparent scarcity of timber there, as in all other parts of this kingdom, so that some course is necessary to be speedily taken to restore and preserve the growth of timber for the future supply of His Majesty's royal navy, and the maintenance of shipping for the trade of this nation. Be it enacted, by the King's most excellent majesty, by and with the advice and consent of the lords spiritual and temporal and commons, in this present parliament assembled, and by the authority of the same :

1. That 10,000 acres, part of the waste lands of the said late Forest of Dean, shall be inclosed and kept in severalty for the growth and preservation of timber, and that it shall and may be lawful to and for His Majesty, his heirs and successors, forthwith to enclose, sever and improve within and out of the parts or places of the waste lands of the said forest, or late Forest of Dean, the whole containing by estimation about 23,000 acres, the full quantity of 10,000 acres of statute measure at sixteen foot [and] half to the perch, whereof the said woodwardship of Lea Baily, containing about 1,100 acres, to be part, and also the grounds called by the several names of Cannop Fellett, Buckholt, Beachinhurst, and Moyrystock (containing about 1,000 acres, heretofore granted to John Gibbon, John Mansil and Ambrose Bavin, some

* Now repealed.

or one of them, and now belonging unto or claimed by Banistree Mainard, esquire, which added to the 10,000 acres shall make up the full quantity of 11,000 acres to be enclosed as aforesaid), to be part. The said 11,000 acres to be set out by virtue of His Majesty's commission to be directed to six or more such persons as His Majesty shall think fit (whereof two, which shall execute such commission, to be justices of the peace for the said county, inhabiting near the parts and places of the said Forest), out of such part and places of the said waste as shall be found or esteemed by the said commissioners, or any three of them, to be most convenient to be inclosed and to be most apt and meet to produce wood and timber for the future benefit of the kingdom, and may be best spared from the use of the commoners and highways of the county, which said inclosures shall be forthwith admeasured by a sworn surveyor and set out and inclosed, butted and bounded, and the quantities, butts and boundaries thereof returned into His Majesty's Court of Exchequer, there to remain of record for ever. And the said inclosure so made and set out as aforesaid to remain in severalty in the actual possession of the Crown for ever, freed and discharged of and from all manner of right, title and pretence whatsoever (excepting of fee deer), according to the purport and intent of this present act, and shall be made and reputed a nursery for wood and timber only.

2. And for defraying the charge of the said inclosures to be made as aforesaid, be it further enacted by the authority aforesaid that the said commissioners so to be authorised as aforesaid, or any six of them (whereof some justices of the peace for the said county inhabiting near the parts of the said Forest to be two), shall by sale of the decayed trees of beech, birch, hawthorn, hazel and holly, and other such like trees not being timber, or that can ever prove timber, now standing or growing in or upon the wastes within the said Forest or late Forest, raise moneys for defraying the charge of making and maintaining the said inclosures, and also for the satisfaction of the claim or interest of Banistree Mainard in the lands aforesaid, which are to be made part of the said quantity of 11,000 acres as aforesaid, in full satisfaction and recompense for the same.

3. And it is hereby declared and enacted that the said lands so set forth as aforesaid shall be fully and perfectly inclosed with sufficient mounds and fences according to the true intent and

purport of this act, within two years after the Feast of Saint
George now next ensuing.

4. And it is hereby further enacted and declared, that at all
times hereafter, whensoever the lord treasurer of England, or
commissioners of the treasury, or chancellor of the exchequer for
the time being, shall, at any time or times hereafter be satisfied
and shall determine that the woods and trees, which shall be
growing on the said 11,000 acres, or any part thereof, so to be
inclosed as aforesaid, are become past danger of the browsing of
deer, cattle or other prejudice, and shall think fit to lay the same
or any part thereof, consisting of 500 acres or more, open and in
common [and] shall cause the same to be so done, That then and
so often it shall and may be lawful to and for the King's majesty,
his heirs and successors, from time to time to inclose in lieu of
so much as shall be so laid open out of the said 11,000 acres, the
like quantity out of any other part of the residue of the said wastes,
to be set out by like commission and admeasurement as aforesaid,
and to be holden, inclosed, freed and discharged of and from all
manner of common, estovers, herbage or pannage and other
rights, excepting fee deer as aforesaid, for so long time as the
same shall remain and continue inclosed according to the purport, direction and intent of this present act to be a nursery for
timber as aforesaid, instead of so much as shall be laid open
according to the direction aforesaid. And whensoever any wood
or timber shall at any time or times hereafter be directed to be
fallen in any part of the wastes of the said late Forest, inclosed
or not inclosed, the same shall be first viewed and allowed to be
fallen by two or more of the justices of the peace for the said
county unconcerned in the premises, and shall not be cut or fallen
until the same be viewed and allowed by such two or more
justices as fit and convenient to be cut and fallen, and that the
said justices shall have marked with a broad arrow and crown
that it may remain to be seen (as they are hereby required and
empowered to do) so many and such trees as are most fit to be
preserved for growth for timber upon every acre intended to be
fallen, and also shall have certified (as they are likewise hereby
required to do unto the lord treasurer or lord commissioners of
the treasury for the time being) the names of the places and number of trees so viewed and allowed to be fallen, and so marked
to be preserved as aforesaid. And if any person or persons shall

at any time or times hereafter, either fell or cut down any wood
or trees upon the premises, or any part thereof, before such
view, allowance and certificate made thereof as aforesaid, contrary to the true meaning of this present Act, or shall after cut
down any of the said marked trees without like allowance, the
person or persons so offending shall forfeit for every tree so fallen
the sum of £20 to him or them who shall inform or sue for the
same in any of His Majesty's courts of record, wherein no essoign,
wager of law or protection shall be allowed to the defendant. And
for further preservation of the said timber growing and to grow
upon the premises, no officer or other person or persons whatsoever shall at any time hereafter have or claim any fee trees out
of the said late Forest upon any pretence whatsoever, but shall
have and enjoy their usual fees in the game of deer of all parts
of the said wastes, inclosed or not inclosed, as formerly they
have had, anything in this act to the contrary notwithstanding.

5. And forasmuch as by former experience it hath been
found that nothing did more conduce to the raising, increase and
preservation of timber and wood within the said wastes than the
execution of the forest laws whilst the said wastes were afforested
and kept under the regard of the Forest, be it therefore further
enacted and declared by the authority aforesaid, that as well the
said 11,000 acres so to be inclosed as all other the waste lands
aforesaid shall be and are hereby reafforested, and shall from
henceforth be governed by forest law, and put under the regard
of the forest to the same effect, and in the same manner, to all
intents and purposes, as the same were in the 10th year of the
reign of the late king Charles of blessed memory, and that all
articles or agreements, and all grants and charters, made since
the 10th year of the reign of the late king Charles, for or concerning the disafforesting the three and twenty thousand acres
aforesaid, or any part thereof, and all the matters, clauses and
things therein contained relating to such disafforestation shall
be henceforth void, so that the said wastes and premises shall be
for ever henceforth deemed and adjudged to be Forest. And to
that end that new elections shall be made forthwith, and from
time to time continued, of all verderers, regarders, and other
officers of and for the governing of the said Forest, according to
the forest law in that behalf.

6. And to the end the said Forest and premises may be per-

N

petually preserved and estated in the Crown for public use as aforesaid, and may not be granted or disposed to any private use or benefit, be it further enacted, that in case any person or persons whatsoever shall presume to take, or shall obtain, any gift, grant, estate or interest of or in the said inclosures or wastes, or any wood or trees growing thereon, or of or in any of the mines or quarries of or within the said inclosures, or any part thereof, every such gift, grant, estate and interest shall *ipso facto* be null and void, and the person or persons so taking or obtaining the same shall be, and is hereby made and declared, utterly disabled and incapable to have, hold or enjoy any such gift, grant, estate or interest.

7. Provided always, nevertheless, that for preventing the destruction of young wood by over-charging the said Forest with deer, it is declared and enacted by the authority aforesaid that in case His Majesty, his heirs and successors, shall think fit at any time hereafter to restore a game of deer within the said Forest or wastes, the same shall not exceed the number of 800 deer of all sorts at any one time there to be kept for His Majesty's game within the said Forest.

8. And to the end some recompense may be made to the persons whose right of common and of herbage within the said intended inclosures is hereby taken from them for the necessary preservation of the said timber as aforesaid, be it further enacted and declared by the authority aforesaid, that it shall and may be lawful to and for all and every the owners, tenants and occupiers of any the several lands (lying within the metes, limits and boundaries of the said Forest, not being part of the said waste ground or inclosures), their heirs, executors and administrators respectively from time to time, and at any time or times hereafter, to cut down and dispose of any of the timber trees, woods or underwoods growing, or which shall hereafter grow, or be in or upon their several or respective lands (lying within the boundaries aforesaid, not being part of the said waste ground as aforesaid), at their own wills and pleasures, without the licences of any justice in eyre or his deputy, and without the license and view of any officer of the said Forest whatsoever, and also without incurring any offence against the forest law or any forfeiture or penalty touching the same, and also to manure and improve the said several lands and tenements by ploughing, assarting, digging, in-

closing, fencing or building upon the same at their wills and
pleasures, and to keep any sort of dogs unexpeditated, and to
hunt and kill any beast of chase or other game in or upon the
said several lands, as if the same were not lying within the bounds
of any forest.

9. And it is enacted by the authority aforesaid that all offences
whatsoever heretofore committed or done by any person or persons whatsoever upon the said lands lying within the said boundaries aforesaid, not within the wastes of the said Forest as
aforesaid, against any of the laws of the forest whatsoever, shall
be and are hereby wholly remitted and discharged.

10. Provided always, and it is hereby enacted and declared,
that all and every person and persons having any right of common
of pasture or of pannage, or any other rights, fees, liberties or
privileges within the said Forest or any part thereof, shall hold
and enjoy the same in the manner following (that is to say):
Their said right of pannage from and after the feast of Saint
Michael the Archangel, which shall be in the year of our Lord
Christ 1687, and not before, and their said right of common of
pasture and all other their said fees, liberties and privileges in and
through such of the said waste ground, and at such time and
times as the same shall not be enclosed as aforesaid the time
of the fence month (that is to say), for fifteen days before and
fifteen days after the feast of Saint John the Baptist yearly and
the time of the winter heyning (that is to say), from the 11th
day of November to the Three-and-twentieth day of April yearly
excepted, under and subject to the forest law, in as ample manner
as he, or they, or those under whom they or any of them might
lawfully claim might have held or enjoyed the same in the tenth
year of the reign of the late King Charles, this Act or any other
thing to the contrary notwithstanding.

11. Saving also unto the inhabitants of and in the parish of
Saint Brevills for the time being lying within the boundaries of
the said Forest their lawful rights and privileges for the taking,
cutting and enjoying the wood growing in a certain place within
the said Forest called Hudnalls as fully and amply as if this Act
had not been had or made, and also saving unto the miners and
persons using the trade of digging for iron ore, coal and ochre in
the said Forest their lawful rights and privileges in all lands and
grounds lying within the perambulation and regard of the said

Forest, other than the said inclosures for the time they shall
continue inclosed, as fully and absolutely as if this act had not
been had or made.

12. Provided nevertheless, that this Act nor anything therein
contained shall make void or null certain letters patents granted
by the King's majesty unto Sir John Wintour, knight, Francis
Finch and Robert Cleyton, esquires, in or about 30th of July, in
the fourteenth year of his now majesty's reign, of certain woods
and ironworks in the Forest of Dean for a certain term of years
yet unexpired.

13. Provided always, that nothing in this act contained shall
be deemed or construed to make void or prejudice a certain lease
for years yet unexpired granted to Thomas Preston, Esquire,
by letters patents under the great seal of certain lands in the said
Forest of Dean called Great and Little Bradleys, Pigslade, Buckholt Moor and Stony Grove now belonging to or claimed by
Dame Mary Stanhope, relict of Charles Stanhope, Esquire.

14. Provided always, and it is hereby declared, that the lands
called or known by the name of Mayly Scot and other lands
heretofore granted unto Sir Edward Villars, knight, deceased, and
his heirs, by letters patents under the great seal of England, bear-
ing date the 28th day of May in the first year of the reign of our
late sovereign lord King Charles the First, shall not be accounted
or esteemed any part of the 23,000 acres which are to be inclosed
or lie waste to the commoners.

15. Provided always, and be it enacted by the authority aforesaid, that if the full and just sum of £1,500 shall not be paid
unto the said Banistree Mainard, his heirs or assigns, by the said
mentioned commissioners, or some other person or persons by
their appointment, for and in lieu of his estate in the lands called
Cannop Fellett, Buckholt, Beechinhurst and Moyry Stocke, on or
before the 24th day of June in the year of our Lord 1669, that
then the said Banistree Mainard, his heirs and assigns, shall and
may have, hold and enjoy all and every the said mentioned lands
in as full and ample manner as any of those persons from whom
he claims did ever enjoy the same or might have enjoyed the
same by virtue of any grant under the great seal of England made
unto them of the premises, anything in this present act to the
contrary in anywise notwithstanding.

16. Provided, and be it further enacted by the authority afore-

said, that the metes and boundaries of the said Forest shall be for ever hereafter taken to extend to such parishes and places only as were commonly used, esteemed and taken to be within the perambulation and regard of the said Forest in the twentieth year of the reign of the late King James and not to any other parishes or places whatsoever, any judgment, ordinance, usage or pretence whatsoever to the contrary notwithstanding.

17. Provided always, and be it further enacted by the authority aforesaid, that any lease or leases made or to be made by His Majesty, his heirs or successors, to any person or persons whatsoever for any term or terms of years not exceeding the term of thirty-one years in possession of the coal mines and quarries of grindstone in the said Forest, or any part thereof, shall be of like force as if this act had never been made, except of such coal mines as are or shall be in any part of the 11,000 acres allotted for His Majesty's inclosure and as shall continue inclosed.

(There is an obvious error in the last sentence. The probable meaning was 'in any part of the 11,000 acres allotted for His Majesty's inclosure so long as the same shall continue inclosed'.)

Appendix III The Dean Forest (Timber) Act 1808*

48 GEO. III, c. 72

An Act for the Increase and Preservation of Timber in Dean and New Forests. [18 June, 1808]

Whereas an Act was passed in the twentieth year of the reign of King Charles the Second, intituled 'An Act for the Increase and Preservation of Timber within the Forest of Dean' : and whereas a certain other Act was passed in the parliament holden in the ninth and tenth years of King William the Third, intituled 'An Act for the Increase and Preservation of Timber in the New Forest, in the County of Southampton'; by which said Acts part of the waste lands in the said Forests of Dean and New Forest respectively were directed to be inclosed and kept in severalty for the growth and preservation of timber, and which said Acts have not been duly put in execution : And whereas from the great and increasing difficulty of procuring a supply of timber from foreign countries, and from the estates of private individuals in the United Kingdom, for the use of the navy, it has become necessary to adopt measures for insuring a more adequate supply of timber in this kingdom, and for this purpose to make more effectual provision for carrying the said recited acts into full and complete execution : And whereas certain inclosures have been made under the said recited Acts in the said Forests respectively; but doubts may arise whether in making some of the said inclosures all the forms of procedure required by the said recited Acts have been strictly complied with; be it therefore enacted and declared by the King's most excellent majesty, by and with the advice and consent of the lords spiritual and temporal, and commons, in this present parliament assembled, and by the authority

* This Act was given a short title by the Short Titles Act 1896, namely, The Dean and New Forests Act 1808. Now in part repealed.

of the same, that certain inclosures in the Forest of Dean, containing plantations of timber, that is to say, the inclosures called and known by the names of Stapledge Inclosure, Speech House Inclosure, Birch Wood Inclosure, and Buck Holt Inclosure, containing about 676 acres, shall be deemed and taken, and are hereby declared to be and shall be held to have been duly and legally made and set out under the said recited Act of the twentieth year of King Charles the Second, and to be effectually inclosed and vested in His Majesty, and to remain in severalty in the actual possession of the Crown, according to the purport and intent of the said last-mentioned Act, during the period of the same remaining so inclosed under the said last-mentioned Act and this Act.

2. [This section relates to certain inclosures in the New Forest only.]

3. And, in order to complete the quantity of 11,000 acres in Dean Forest, and 6,000 acres in New Forest, to be inclosed and kept in severalty for the growth and preservation of timber, according to the true intent and meaning of the said recited Acts; be it enacted, that it shall be lawful for His Majesty, his heirs and successors, from time to time to inclose, sever, and improve within and out of the waste lands of the said Forest of Dean and New Forest respectively, in whole or in part, such quantity of lands in the whole as shall, together with the quantity already in inclosure, or which shall be inclosed as aforesaid in the said Forests respectively, make up the said quantities of 11,000 acres in the Forest of Dean, and 6,000 acres in the New Forest, and so that there shall not be more than 11,000 acres in the Forest of Dean, and 6,000 acres in the New Forest, inclosed and held in severalty as aforesaid at one and the same time; and such inclosures shall be made under and by virtue of commissions to be granted and issued by His Majesty for that purpose, and each of such commissions shall be directed to six or more such persons as His Majesty shall think fit, whereof two in each commission shall be justices of the peace for the county within which the Forest in which the inclosure shall be made shall be situate, and shall not be officers of such Forest; and such inclosure shall be set out and made from and out of such parts or places in the said Forests respectively as shall be found or ascertained by the said commissioners, or any three or more of them, to be most

convenient to be inclosed, and to be best adapted for the growth
and produce of timber, and may be best spared from the commons and highways of the respective counties; which said inclosures shall be admeasured by a sworn surveyor, and set out
and inclosed, butted and bounded, and the quantities, butts and
boundaries thereof returned into His Majesty's Court of Exchequer, there to remain of record for ever; and the said inclosures so made and set out as aforesaid shall remain in severalty
in the actual possession of the Crown, freed and discharged of
and from all rights of common, and of and from all manner of
rights, titles or pretences, or privileges or claims whatsoever, during the period of the same remaining so inclosed for the growth
and preservation of timber, and until the same or any part thereof shall be laid open under the provisions of the said recited Acts
and this Act, according to the purport and true intent of the
said recited Acts and of this Act, and shall be made and reputed
a nursery or nurseries for wood and timber only.

4. And be it further enacted, that at all times hereafter, whenever the lord high treasurer or commissioners of the treasury, or
chancellor of the exchequer for the time being, shall be satisfied,
and shall determine that the woods and trees which shall be growing within any of the said inclosures, whether made before the
passing of this act, and hereby confirmed, or to be made under
and by virtue of this act, are become past danger of browsing of
deer, cattle, or other prejudice, and shall think fit to lay the same
or any part thereof open and in common, and shall cause the
same so to be done, that then and so often it shall be lawful for
His Majesty, his heirs and successors, from time to time to inclose,
in lieu of so much of the inclosures in either Forest as shall be so
laid open, the like quantity out of any other part of the residue of
the wastes of the same Forest, to be set out by like commission
and admeasurement as aforesaid, and to be holden, inclosed, freed
and discharged of and from all manner of common and other
rights as aforesaid, for so long time as the same shall continue
inclosed, according to the direction, purport and intent of the
said recited Acts or this Act, to be a nursery or nurseries for
timber as aforesaid, instead of so much as shall be laid open
according to the direction aforesaid.

5. And, for the making and maintaining the said inclosures
so set out and made as aforesaid, and for defraying the charges

thereof; be it further enacted, that the said commissioners so to
be appointed, under whose authority any inclosure in either of
the said Forests shall be made, or any three of them, with the
assistance of one of the purveyors of His Majesty's navy, shall
from time to time set out so many decayed trees in such Forest,
not being ship timber, as shall be necessary to make and maintain the said inclosure.

6. And, to the end the said inclosures may be preserved in the
Crown for public use as aforesaid; be it enacted, that in case
any person whatever shall presume to take or obtain any gift,
grant, estate or interest of or in the said inclosures, or any wood or
trees growing thereon, every such gift, grant, estate or interest
shall *ipso facto* be null and void, and the person so taking the
same shall be utterly disabled and incapable to have, hold or
enjoy any such gift, grant, estate or interest, and also shall forfeit
treble the value of any such gift or grant to him who shall first
sue for the same in any of His Majesty's courts of record at West-
minister by action of debt, wherein no essoign or wager of law
shall be allowed to the defendant.

7. And be it further enacted, that every person who shall wilfully destroy or take away, or shall break down any fence or inclosure, or any part thereof, made for the protection of any nurseries of wood and timber as aforesaid, shall for the first offence
forfeit the sum of £10, and for the second offence the sum of
£20, and for the third offence shall be deemed guilty of felony,
and may be transported to any part beyond the seas for the term
of seven years, or be subject to such other punishment by fine,
imprisonment or otherwise, as the court before which such person shall be convicted may direct; and such penalties shall and
may be recovered, and on non-payment thereof, the person who
shall forfeit the same may be committed to prison, in the manner
and for the same periods as is specified in an Act passed in the
sixth year of the reign of his present majesty, intituled 'An Act
for the better Preservation of Timber Trees, and of Woods and
Underwoods, and for the further Preservation of Roots, Shrubs
and Plants', in relation to the penalties of £20 and £30 respectively, for wilfully cutting or breaking down any timber
under the said Act.

Appendix IV Forest of Dean Byelaws, 1929

Byelaws made by H.M. Forestry Commissioners in pursuance of the Forestry Act, 1927

The following acts in the Forest of Dean are PROHIBITED except in so far as they may be authorised in writing by the Forestry Commissioners or the Assistant Forestry Commissioner for England and Wales or the Deputy Surveyor in charge of the Forest, and any person who does any of the following unauthorised acts shall, on summary conviction, as in manner provided by the Forestry Act, 1927,* be liable to a fine not exceeding Five Pounds, and in case of a continuing offence to a further fine not exceeding Ten Shillings for each day during which the offence continues :

(a) lighting any fire, or burning or setting fire to any timber, tree, shrub, brushwood, gorse, heather, furze, turf, grass, fern or other substances therein, whether growing or not; or dropping or leaving any lighted match, tobacco or cigarette; or

(b) placing or leaving in the Forest (except in such places as may be allotted for the purpose by the Forestry Commissioners) or in any lake, pond, drain or watercourse therein any glass, tins, rubbish, paper, filth, dead animals, refuse or other objectionable matter; or

(c) damming, obstructing or restraining the flow of any drain or watercourse; or

(d) removing or injuring any post, chain, railing, fence, gate, notice board, building, bridge, culvert or other matter or thing belonging to the Forestry Commissioners, or defacing or disfiguring the same by posting or affixing in any way any bill, placard or notice, or by cutting, stamping, writing or marking thereon; or

(e) cutting, digging up, felling, breaking, removing or doing any injury to timber or to any tree, branch, shrub, brushwood, gravel, sand, clay, loam or other substances,

* Since superseded by the Forestry Act 1967

gorse or furze; or digging up wild flowers, heather, turf, grass, fern or other growing plants; or

(f) catching, netting, trapping, chasing or shooting any bird, game, fish or animal (except rats and other vermin), or attempting to do so, or taking birds' eggs or nests; or allowing dogs to worry or chase any animal or bird; or

(g) (except in places duly allocated for the purpose by the Forestry Commissioners and subject to such regulations as may be made by them in respect thereof) encamping, or erecting, placing or leaving any tent, booth, swing, pole, clothes line or other erection whatsoever, or any motor car, motor cycle or charabanc; or

(h) plying for hire, off the public roads, with or letting out any horse or other animal, or any motor car, motor or other cycle, charabanc, wagon, carriage or other wheeled vehicle; or

(i) (without prejudice to the Forestry Commissioners' right and power to control grazing over the whole Forest and without prejudice to the privileges which have been enjoyed by the local stock owners) turning out in the enclosures to graze or feed or allowing or suffering to remain therein any cattle, horse, mule, pig, sheep, goat, ass, goose, duck, fowl or other animal; or

(j) laying down any pipe or drain, or digging any hole for the purpose of discharging or by any means whatever directing or discharging or allowing to be discharged any sewage or other offensive liquid; or

(k) interfering with, obstructing or annoying any person who, with the consent of the Forestry Commissioners, is engaged in riding, shooting or fishing, or any person lawfully and peacefully using the Forest; or

(l) assaulting, resisting, or aiding, or inciting any person to assault or resist any Officer of the Forestry Commissioners or other person in the execution of his duty or the lawful exercise of any authority under these Byelaws or otherwise.

Nothing in these Byelaws shall take away, abridge or limit any remedy now existing by way of indictment or otherwise, or shall interfere with or prejudice the powers of the Forestry Commissioners, the Court of Verderers or of any Authority legally existing for preventing or punishing any offences whether specified in these Byelaws or not, or the rights and powers of the Forestry Commissioners over the Forest of Dean.

The Officers of the Commissioners are empowered to exclude or remove from any part of the Forest of Dean any person who commits an offence against these Byclaws or against the Vagrancy Act, 1824.

Dated the 19th day of February, 1929.

The Official Seal of the ⎫
Forestry Commissioners ⎪
was affixed to these Bye- ⎬
laws in the presence of ⎭

A. G. HERBERT,
Secretary to the Forestry Commissioners.

Appendix V Inclosure Commissioners appointed 20 November 1962

ELIZABETH the SECOND by the Grace of God of the United Kingdom of Great Britain and Northern Ireland and of Our other Realms and Territories Queen, Head of the Commonwealth, Defender of the Faith, To Our Minister of Agriculture Fisheries and Food for the time being, The *Right Honourable Benjamin Ludlow Bathurst Viscount Bledisloe*, of Lydney Park in the County of Gloucestershire, QC, *Arnold Cooper* of The Nook, Parkend, Lydney in the said County, Justice of the Peace for the said County, Esquire, *Albert Brookes* of 12 Highbury Road, Bream, Lydney in the said County, Justice of the Peace for the said County, Esquire, *John Rooke Johnston* of Savage Hill, Newland, Coleford, in the said County, Esquire, OBE, Justice of the Peace for the said County, *Morgan Philips Price* of The Grove, Taynton in the said County, Esquire, MA, Justice of the Peace for the said County, FRGS, (Miss) *Miriam Joan Kerr* of The Barn House, Newnham in the said County, Justice of the Peace for the said County, *Cyril Edwin Hart* of 'Chenies', Coleford in the said County, Esquire, MA, PhD, FRICS, *Oliver Guy Oakey*, of Mireystock House, Lydbrook in the said County, Esquire, *John Hylton Watts*, of the Rocklands, Lydney in the said County Esquire, *John Robert Haines* of Bastion House, Brunswick Road, Gloucester in the said County Esquire, *Francis Geoffrey Little*, of May Lawn, Mitcheldean in the said County, Esquire, Justice of the Peace for the said County, and the Deputy Surveyor of the Forest of Dean for the time being GREETING : WHEREAS by an Act of Parliament passed in the Twentieth year of the Reign of King Charles the Second, entitled 'An Act for the increase and preservation of timber within the Forest of Dean' it is enacted and declared that Eleven thousand acres part of the waste of the said Forest should be inclosed and kept in severalty for the growth and preservation of Timber for the Navy AND THAT whenever the Lords Commissioners of the Treasury should be satisfied that the Woods and Trees growing in

any inclosure made by virtue of the said Act were become past
danger of browsing of Deer, Cattle, or other prejudice and should
think fit to lay the same or any part thereof open and in common then and so often it should be lawful for His Majesty, His
Heirs and Successors to inclose in lieu of so much as should be
laid open the like quantity of the waste of the said Forest to be
free from all common and other rights for so long as it should
remain inclosed AND WHEREAS by an Act of Parliament
passed in the Forty-eighth year of the Reign of King George the
Third chapter seventy two the powers given by the before mentioned Act were revised and confirmed AND WHEREAS it hath
been made to appear unto us by the Lords Commissioners of
Our Treasury upon a representation made to them by the Commissioners in charge of the said Forest that it is expedient that
certain portions of the waste land of the said Forest not exceeding Five thousand acres be inclosed KNOW YE THEREFORE
that we very much confiding in your fidelity industry and pro-
vident circumspection have assigned you to be Our Commissioners and by these presents do give to you or any three or more
of you (provided two of you who shall execute this our Commission are Justices of the Peace for the said County of Gloucester not being Officers of the said Forest) full power and authority
to cause such parts of the open waste land of the said Forest as
shall be found or ascertained by you or any three or more of you
to be most convenient to be inclosed and to be best adapted for
the growth and preservation of the Timber to the extent in the
whole of not exceeding Five thousand acres to be admeasured
by a Sworn Surveyor and set out and inclosed for the growth
and preservation of timber as you or any three or more of you
shall deem proper for that purpose to be butted and bounded in
the manner required by the before mentioned Act of Parliament
passed in the Forty-eighth year of the reign of King George the
Third and that in so doing you or any three or more of you
shall in every respect obey fulfil perform and execute the powers
authorities and orders which are directed limited and appointed
in and by the said Acts of Parliament PROVIDED ALWAYS
that there shall not be more than Eleven thousand acres of the
waste of the said Forest inclosed and held in severalty as aforesaid at one and the same time AND by virtue of these presents
we hereby give you or any three or more of you full power and

authority to certify and report to the Lord Chief Justice of England and the rest of the Judges of the Queen's Bench Division of the High Court of Justice from time to time as may seem expedient to you or any three or more of you the quantity or quantities of the open waste land of our said Forest not exceeding in the whole Five thousand acres which may from time to time have been by you or any three or more of you set out and inclosed as aforesaid together with the butts and boundaries thereof to the intent that the said Certificates and Reports or Certificate and Report may be from time to time enrolled on the part of Our Remembrancer in Our Supreme Court of Judicature AND THEREFORE WE COMMAND YOU or any three or more of you (provided that two of you are Justices as aforesaid) diligently to attend in and about the premises so as when you or any three or more of you as aforesaid have executed this our Commission touching Our said Forest and have caused such part or parts of the open waste land thereof not exceeding the said quantity of Five thousand acres to be admeasured by a Sworn Surveyor and set out inclosed butted and bounded with such designations and descriptions as to you or any three or more of you shall seem convenient and fitting for Our Service and interest and have done such other matters and things relating thereto as shall be conducive to and necessary for the purposes aforesaid and agreeable to the tenor intent and meaning of the said recited Acts of Parliament and of this Our Commission that then you by whom this Our Commission shall be executed DO return the same and CERTIFY and REPORT your whole proceedings in the premises to the Lord Chief Justice of England and the rest of the Judges of the Queen's Bench Division of the High Court of Justice at Westminster as soon as may be under your hands and seals or under the hands and seals of any three or more of you by whom this Our Commission shall be executed as aforesaid to the intent that the same may be Enrolled on the part of Our Remembrancer in Our Supreme Court of Judicature that thereupon right may be done to Us in the premises and such further directions given herein as shall seem just according to the said Acts of Parliament in that behalf made and provided IN WITNESS whereof we have caused these Our Letters to be made Patent WITNESS Hubert Baron Parker of Waddington Lord Chief Justice of England the Twen-

tieth day of November in the eleventh year of Our Reign BY
WARRANT of the Lords Commissioners of Our Treasury dated
the eighth day of October One thousand nine hundred and
sixty two.

(Signed) Claude Grundy
Queen's Remembrancer

Appendix VI Wild Creatures and Forest Laws Act 1971

An Act to abolish certain rights of Her Majesty to wild creatures
and certain related rights and franchises; to abrogate the forest
law (subject to exceptions); and to repeal enactments relating to
those rights and franchises and to forests and the forest law;
and for connected purposes.

BE IT ENACTED by the Queen's Most Excellent Majesty, by and
with the advice and consent of the Lords Spiritual and Temporal,
and Commons, in this present Parliament assembled, and by the
authority of the same, as follows :

   1.—(1) There are hereby abolished—

     (a) any prerogative right of Her Majesty to wild creatures
       (except royal fish and swans), together with any preroga-
       tive right to set aside land or water for the breeding,
       support or taking of wild creatures; and

     (b) any franchises of forest, free chase, park or free warren.

   (2) The forest law is hereby abrogated, except in so far as it
relates to the appointment and functions of verderers.

   (3) Any right of common originating in the forest law shall
be free of restriction by reason of the fence month or the winter
heyning or any payment in place of it, but the foregoing provision
shall not affect the suspension or exclusion of any such right for
the time being effected by or under any enactment or any limita-
tions or restrictions for the time being imposed by or under any
enactment on the exercise of any such right.

   (4) The enactments mentioned in the Schedule to this Act
(being enactments which, or parts of which, are made unnecessary by subsections (1) and (2) above or, apart from those
subsections, are no longer of practical utility) are hereby repealed
to the extent specified in the third column of that Schedule.

   (5) Except as provided by subsection (3) above, no existing
right of common or pannage originating in the forest law shall
be affected by the abrogation of the forest law or by the repeal
by this section of any enactment giving or confirming that right.

   (6) Notwithstanding the abrogation by this section of the

o

forest law or the repeal by this section of the Dean Forest Act
1667, verderers in the Forest of Dean shall continue to be elected
and hold office as at the passing of this Act.

(7) The repeal by this section of section 13 of the Act 1 & 2
Geo 4. c. 52 (powers of purchasers of forestal or other rights
held in right of the Duchy of Lancaster) shall not affect the
operation of that section in relation to any existing power to
depute or appoint gamekeepers.

2.—(1) This Act may be cited as the Wild Creatures and
Forest Laws Act 1971.

(2) The partial repeal by this Act of section 2 of the Night
Poaching Act 1828, extend to Scotland, but except as aforesaid
this Act does not extend to Scotland.

(3) This Act extends to Northern Ireland and shall, as respects
matters within the powers of the Parliament of Northern Ireland,
be subject to alteration by that Parliament as if it had been an
Act passed before the day appointed for the purposes of section 6
of the Government of Ireland Act 1920.

SCHEDULE
Enactments Repealed

(so far as they relate to forest law in general and the
Forest of Dean in particular)

Statute, etc	Title, short title or subject	Extent of repeal
25 Edw 1. (1297).	The Charter of the Forest.	The whole statute, so far as unrepealed.
25 Edw 1. (1297).	(Confirmation of the Charters.)	In chapter 1, the words 'and the Charter of the Forest', where first occurring, and the words 'and the Charter of the Forest for the wealth of our realm'.
33 Edw 1. (1305).	An Ordinance of the Forest.	The whole statute.
34 Edw 1. (1306).	An Ordinance of the Forest.	The whole statute, so far as unrepealed.
[Of uncertain date.]	The Customs and Assize of the Forest.	The whole statute.
1 Edw 3. Stat 2. (1327).	(Botes in forest.)	Chapter 2.
25 Edw 3. Stat 5. (1351).	(Limit on demand of puture in forest.)	Chapter 7.

Statute, etc	Title, short title or subject	Extent of repeal
7 Hen 4. (1405).	(Confirmation of Liberties.)	The words 'and the Charter of the Forest'.
4 Hen 5. Stat 2. (1416).	(Confirmation of Charters and Statutes.)	The words 'and the Charter of the Forest'.
16 Chas 1. c. 16.	The Delimitation of Forests Act 1640.	The whole Act.
19 & 20 Chas 2. c. 8.	The Dean Forest Act 1667.	The whole Act, so far as unrepealed.
48 Geo 3. c. 72.	The Dean and New Forests Act 1808.	The preamble. Sections 1 and 2. In section 3 the words from the beginning to 'be it enacted that'; the words 'and New Forest respectively'; the words 'in the said forests respectively' in both places; the words 'and six thousand acres in the New Forest', in both places; the words from 'and the quantities, butts and boundaries' to 'of record for ever'; and the words 'the said recited Acts and', in both places. In section 4 the words from 'the lord high treasurer' to 'shall determine that'; and the words 'the said recited Acts or'. Sections 5 and 7.
10 Geo 4. c. 50.	The Crown Lands Act 1829.	The whole Act, so far as unrepealed.
6 & 7 Will 4. c. 3 (1836).	An Act for vesting the office of constable of the castle of St Briavels in the First Commissioner of His Majesty's Woods, Forests, Land Revenues, Works and Buildings; and for vesting the office of keeper of the forest of Dean in the county of Gloucester in the Commissioners of His Majesty's Woods, Forests, Land Revenues, Works and Buildings.	The whole Act.

Statute, etc	Title, short title or subject	Extent of repeal
1 & 2 Vict c. 42.	The Dean Forest (Encroachments) Act 1838.	The whole Act, so far as unrepealed.
5 & 6 Vict c. 65.	The Dean Forest Act 1842.	The whole Act.
7 & 8 Vict c. 13 (1844).	An Act to extend until the 1st day of January 1845, and to the end of the then next session of Parliament the time within which conveyances may be made on behalf of the Crown of and disputes settled with regard to encroachments in the forest of Dean.	The whole Act.
24 & 25 Vict c. 40 (1861).	An Act to make further provision for the management of Her Majesty's forest of Dean, and of the mines and quarries therein and in the hundred of Saint Briavels in the county of Gloucester.	Section 25.
29 & 30 Vict c. 70 (1866).	An Act to extend the provisions for the inclosure, exchange and improvement of land in certain portions of the forest of Dean called Walmore Common and the Bearce Common, and for authorising allotments in lieu of the forestal rights of Her Majesty in and over such commons.	The whole Act, so far as unrepealed.
33 & 34 Vict c. viii.	The Abbot's Wood (Dean Forest) Act 1870.	The whole Act, except section 9.
46 & 47 Vict c. lxxxvii.	The East and West Dean (Highways) Act 1883.	The whole Act.
6 Edw 7. c. cxix.	The Dean Forest Act 1906.	Section 1.
9 & 10 Eliz 2. c. 55.	The Crown Estate Act 1961	In Schedule 2, paragraph 2(a).

Index of Subjects

Page references to illustrations are printed in italic.

The following group-headings should be noted: Acts, Animals, Clergy, Forest, Forest Officials, and Religious Houses.

Acorns, 19, 22, 118, 201
Acts, Laws, *chronologically*:
  Assize of Woodstock (1184), 21, 22
  Magna Carta (1215), 22
  Charter of the Forest (1217), 21, 22, 23, 24, 79, 82
  Consuetudines et Assise de Foresta (1278), 24
  Charter of the Forest, confirmation (1297), 194
  Ordinance of the Forest (1305), (1306), 194
  Act for the Deafforestation etc of the Forests (1653), 105
  Act to mitigate forest law in Dean (1657), 106
  Dean Forest (Reafforestation) Act 1667, 108, 194, 206
  Dean Forest (Timber) Act 1808, 135, 195, 214
  Commission Act 1831, 136
  (Encroachments) Act 1838, 136, 193, 198
  (Mines) Act 1838, 136, 193, 201
  (Encroachments) Act 1844, 137
  (Amendment) Act 1861, 145
  Crown Lands Act 1829, 136, 193, 196, 198
  Dean Forest Act 1906, 149
  Forestry Act 1967, 193, 199
  Wild Creatures and Forest Laws Act 1971, 190–201, 225–8; *and see* Forest law, Common law
Afforestation, *see* Forest
Agistment, *see* Animals
Agriculture, 19, 61
Alehouse, 101
Animals,
  boar, pig, swine, 19, 20, 22, 29, 36, 38, 73
  cat, 37
  cattle, 19, 23, 28
  deer, 19, 20, 22, 27, 28, 29, 36, 37, 38, 73, 85, 86, 109, 110–14, 138, *185*, *187*, 195, Ch 7
  browsing, 27, 103

  fawning, *see* Defence month
  fee-, 40, 137, 139
  red, 20, 36, 176, 177
  roe, 20, 36
  fallow, 20, 36
  gifts, 36
  close seasons, *see* Defence month, Winter Heyning
  not to exceed 800, 108, 178, 179, 210
  methods of catching, 59, 181
  leap-gates, 71
  population, 138, 185, 186
  sustenance, 20, 27, 37, 76, 103
  removal, 180
  return, 185, 186
  dog, 29, 38, 59, 81
  lawing of, 81
  fox, 27, 37
  goat, 29, 53, 82, 118
  hare, 37
  horse, 19, 23
  oxen, 26, 53
  sheep, 19, 29, 82, 118, 201
  wolf, 27, 37, 58
  commonable, 29, 201
  uncommonable, 29, 201
  agistment, 28, 36; *and see* Agister
  drifts, 28
  gamekeeper, 172
  snares, nets, traps, 59; *and see* Forest, Hunting, Venison
Arms, 27, 29, 59, 75, 110
  arrows, 27, 59,
  bows, 27, 59
  crossbows, 59, 75
  guns, 110–14
  quarrels, 75, 83
  shot, 110–14
Arrows, *see* Arms
Assarts, 21, 22, 29, 60, 61, 86
Attorneys, 48
Attorney-General, 98, 115, 119

Bailiwicks, 26, 27, *47*, 93
  Abenhall, 26, 27, 37, 61
  Bearse, 26
  Bicknor, 26

Index of Place Names

236 Index of Place Names

Index of Personal Names